Building Walls

Building Walls

Excluding Latin People in the United States

Ernesto Castañeda

LEXINGTON BOOKS
Lanham • Boulder • New York • London

Published by Lexington Books
An imprint of The Rowman & Littlefield Publishing Group, Inc.
4501 Forbes Boulevard, Suite 200, Lanham, Maryland 20706
www.rowman.com

6 Tinworth Street, London SE11 5AL, United Kingdom

British Library Cataloguing in Publication Information Available

Library of Congress Cataloging-in-Publication Data

ISBN 9781498585651 (cloth : alk. paper)
ISBN 9781498585675 (pbk: alk. paper)
ISBN 9781498585668 (electronic)

♾™ The paper used in this publication meets the minimum requirements of American National Standard for Information Sciences—Permanence of Paper for Printed Library Materials, ANSI/NISO Z39.48-1992.

Printed in the United States of America

This book is dedicated to the memory of all those who have died in the borderlands in search of a better life.

Contents

PART III: IMMIGRATION AS AN EXPERIENCE

Acknowledgments

A conversation with the brilliant Cecilia Menjívar produced the idea for this book. I thank Sarah Craig, Courtney Morales, and Lexington Books for their support of this project. I deeply thank Celia Lacayo for her feedback on the first version of the full manuscript; her wise suggestions helped strengthen the book. I have been working on some of these chapters for over a decade; some were written in 2018. Together they offer an overall picture about what is new and what is old about anti-Mexican and anti-immigrant words and policies.

Many people have provided invaluable help on the various chapters in this book. Maura Fennelly helped me finish the introductory and concluding chapters in prompt fashion and provided editorial feedback on all chapters. Parts of the introductory chapter build on conversations with Salvador Vidal-Ortiz and Juliana Martinez about who, when, and where is Latin*. (I use the asterisk because in Windows DOS operating system, the asterisk stands for a wildcard. Searching for Latin* would provide files with all possible endings thus including Latin, Latino, Latinas, Latinx, etc.). The conclusions here are mine. Salvador and Juliana bear no responsibility for the terms used. The introduction and conclusion contain revised portions of a review I wrote of Michael Dear's *Why Walls Won't Work*.

Partha Chatterjee, Richard Sennett, Craig Calhoun, and the members of the NYLON network provided feedback and encouragement on the theoretical Chapter 2, "Migration and Its Challenges to Political Theory and Nationalism." I also presented Chapters 2, 3, and an overview of the book at the Department of Philosophy, Universidad Panamericana, Mexico City, in August 2018. I thank Ma. Elena García Peláez Cruz, Luis Xavier López Farjeat, José Luis Rivera, Enrique Camacho, Cecilia Coronado, Alfonso Gánem, Carla Adell, and Gustavo Andrade for their feedback and engagement with the project.

I thank the late Charles Tilly, the late Allan Silver, Gil Eyal, and Peter Bearman for critical comments on early versions of Chapter 3, "Boundary Formation: Nationalism, Immigration, and Categorical Inequality between Americans and Mexicans." I also appreciate the questions and suggestions from co-panelists and audiences at Lineae Terrarum: International Borders Conference, organized by Tony Payan at the University of Texas at El Paso in March 2006; the American Sociological Association's annual meeting August 2008; and the Inter-Ivy Sociology Symposium, Princeton University March 2008, and especially the respective discussants—Josiah Heyman, Nestor Rodriguez, and Douglas Massey—who provided insightful and supportive comments.

Alexandra Delano helped edit and publish a Spanish version of Chapter 4, "Border Vigilantes at the University: Anti-immigrant Discourse and Ideological Campaigns." The earlier version of this chapter was published as Castañeda, Ernesto. 2006. "Los Minutemen en la universidad: el debate migratorio actual y los debates ideológicos pasados." *Estudios de Política y Sociedad*. Vol. 2, No. 3. pp. 29–39, for which I am the copyright holder. Emmanuel Gardea, Sarai García, and Citlali Castillo aided with the translation into English. Philip Alig and Susana Arzate helped update the text. This is a fully revised and extended version of that article.

It was a pleasure to work with Dennis West, who wrote and researched the bulk of Chapter 5, "Fronting the White Storm." My former student and co-author Catherine Harlos wrote the first version of Chapter 6, "Anti-Immigrant Online Comment Sections in the Aftermath of Trump's Election."

For their help with Chapter 7, "Different Understandings of the Border Wall: The Social Meanings of the Wall for Border Residents," first and foremost, I thank the students enrolled in my spring 2013 Methods of Research course offered by the Department of Sociology and Anthropology at the University of Texas, El Paso. While only a number of testimonies and photographs were used in this text, all the students' perspectives were useful in writing the text and doing the analysis. I thank my teaching assistants Jorge Hernandez and Curtis Smith for help with the logistics of conducting group ethnography. I thank Itzel Rosales, Miguel Zuniga, Brian Diedrich, and Jonathan Klassen for their help with this project as undergraduate research assistants. I also thank Benita Heiskanen, Andrae Marak, Jeanne Grant, and Howard Campbell for useful suggestions that improved the text originally published as "The Socially Polysemantic Border: Positionality and the Meaning of the Fence." *The Middle Ground Journal: World History and Global Studies.* Number 8, pp. 1–29 for which I hold the copyright. This book includes a revised version of the article.

The research behind Chapter 8 was funded by a grant from the *Programa de Migración y Salud* (PIMSA) Binational Health Program, administered through the School of Public Health at the University of California, Berkeley. I thank all the members of this three-city study for their help with research design and implementation. Beyond my co-authors Natali Collazos, Eva Moya, and Silvia

Chávez-Baray, they also include Oscar A. Esparza, Leticia Calderón Chelius, Griselda Villalobos, Itzel Eguiluz, Edna Aileen Martínez, Karen Herrera, Tania Llamas, Marcela Arteaga, Laura Díaz, Maribel Najera, Nancy Landa, and Virginia Escobedo. Natali Collazos's data analysis and drafting of the paper was supported by American University's College of Arts & Sciences Undergraduate Summer Scholarships 2016. Citlali Castillo, Cynthia Cristobal, Sofia Hinojosa, and Celine-Marie Pascale provided feedback and support writing this chapter. My AU writing group colleagues and friends Nicole Angotti, Michael Bader, Molly Dondero, Randa Serhan, Rachel Sullivan Robinson, Kirsten Stoebenau, and Nina Yamanis provided useful feedback on this chapter, future directions for that project, and on the book proposal. All shortcomings remain my own.

Robert Smith, Federico Besserer, Leslie Martino, Cid Martinez, Silvia Domínguez, Thomas Soehl, Steven Gold, Pamela Anne Quiroz, Rene Flores and a number of anonymous reviewers provided feedback for Chapter 9, "Invisible New Yorkers: Boundaries, Interethnic Networks, Immigrant Integration, and Social Invisibility," on the boundaries and networks of Mexicans in New York.

The students in Fall 2017 Borders, Migration, and Globalization complex problems freshman seminar at American University provided critical and editorial input on many chapters: Amber Shemesh, Veronica Robertson, Chloe Bambara, Citlali Castillo, Molly Dee, Lauren Ferrier, Alyssa Hugel, Daniela Jallath, Minwoo Kang, Samantha Liptak, Bailey O'Donnell, Grace Shanahan, Emilia Turrisi, Jack Boone, Anthony Baron, and Colby Parkinson. The Fall 2018 Borders, Migration, and Globalization students Chase Dexter, Gabriela Garcia-Astolfi, Sahiba Madan, Samantha Lord, Timothy Ryan-Liss, Juan Pelaez-Barboza, Alyssa Bursie, Emily Fontaine, Nikolaos Theodoratos, Kayla Baldie, Joseph Rose, Anupama Paul, Samuel Blodgett, Sage Coates-Farley, Ariel Krysmalski, Josephine Flanagan, Gabriel Cabanas, Gavin Meyer, and Amber Shemesh—also edited chapters and offered their candid feedback. They did not always agree with my arguments and conclusions; thus, they helped strengthen the text. Students from The Rise of Critical Social Thought course also gave feedback on some of the ideas and chapters. I thank all of them for their assistance and criticisms. Hannah McNamara, Liza Sweitzer, Diego Aleman, Cynthia Cristobal, Abigail Mitchell, and Dennis West helped to edit various chapters. Maura Fennelly and Lesley Buck helped to make all chapters more readable.

I thank my parents, Ernesto and Ma. Elena; my sisters Mónica and Claudia; and my brothers-in-law Nils and Guillermo. I thank Madelaine and Arthur Warren for their support through all the years that I have been working on this and other books. Special thanks to Lesley Buck and our children, Ernesto and Alexander.

Washington, D.C., January 2019

Part I

CATEGORICAL THINKING

Chapter 1

The Historical and Contemporary Exclusion of Latin People from the American Identity

Ernesto Castañeda and Maura Fennelly

Despite common beliefs, everyday talk, and misleading genetic ancestry tests, there is no scientific basis behind race (Golash-Boza 2018, 2016a, Morning 2011, Gannon 2016, Castañeda 2018c). Race is a social construction; individuals have more genetic commonalities than differences because we are all part of the same species. Genetic differences between individuals are less than 0.1 percent of their total genomes (Chou 2017). It is ludicrous to fixate on observable phenotypical things such as hair, eye, or skin pigmentation to extrapolate from them intelligence or morality. Nonetheless, when people believe that race is real, acting on this belief results in meaningful differences of perceived human worth, employment preferences, discriminating policies and institutional practices (Golash-Boza 2018). Thus, the consequences of racialization are substantial for groups of people and produce what Charles Tilly calls durable categorical inequality (Castañeda 2018c, Tilly, Castañeda, and Schneider 2017).

Omi and Winant "argue that race has been a master category, a kind of template for patterns of inequality, marginalization, and difference throughout U.S. history" (2015, viii). Race is about "making up people" (Mills 2008), and herding individuals into racial categories. This is not an easy process free of ambiguities (Omi and Winant 2015, 105). Omi and Winant "emphasize the fundamental instability of the race concept" (Omi and Winant 2015, x) as race is constantly in formation. Racial categorizations have never been purely descriptive, scientific, or neutral processes. Rather, "practices of distinguishing among human beings according to their corporeal characteristics became linked to systems of control, exploitation, and resistance. Since race and racism involve violence, oppression, exploitation, and indignity, they also generate movements of resistance and theories of resistance" (Omi and Winant 2015, 3). Omi and Winant call for "an awareness that the concept of race is subject to permanent political contestation" (2015, ix). We see racial conceptions challenged and transformed by both oppressed and oppressing groups.

After World War II and the civil rights legislation, there was a decrease in discourses based on scientific racism to justify group inequalities. Instead, there was a rise in discourses about cultural differences resulting in different group outcomes. Lévi-Strauss argues that soon after Nazism and the Holocaust and the delegitimation of racial purity and ethnic cleansing quests, the concept of "culture" had often taken the place of "race" in exclusionary discourses used to explain differences and the supposed intrinsic inferiority of certain groups (Lévi-Strauss 2007 [1952]). Today, individuals may attribute multi-generational cultural differences to biology, conflate race and culture, and treat people of different nationalities and ethnic groups as perpetually inferior (Lacayo 2017). Racist conceptions have taken many ideological and practical forms during American and European history (Kendi 2016), but they all have served to justify the extreme exploitation and social exclusion of particular human groups. Racism is not only about individual beliefs, but about systems of differentiation and oppression (Bonilla-Silva 2017, 1997).

ARE MEXICANS A RACE, A CULTURE, OR AN ETHNICITY?

Racialized relations between U.S. and Mexican citizens occur in the historical shadow of U.S. imperialism and its Manifest Destiny (Hahn 2016). Territorial expansionism was justified by racist theories. Some "scientific racists" of the 1840s had a theory about the weather and the natural environment shaping the physical and cultural characteristics of different "nations." Zeke Baker calls this "racial climatology" (Baker 2018, 749). He cites Samuel Forry:

> It requires not the gift of divination to foresee the destiny of Mexico and the States south of it, whose inhabitants, enervated by climate, conjointly with other causes, will yield, by that necessity which controls all moral laws, to the energetic arm of the Anglo-Saxon. (Forry 1842a:22, cited in Baker 2018, 752)

These are not marginal opinions by an outsider. Forry was influential at the time; he published in medical and scientific journals such as the *New York Journal of Medicine*, the *New York Lancet*, as well as in the *American Biblical Repository*. He was a pioneer in meteorology, vital statistics, and military personnel management and was part of the intellectual debates about racial definitions, differences, and origins (Baker 2018). The U.S.-Mexico war—partly based on racist arguments that only Lincoln and a few others opposed—took place between 1846 and 1848, only a few years after the publication of Forry's book. As the borderlines shifted and their lands changed political jurisdiction once again, some *Mexicanos* became part of the U.S. population as a colonized minority and later others did it through immigration.

Immigration has always been a fact of life. The terms immigration problem or immigration policy were not present in the U.S. press before 1900 (Benton-Cohen 2018, 18). As historian Katherine Benton-Cohen argues, it was the fact-finding congressional Dillingham Commission on immigration—headed by a couple of immigration restrictionist congressmen—and its 1911 book *The Immigration Problem: A Study of American Immigration Conditions and Needs* that first framed immigration as a "problem" and the idea that it was up to the federal government to fix it. This understanding was the result of Progressive Era bureaucratic thinking that experts could solve social problems (Benton-Cohen 2018, 2).

Immigration policy in the United States has been marked by contradictions between the desire for economic and territorial growth by increasing the non-indigenous population and racist worries about different groups outnumbering Anglo-Saxons or curtailing their cultural, political, and economic dominant influence,

> The anti-Irish nativism of the 1850s did not yield federal restrictions (though some state and local barriers to the Irish existed). . . . In 1864, when the North desperately needed more laborers, President Abraham Lincoln inserted a new plank into the Republican Party's platform, stating that "foreign immigration, which in the past has added so much to the wealth, development of resources, and increase of nations, should be fostered and encouraged by a liberal and just policy." That year, Congress passed a bill to encourage immigration, the only one of its kind in American history. . . . The Chinese Exclusion Act of 1882, which barred only workers, became the first federal law to forbid immigrants on the basis of race and class. . . . The Immigration Act of 1882 marked the moment when "the Federal government first took control of immigration" from the piecemeal oversight of the states. . . . Most important, until 1921, no numerical quota for immigrants existed anywhere in federal statute. Before Chinese exclusion, there was no such thing as an illegal alien. (Benton-Cohen 2018, 16–17)

Therefore, it is anachronistic to talk about historical European immigrants as coming to the United States "legally," as contemporary immigration restrictionists do (see Part II).

Seasonal workers from Mexico met some of the labor demand left by the exclusion of the Chinese and Japanese (Ngai 2004). The federal government did not try to count land-crossings through the southern border until around

1908, and "although Mexicans faced all kinds of discrimination, they were legally white and eligible for citizenship under U.S. law; the Japanese were neither" (Benton-Cohen 2018, 62). Benton-Cohen writes that in 1900 Mexicans belonged in an overlapping category between legal whiteness and social inferiority (Benton-Cohen 2018, 12). The Mexican Revolution (1910–1920) resulted in increased emigration. In the 1920s as quotas limited eastern and southern European immigrants, Mexican labor in the Southwest increased: "Mexicans began to assume a greater real and symbolic importance in immigration debates. As eugenics rose in influence, racialized denunciation of Mexicans became more frequent. Nevertheless, Mexicans would not have a numerical limit until the Hart-Celler Act of 1965" (Benton-Cohen 2018, 240). Those small quotas have largely created the current issue of undocumented migration.

While the United States has been settled by people coming from many parts of the world, newcomers from new parts of the world are looked down upon. Historically non-slaved groups that are now considered "white" were excluded and racialized, yet

> being of "Irish race" never equated to the legal and social inequalities of being African American. . . . An Italian could be discriminated against on the basis of race but still benefit from being white. The word "race" was both ubiquitous and contested in the Dillingham Commission's era because ideas about science, heredity, and acquired characteristics were fluid and undergoing great passionate debate. Some people used it simply to refer to a group united by custom, geography, and appearance; others, to claim that one group was biologically inferior or superior to another. Some—influenced by scientific racism and, especially by 1910s, eugenics—made claims about hereditary characteristics of body, intelligence, and morality that fueled the exclusion of southern and eastern Europeans with the quota laws in the 1920s. . . . A more restrictive immigration policy, in Ward's [Harvard climatologist and eugenics's early enthusiast] view, was essential to the "prevention of the unfit" in the United States. (Benton-Cohen 2018, 12–13)

Despite its popularity and political convenience, the idea of race has never been fully settled because it cannot be.

Brown Exclusions

Theoretically and empirically exploring the long and systematic exclusion of Mexicans as it is embedded in political and social theory, in public debates, and in everyday practices is a largely understudied process in the scholarly literature, which instead tends to focus on the black/white binary. This book illustrates narratives, processes, and mechanisms that have been mobilized to exclude people with roots in Latin America and the Caribbean from enjoying equal economic opportunities and full political participation in the United States. Through different methods and approaches, this book describes the exclusion and racialization of people with origins in Latin America residing within the United States at different historical periods and in different locations. But, how should we call these people? What can we call the processes that group them as "others" without "othering" them in the process of denouncing their categorical exclusion? The answer has to be provisional, a theoretical shortcut, an ideal type; and we most often go back to the context to remember who in particular we are talking about.

Demographic Profile

According to the U.S. Census Current Population Survey 2016, there were 56.9 million Hispanics in the United States, of which 37 million (86.5 percent) are U.S.-born, 7 million are naturalized citizens, and 13 million are non-citizens, the majority with green cards, visas, and work permits (U.S. Census Bureau 2018b). The respective national origins are 35.8 million of Mexican origin, 5.4 Central American, 5.2 Puerto Rican, and 2.1 Cuban (U.S. Census Bureau 2018a). Puerto Ricans are U.S. citizens by birth, and until January 12, 2017, Cubans had immediate immunity when reaching American coasts because they were officially perceived as leaving an undemocratic enemy regime. Therefore, the great majority of Hispanics in the United States are "legal" and of Mexican descent.

Hispanic

While "race" still underlines biological descent, ethnicity is often used more to refer to cultural commonalities (Hattam 2007, Golash-Boza 2018). Following court precedents that declared Mexicans as white (Benton-Cohen 2018, 62), and striving to be post-racial while allowing for self-differentiation, demographers and staff in the the U.S. Census Bureau do not *racialize* Latinos by referring to them in official documents and census forms as an "ethnicity" whose members can belong to different "races." Thus, government officials and researchers who rely on census data often write reports using mutually exclusive categories such as non-Hispanic whites, non-Hispanic blacks, and Hispanics. They could also run statistics on white Hispanics, black Hispanics, Asian Hispanics, Native American Hispanics, and so on. These are technical terms correctly used by government reports, health researchers, and demographers because they derive from definitions used in the decennial census and population surveys. Nonetheless, many individuals answering these census questions often have a hard time understanding why and how to choose a racial category and whether they are Hispanic. So, we also have categories like Other, Mixed race, as well as unanswered questions and lower response rates.

In other words, the Census decouples "race" from being Hispanic, which it considers an "ethnicity" because it recognizes that Hispanics may share a language, culture, heritage, or identity and have different skin colors and phenotypes. Thus, the Census as of 2018 constructs categories such as non-Hispanic Whites, non-Hispanic Blacks, Hispanics, Asians, Mixed-race, and other categories based on the combination of these two questions, in practice creating race-like mutually exclusive categories from terms and questions that hardly match everyday terms that people use to self-identify. This is not a technical error that "better" questions could easily fix; rather it shows the fluidity, complexity, and arbitrariness of belonging, or being considered to belong, to a particular ethnoracial category. There is not a true difference between ethnicity and race when people consider them both as natural, immutable, or essential characteristics; and given that they both result from a process of categorization, I will often use the term ethnoracial not to give primacy to one chimera over the other as we should not reify either.

The U.S. Census has changed racial and ethnic definitions and categories throughout the years (Loveman and Muniz 2007). But how did the Census Bureau begin using the term Hispanic? In the 1960s Mexican-Americans, Cuban-Americans, and Puerto Ricans lived in different parts of the United States, had different political agendas, did not identify with each other, would answer "white" in census questionnaires, and identified with their particular countries of origin (Mexico, Cuba, Spain, Puerto Rico, Dominican Republic) (Mora 2014a, 3). Some populations in New Mexico used the terms Spanish and Hispanic to underline their Spanish origins (Gómez 2007). In New York, Spanish and Hispanic were used as a pan-ethnic term to denote the linguist and cultural group formed by immigrants from Spain and the Spanish-speaking Caribbean living there since the early 1800s, and who participated in literary and cultural societies (Haslip-Viera 2010). Nonetheless, the adoption of the term Hispanic to signify a U.S.-wide community came before the identity existed and before the popular use of the term (Mora 2014a, 169). The term Hispanic was first used in the 1980s Census (Tienda and Ortiz 1986). The category was proposed by a network of state and non-state actors such as the National Council of La Raza, Univision, the Census Bureau, and the Cabinet Committee on Opportunities for Spanish-Speaking People (CCOSSP) (Mora 2014b, xii). The term was created instrumentally with a purposely ambiguous definition to be applicable to as many individuals as possible (Mora 2014b, 5). There is no legal litmus test to be Hispanic or not. For the Census Bureau "Hispanic refers to people whose origin is Mexican, Puerto Rican, Cuban, Spanish-speaking Central or South American countries, or other Hispanic/Latino, regardless of race." The definition is circular and purposely open. To this day, one can call oneself Hispanic whether born in the United States, Latin America, or the Iberian Peninsula; if one has one or two parents with that origin, or, one grandparent is Hispanic; if one is married to a Hispanic; if one has Hispanic children; or if one simply chooses to identify as a Hispanic (Passel and Taylor 2009). As an "identity" it is open to individual adoption and to political use when used collectively to reduce categorical inequality or to combat group stigma.

Therefore, some people prefer to use the term Latino to refer to themselves in reaction to what they see as top-down externally imposed labels. Thus, since 2000 the U.S. Census lists Hispanic and Latino as synonymous or interchangeable terms. "Latino" and "Hispanic" could be seen as pan-ethnic labels that *racialize* a large number of people in the United States as a "multiracial ethnic group." These terms sometimes assume and overstate a common culture and language among people from many different nation-states and of different immigrant generations. Indeed, some of the countries of origin are highly nationalistic, for example, Colombia, Mexico, Argentina, the Dominican Republic (Rippberger and Staudt 2002). Recent-immigrant arrivals tend to identify primarily with people from their own community and from their country of origin, although that identity is framed by what they have in mind as an "imagined community" (Anderson 2006) because often they had limited contact with people from outside their region of origin before migrating. For example, many Mexicans from the Mixteca region who now live in New York City rarely visited or met people from outside their hometowns and neighboring areas until they arrived in New York. This was also common for Italians who had local or regional identities like Sicilian and only became "Italian" in the diaspora.

The labels of "Hispanic" or "Latino" are commonly used in media, public debates, and in social science literature to talk about often misunderstood groups of "others." At the same time, these labels have become accepted by these groups. Those socialized in the United States, those more integrated and politically active are more likely to use the terms and fight over what term to use and what are the political and symbolic implications (M. de Onís 2017). This may be similar to the manner in which former generations embraced the term Chicano (Guzman 1971, Vasquez 2005 [1970]) or in which others embrace the term Latino. Some people use the terms as synonymous, and others prefer one over the other. Puerto Rican anthropologist Arlene Dávila writes that by the 1970s, the term Hispanic was seen to be contrary to the cultural nationalism that accompanied larger struggles for civil empowerment by both Chicanos and Puerto Ricans and thus a denial of their identity and a rejection of their indigenous and colonized roots. Ironically, it was shortly after these cultural struggles that the U.S. government coined the official designation of "Hispanic" to designate anyone of Spanish background in the United States. This explains why Latino activists generally regard "Hispanic" as a more politically "sanitized" terminology than "Latino/a," even though both terms are equally guilty of erasing differences while encompassing highly heterogeneous populations and can be as equally appropriated for a range of politics. (Dávila 2012, 15)

This is indeed an example of a definitional struggle (Mora 2014a) with groups of individuals, interests, and causes favoring one term over another, as well as a way to broker between groups and depoliticize thorny issues. Thus, in the late 1960s and early 1970s, the CCOSSP

focused on rearticulating the demands of Mexican Americans and Puerto Ricans alike. Specifically, the committee concentrated on issues that best fit the institutional capabilities of the federal government, such as bilingual education, housing, unemployment, and the administration's agenda—particularly minority entrepreneurship. As a result, it never addressed the more militant and abstract questions of Chicano and Puerto Rican self-determination. And by claiming to cater to the Spanish-speaking population as a whole, CCOSSP could skirt the more radical ethnic-specific issues like Mexican American land grant claims and Puerto Rican independence. (Mora 2014b, 47)

So, on the one hand, we have the interest of politicians, bureaucrats, civic organizations, and self-appointed leaders and representatives, a new cadre of experts presenting a new term, identity, and type of American citizen. While on the other hand, we have a competing set of popular meanings, understandings, and self-identifications by regular people with ancestry in Latin America or the Caribbean.

Chicano

The term Chicano or Xicano is an abbreviation of Mexicano (Guidotti-Hernández 2017, 142). Chicano activists associate the term with the Aztec civilization and with the story of Aztlan (Bebout 2016, Chapter 2). The term did not catch on among Texan-Mexicans (Limón 1981). For example, most people in El Paso are of Mexican descent, and most arrived into the city in the past decades, yet "Mexican Americans and Mexican nationals feel that they are quite different from each other. Additionally, . . . Mexican Americans display interethnic distinctions among themselves" (Vila 1998, 185). In the early 1990s, only 1 percent of El Pasoans called themselves Chicano (Staudt 1998, 47). In surveys we conducted in the early 2010s (Loza, Castañeda, and Diedrich 2016), we also found a very small percentage of El Pasoans identifying as Chicanos. Sociologist Pablo Vila argues that this is because of the symbolic struggle or contested meaning of the term Chicano, which has not reached a semiotic closure. Chicano can mean:

- "militants who want to preserve their Mexican heritage" often through the Chicano movement;
- "Any person of Mexican descent living in the United States";
- Poor Mexican-Americans;
- *Cholos*, "members of a working-class youth subculture" in the Southwest. Because of their dress and manner of speaking, they are often wrongly assumed to be members of gangs;
- "Mexican Americans losing their Mexican roots";
- "Uprooted Mexican Americans who are neither Mexican nor American";
- English-dominant Mexicans;
- U.S.-born Mexicans;
- "A term whose moment has passed";
- A derogatory term (list quoted and adapted from Vila 1998).

Therefore, the meaning of the term Chicano depends on the person speaking, the interlocutor, and the geographical and socio-historical contexts.

Regional Differences

In the same way that the term Chicano has a history rooted in California (Guzman 1971, Chávez 2002), there are important regional differences for what terms are used to designate people with origins south of the border. For decades *Mexicans, Hispanics,* or *Latinos* referred to people of Mexican origin in the Southwest (Guzman 1971) but as Mexicans have moved to new destinations, including New York, Mexicans are now almost everywhere in the United States (Massey 2008), and other Latin groups have followed a similar path of dispersion through time.

In New York City, for a long time, the terms Spanish, Hispanic, Latin, or Latino meant people of Puerto Rican, Cuban, or Spanish Caribbean origins. Puerto Ricans used to be concentrated in East Harlem, aka El Barrio; Bushwick; and in other neighborhoods where they had considerable political clout (Dávila 2004, Marwell 2007). Dominicans are also concentrated in certain neighborhoods in Northern Manhattan, specifically in Washington Heights, and are also well organized politically (Kasinitz, Mollenkopf, and Waters

2004). Mexicans in New York City are a group "coming of age" (Smith 2006), little by little gaining the political influence of Puerto Ricans. While many Mexicans in New York are not citizens, and thus cannot vote, and are not concentrated in a neighborhood, they still hold a certain political influence.

When referring to Latinos in New York, this group was traditionally formed by Puerto Ricans, then Dominicans, followed by Mexicans as the most numerous groups. Significant numbers of Central and South American citizens have also migrated to the New York metropolitan area in recent years. All Puerto Ricans are "legal" as residents of a U.S. territory; they acquire automatic citizenship at birth. Nonetheless, people speak Spanish in Puerto Rico, and many of those born on the island see themselves as Puerto Ricans first, and then as Latinos or Americans. Puerto Ricans have been in New York since the early 1900s. Historically, Puerto Ricans were also seen as contentious, especially in the sixties when they organized and rioted following police abuses in 1965 and 1967. Puerto Ricans had a radical organization—the Young Lords—modeled on the Black Panthers (Schneider 2014, Gutiérrez 2016, 41); but I argue that the relatively successful minority/immigrant incorporation in the United States following the institutionalization of the civil rights movement and the co-optation of political elites also serves to explain the de-radicalization of Puerto Rican organizations in the mainland. Some use the term Nuyorican or Boricua to designate Puerto Ricans born in the United States or pro-independence Puerto Ricans (Guidotti-Hernández 2017, 144). But, the context, who is speaking to whom, and individual preferences matter.

Latino-Americans

Non-Hispanics sometimes use the terms Hispanic-Americans, Latino-Americans, or Latin Americans as a parallel to African-Americans, Asian-Americans, or even Italian-Americans, yet *Latinoamericanos* in Spanish or Latin Americans are terms most often used by people in Latin America and the United States to refer to people born and living in Latin America. Furthermore, many people living in the Americas consider themselves Americans since they consider America the correct geographical name for the hemisphere that is not just the United States or North America, but also Central America and South America. In Mexico people are taught in school that geographically speaking Mexico is part of North America. The name of the North American Free Trade Agreement (NAFTA) also framed the area in these terms. For decades people from Latin America trying to identify with people from Latin America have used the words Latino in Spanish or Latin in English.

Mexicans are the largest group in the United States, but important numbers of people from Latin America and the Caribbean have arrived in the United States and shaped what it means to be Latin in their specific communities of destination. Clustering by outsiders, as well as real cultural commonalities, most importantly language, brings people from different Latin American countries together and contributes to the formation of a real pan-ethnic "Latino" identity that before existed only in the imagination of Thomas Jefferson, José de San Martín, Simon Bolivar, and other early proponents of independence from European colonial Empires and pan-Americanism, the union of all of the Americas.

The identification of people living in Latin America, who have never migrated, with a Latin background exists but is rather abstract and mainly works in contrast to other large groups such as Anglos, Saxons, Scandinavians, Africans, Asians, and Arabs (Gobat 2013). Napoleon proposed and pushed for the use of the term *l'Amérique latine* with colonial designs in the area (Phelan 1968). In the adoption of this term, Napoleon succeeded in building a divide between Canada, the United States, and the rest of the countries in the American continent that had officially adopted European languages derived from Latin (Spanish, Portuguese, Italian, and French). Napoleon did this in an overt attempt to curtail the influence of the Monroe Doctrine, and the idea of the "manifest destiny" of the United States in the Americas and the Caribbean. Imperial France also had colonial designs and supposedly cultural claims going back to the Roman Empire expanding from Latium (Lazio, Italy). Since French culture, language, and peoples were colonized and influenced by Latin language and people, the French empire would be a more logical overseer of colonies that had a previous connection to the fellow Mediterranean Latin Spanish and Portuguese Empires. In other accounts, it was revolutionaries who took the term *Latinoamericanos* because they were inspired by the Enlightenment ideas and the French Revolution (Gutiérrez 2016, 34).

The word Hispanic comes from Hispania, which was the name that Romans gave to their cities and colonial territories in the Iberian Peninsula. So, both of the terms Latin and Hispanic are referents to the Roman Empire. Lately, some millennial blogs and videos circulated on social media try to settle and provide proper definitions of Hispanic focusing on the Spanish language and of Latino as relating to Latin America and thus including Brazilians and maybe Portuguese, but things are not that clear-cut.

Latinidad

In a cultural twist, some academics and activists talk about Latinidad as the cultural elements of this ethnic group, thus as the real "stuff" behind the Latin identity. Yet, what practices are encompassed in Latinidad vary depending on the individual and context, so this term does not resolve the ontological issue. Latinidad probably appeared in Chicago in the 1970s to create a political coalition between Mexicans and Puerto Ricans (Gutiérrez 2016).

Latinx

For some, the problem with the Spanish term Latino is that it favors an androcentric (male-centered) approach to name this collective (Vidal-Ortiz and Martínez 2018). There is no denying that LGBTQ and trans individuals of color face multiple simultaneous exclusions. So, there is a debate about whether to write Latino/a/x, Latino@, Latine, Latinex, or LatinX.

Ethnic studies departments were created as a result of student-led social movements within universities, for example, the Third World Liberation Front movement at the University of California, Berkeley in 1968 and 1969. Latinx is equally used as a political act like many of these other terms were used before, but the majority of this population has not caught up on the use of Latinx, and it is yet to be seen what new term catches on beyond social media, activist circles, and college students. Some argue it may become another acceptable option to use, but it will unlikely replace other terms completely.

Some scholars see the use of LatinX as an imposition (Trujillo-Pagán 2018). As Eric Morales writes,

> The term Latinx "does not correspond to Spanish syntax and this will prevent Spanish dominant people from identifying with it, creating a larger schism between recent Latino immigrants and American born Latinos. Additionally, there is something incredibly condescending for an English speaker to tell recent immigrants that Spanish is a gendered and patriarchal language but not to worry, because they can fix it with a term that does not conform to Spanish grammar. On top of that, any interpretation of Spanish as a patriarchal language requires a very superficial reading of the language." (M. de Onís 2017, 82)

Individuals are free to identify as Latinx and use the term, but I think it is premature and a bit forced to use the term for the whole population.

Latin people

As a couple of people have suggested online, I hereby propose the use of the term Latin people. It keeps the references to a series of people related to their current or former use of Spanish and/or Portuguese as Romance languages derived from the Latin language. But unlike the Spanish versions of the word, which attribute gender and number, in English Latin can be used to describe single, plural, and all genders. Therefore, it is not only less sexist and more inclusive than Latino, but it is also within the parameters of common English spellings, characters, and grammar. Furthermore, I use Latin as an adjective and not as a noun. This way, it does not carry a number or gender. This way a person is not "a Latin," but rather "a Latin person" because someone is a person first and Latin second. Latin is used as a modifier rather than as a term denoting an all-encompassing ontology around a nebulous cultural categorization. Past geographical place of residence or family origin should not be used as the most important ontological characteristic of a person or group. There is no reason why origin or ethnicity should be characterized as more primordial than humanity or other traits. Thus, I talk about Latin people or peoples in order to be inclusive of different gender and sexual orientations of individuals as well as differences by physical appearance, disability, age, and national origin. The context makes it clear that we are not talking about the Latin language.

Throughout this text, I will use the term Latin people to refer to Latinos across the United States of which, as discussed earlier, they are mainly citizens or legally in the United States and are often, but not always, of Mexican descent. I use the term Mexican when people were born in Mexico or are of Mexican origin. Sometimes I use Mexican-American to denote the second and later generation immigrants with roots anywhere in Mexico. The context determines which term is most appropriate, yet it is never perfect.

Latin individuals see national and local identities as relevant. Despite these caveats, this constructed pan-ethnicity reflects the views of non-Latin people. If a strong group identity is to form fully, it will be the result of a performative effect of categorizations from artificial census categorizations, and in response to perceived common threats. The Latino category could be strengthened as part of a process of reaction formation (Portes and Rumbaut 2014) against the growing anti-immigrant discourse, and the increase in deportations and racial profiling in the United States. Undocumented Latin immigrants often prefer to keep a low profile to avoid problems, and while seen as model employees, there are instances of collective action, especially in reaction to policies that target Latinos like the proposed Sensenbrenner law that resulted in a record number of participants in the immigrant rights marches of May 1, 2006. Nevertheless, ethnic and pan-ethnic labels and identities are indeed successes in blurring internal boundaries. The terms Hispanic or Latino as used in the United States today do transcend national origins. The term Mexican-American blurs the boundary between Mexican and American. As I argue, processes of inclusion and exclusion happen simultaneously (Castañeda 2018b).

The purpose here is to use labels like Latin people as categories to analyze the views that people who are not part of these groups may have of them given that 1) outsiders often lump them together in a category; 2) in the case of people of Latin American and Caribbean roots, they use the term Latino as a new political identity banner under which different people choose to organize politically in the United States; and 3) Latino, in Spanish, is a term that people born in Latin America use when referring to themselves along with other people from Latin America.

In the rest of the book, I will not use the term Hispanic often since for outsiders it is synonymous with Latino, and many insiders find Hispanic racist or offensive since it appears to underline Spanish racial, cultural, and linguistic roots over Native American ones. At the same time, the use of the term Latino or Latin here does not imply to deny that history or roots but embraces the often *mestizo* identity of mixed racial ancestry that many Latinos have. This is not to say that there is no racism in Latin America (Levitt 2001, Telles 2004) or that the concept of mixed ancestry has not created complications for the integration of Latin people throughout U.S. history (Gómez 2007, Rodriguez 2007).

What Can We Learn from the Existing Literature?

The U.S.-Mexico border was a space of controversy and tension well before the 2016 election. The line separating the two countries has always been politicized. The Border Patrol was born in 1924 (Hernández 2010), and water disputes, cultural exchanges, intermarriage, and the many wars waged against Native Americans in the region preceded it (Dear 2013). In less than thirty years, residents in the region went from being subjects of the Spanish crown to being Mexican citizens, then to Texas citizens, and then U.S. citizens when Texas was annexed by the United States.

Mexico gained independence from Spain in 1824. The first Mexican president, Guadalupe Victoria, oversaw the establishment of a federal system, the opening of international trade, and the encouragement of the migration of people from Europe and the eastern United States into an area of Mexico that later became the current U.S. state of Texas. On March 2, 1836, Anglo-Texan elites declared independence, which lasted until Texas was annexed to the United States in 1845, leading to the Mexican-American War (1846–1848). The 1848 Treaty of Guadalupe Hidalgo ended the Mexican-American War and marked the birth of the border region as such and the growth of twin cities, often next to military posts, along the newly drawn borderline. With the 1853 Gadsden Treaty, Mexico transferred an area including Yuma, Tucson (now Arizona), and Mesilla (now New Mexico) to the United States. In the late 1800s those in charge of surveying the border and building border monuments—white obelisks marking the end of one country and the start of another—suffered many challenges to reflect a line in a map into a rough terrain (Dear 2013).

The borderlands became an open frontier inhabited by those looking for a new life. Few observers in the early 1800s would have imagined that this mountainous desert region would experience a population explosion, yet by 1910 the Mexican border states had 10 percent of Mexico's population, and 7 percent of the U.S. population lived in the U.S. border states of California, Arizona, New Mexico, and Texas. After the Mexican Revolution of 1910, around 10 percent of the Mexican population moved to the United States. After the Great Depression, the United States deported many Mexicans and Mexican-Americans; many of the deportees stayed in the borderlands. This reoccurred with the guest worker Bracero Program (1942–1964) and then the massive deportations through Operation Wetback in the 1960s, and again after the recent recession and a historical number of deportations (Golash-Boza 2015).

In 2000, the six states on the Mexican side of the border had a population of over 22 million, around 16 percent of Mexico's population. The U.S. border states had a population of over 67 million, around 21 percent of the U.S. population. Besides the demographic importance of the border, much international trade continues to pass through the region. In the early 2000s, there were 290 million legal crossings, including 100 million vehicles, and U.S. Customs collected more than $20 billion in fees and duties annually (Dear 2013, 73). Despite the violence, in 2010, trade between Ciudad Juarez and Texas grew by almost 50 percent to more than $71 billion (Dear 2013, 163). Overall U.S.-Mexican trade totaled $400 billion in 2010 and $534 billion in 2014 (Dear 2013, 152).

This trade has increased at the same time that human mobility is increasingly monitored and the border increasingly militarized. In the 1990s, Operation Hold the Line in El Paso, Texas, and Operation Gatekeeper in San Diego County, California, started the heavy policing of the borderline and the building of the fence, using temporary metal landing strips used during the Vietnam War. Besides humanitarian concerns and doubtful effectiveness, Dear (2013) cites fiscal concerns around the fencing and policing of the border.

With more than 20,000 officers, the U.S. Border Patrol has become the fastest growing federal employer (Dear 2013, 108). Although the border is almost 2,000 miles long, over $2 billion has been spent on fencing 700 miles, with costs in some areas of more than $16 million per mile. Additional vehicle barriers cost around $1 million per mile. Maintaining the fence over the next 20 years is estimated to cost $6.5 billion (Dear 2013, 107). The fence was only part of the $12 billion budget of the George W. Bush administration's Secure Border Initiative. A $20.6 million contract given to Boeing to test a virtual border was unsuccessful, yet Boeing secured a $1.1 million contract to build towers with cameras, sensors, and radars (Dear 2013, 117). Furthermore, "in 2008, approximately 442,000 detainees passed through ICE's 32,000 detention beds at the cost of $2.4 billion per year" (Dear 2013, 112). Up to 25 percent of those deported were permanent legal residents, and despite the rhetoric, most of them had no criminal records (Dear 2013, 114–15).

Contrary to what one often hears in the media, towns on the U.S. side of the U.S.-Mexico border are safe, peaceful, bicultural places (Castañeda and Heyman 2012). This is important to remember at a time when so many fears and insecurities are projected onto the border. As Dear writes, "The US–Mexico borderlands are among the most misunderstood places on earth. The communities along the line are far from the centers of political power in each nation's capital" (Dear 2013, 1). They are seen as epicenters in the fight against drug trafficking and undocumented migration, yet these issues come from outside the border. Border communities have experienced a heavy and disproportionate burden to enforce national policies to manage migration and to keep the drug trade underground. The cost of trying to seal the border is enormous, but its efficacy minimal. The burden of the war on drugs has also been placed heavily on Mexico. Furthermore, the violence did not "spill over" into the United States, and it is unlikely it will.

Many politicians use the border as a symbol of separating us and them, Americans and Mexicans, and other individuals from Latin America (Staudt and Spener 1998). This demarcation and othering has material consequences. While many Americans advocate for Latin immigrants, there is still a sizable portion of the electorate who demands walls to be built. Such anti-Mexican rhetoric and legislation in the country affects many Latin peoples (Cervantes-Soon 2014) because anti-Mexicans can rarely differentiate between immigrants and U.S.-born brown Latin individuals. As Jimenez (2010) discusses, the continuous Mexican migration that the United States experienced for many decades meant that Mexicans replenished ethnic cultural practices, including the use of Spanish, but they also help frame Mexicans as eternal outsiders to the American body-politic no matter how many generations they have been in a territory. This then affects others who may look Latin in the eyes of nativists.

Anti-immigrant policies add to this exclusion and prejudice. Anti-immigrant legislation influences Americans' views on Latinos. René Flores analyzes Arizona's SB 1070, a bill which "required police to check the immigration status of those arrested or stopped and made it a crime to transport or harbor unauthorized immigrants" (Flores 2017, 334), looking at 250,000 tweets by Arizona residents. He compares tweets made three months before the passage of the bill and three months afterward and finds that tweets were 37 percent more negative toward Mexicans and Hispanics after the bill was enacted than before. This illustrates how such discriminatory immigration policies impact public discourse surrounding Hispanics and Mexicans in America. The approval of increased use of surveillance and detention of Hispanics in the state relates to the othering and understanding of "American" as "not Mexican."

Effects on the Education of Children and Youth

Latin millennials also reckon with their own identity in finding themselves as part of a race and ethnicity (Flores-González 2017). Latin children navigate many legal and social barriers and challenges in education (Osorio 2018). Latin children's experience with education in the United States also reveals the group's marginalization. The Supreme Court case of *Plyer v. Doe* (1982) looked at a law in Texas passed in 1975 that prohibited undocumented immigrant children from attending public schools throughout the state. In 1977, Plyer, who was the city of Tyler, Texas's superintendent, was forced to follow a school board decision to no longer allow undocumented children to attend the schools due to a fear of having too many immigrants in the town. The Supreme Court ultimately ruled that states cannot bar students from a public education based on their immigration status (Lepore 2018). Although the 1970s Texas law was overturned, Latin and Hispanic children in the United States often struggle with being accepted by their classmates. This is especially the case when the students are undocumented (Gonzales 2011, 2015). Sandra Osorio uses Latino Critical Race Theory to look at how Latino children experience belonging in the United States and found that "even though they were all US citizens, their experiences were complicated by race, citizenship status and language because their parents were undocumented" (Osorio 2018, 101).

Claudia Cervantes-Soon (2014) had the opposite experience as a researcher earning her Ph.D. while commuting every day from her hometown of Ciudad

Juárez, Mexico. She did fieldwork at a school in Juárez and had her identity challenged daily. Many of the students saw her as someone who looked just like them, but they knew she was receiving an advanced degree in the United States. Her privilege of being able to leave the town and work toward a Ph.D. made her different from the children and the other residents of the town. The Mexican students called Cervantes-Soon "la gringa" and she witnessed how she was defined as an outsider entering a marginalized space, despite coming from the same town. Cervantes-Soon's feeling of exclusion due to her dual life in the United States emphasizes how once it is crossed, the border creates symbolic differences between "us and them."

The work of Nilda Flores-González looks at how Latino youth in the United States find where they belong in a country that is often exclusionary. In one study, she and her colleagues interviewed 157 foreign and U.S.-born Latinos aged 14–28. They found that most of the interviewees identified as Latino, Hispanic, or by their national origin. Few identified as black or white. She finds that they "come to construct their identities through their experiences as racial subjects" (Flores-González, Aranda, and Vaquera 2014, 1846). They propose that youth "do race" when they do not feel like they belong to a general group or when their identity is not celebrated.

Flores-González conducted more in-depth interviews with second-, third-, and fourth-generation Latino millenials in Chicago to understand their sense of self (Flores-González 2017). She found that most referred to being Latino as an "ethnorace." They saw their position in the U.S. hierarchy as between blacks and whites; they felt that they were more privileged than black Americans, but far less privileged than whites.

Latinos, especially youth, struggle to feel a sense of belonging in the United States. With state bills allowing for discrimination and profiling of Latinos, which in turn fuel more anti-Hispanic and anti-Latino sentiment, it is not surprising for Latino immigrants and their children to feel unwelcomed. Critical Race Theory helps researchers understand the effects of racialization (Delgado and Stefancic 2017).

American identity often is associated with whiteness, which explains animosity among non-white immigrants entering and living in the country. Lee Bebout (2016) shows how representations of Mexico and Mexicans have been used to construct whiteness. While Critical Whiteness Studies have largely grown in relation to African-American Studies and the black-white binary, in certain times and places whiteness is constructed in relation to Mexicanness. For example, since the early 1980s "cultural workers of the political Right" such as Pat Buchanan have adapted the idea of a Reconquista of Aztlán, as dreamt by Chicano radical activists, as a cornerstone of their anti-immigrant cultural threat polemics.

Celia Lacayo finds that whites, mainly conservative professionals, in Orange County, California, prefer to live in predominantly white neighborhoods and say they would feel uncomfortable living in a mostly Hispanic neighborhood (Lacayo 2016, 8). She writes,

> Thus, Latinos face a unique racialization. Unique in the sense that, unlike Blacks, Latinos are assumed to be "illegal" and, unlike Asians, they are seen as inferior. In other words, white respondents differentiate between minority groups, where they perceive Asians to be smart and successful, unlike Latinos. They attribute this to culture/race not class. (Lacayo 2016, 14)

As Lacayo argues, the category of Latinos includes both immigrants and ethnoracial minorities. This group must

> cope with being perceived as a perpetually foreign "invader," it also must deal with the labels and perceptions that come with being a racial minority, including being perceived as uneducated, criminal, and welfare dependent. This dual racialization is described by whites as unique to Latinos (Flores-González 2010). But more important, whites characterize both Latino immigrants and Latinos in general as inferior, rendering them a racial group regardless of immigrant status and generation. . . . Overall, the sentiments of whites in this sample toward Latinos were not only nativist and negative but also racist. They revealed that whites categorize Latinos as a racial group and clearly render them as nonwhite. Although Latinos are a heterogeneous group with significant differences in class, generation, status, and national origin, whites exhibit racialized attitudes toward Latinos that have a homogenizing effect. (Lacayo 2017, 576)

Despite legal definitions and census categories, Lacayo argues that, at least in California, Latin people are racialized. Other scholars also make this argument (Feagin and Cobas 2015, Armenta 2017, Aranda and Vaquera 2015). Yet, a study finds that individuals ascribed to be Mexicans face more discrimination than others perceived to be white or Latino (Vargas et al. 2016).

Building Walls: Drawing Lines between Peoples

Popular discussions around immigration are fraught with tension, false information, and a lack of consensus. Donald Trump's ascent to the presidency of the United States was in part due to his divisive rhetoric and policy promises on immigration. While his claims to "build a wall" may appear extreme and hateful to many, they are appealing to a large portion of the American electorate. The power of the presidency allows Trump to implement a travel ban barring certain immigrants and refugees from entering the United States (Tilly, Castañeda, Wood 2019).

However, the United States still functions as a democracy. There is a large amount of resistance to Trump's immigration policies by citizens and lawmakers on the national, state, and local level. Yet, there are also anti-immigrant factions throughout the country that do want a concrete border wall to be built along the U.S.-Mexico border.

This book focuses on the relationship between Americans and Latin people, mainly Mexicans; while the focus on Mexican-origin individuals is not ideal this is pertinent since outsiders think of Mexicans and Latin individuals as basically the same. Some Americans see using the term Hispanic or Latino as the politically correct way to refer to a "Mexican," which was historically seen as derogatory (Gutiérrez 2016, 32). The partial assimilation and exclusion of this group have been constant processes. The rhetoric and policies implemented by President Trump are blunt and extreme and have singled-out Mexicans, but they do follow many of the actions taken by previous presidents, including President Barack Obama. It is important that we are aware of how these policies reflect social views toward immigrants and Latin individuals as an ethnoracial minority.

This book focuses on the relationship between Mexicans and Americans for several reasons. First, in terms of immediate geographic boundaries, the United States shares a long border with Mexico and a long history of immigration (Garip 2017). Although Mexican individuals' reasons for leaving Mexico are all unique, there are common reasons that are often ignored, which lately increasingly include escaping violence from the war on drugs, as is the case for Central Americans.

Interviews with migrants talking about poverty, violence, or lack of social mobility in their towns of origin are almost entirely absent from the media and news cycle. Instead, stereotypes portraying Mexican migrants as uneducated, impoverished, unfit, violent, and "bad hombres" dominate American discourse. Yet, these patterns of judgment and prejudice toward Mexican migrants are not unique to American culture. The international system of nation-states has looked to produce homogenous cultures within political boundaries and gives national governments the legal right to determine who does or does not have a right to reside in a country. Yet migrants can become in themselves political actors especially when they organize around social movements fighting their categorical exclusion. As the anthropologist and political theorist Partha Chatterjee (2004, 59–60) explains, when these populations ask for permission to stay, making legal or political claims on the state, they enter the field of the political. Migrants enter the political sphere when seeking legal status.

National identity plays a large role in determining who the government wants, or does not want, in the country. Often states seek to create and support a homogenous population. The "us" versus "them" rhetoric depends on othering a certain group of migrants who are constructed as different than most individuals in a region. The categories created are artificial, but that does not mean they lack significance. Despite the social construction of race and the artificiality of national borders, citizens are often unable to recognize that such "othering" is part of states' apparatuses to produce a national identity and control a population, territory, and resources.

Philosopher and political theorist Hannah Arendt discusses this national push for homogenization throughout her seminal *Origins of Totalitarianism*. She posits:

> The reason why highly developed political communities, such as the ancient city-states or modern nation-states, so often insist on ethnic homogeneity is that they hope to eliminate as far as possible those natural and always present differences and differentiations which by themselves arouse dumb hatred, mistrust, and discrimination because they indicate all too clearly those spheres where men cannot act and change at will. The "alien" is a frightening symbol of the fact of difference as such. (Arendt 1958, 301)

Arendt points to a common phenomenon of fearing those who appear different than the self. Individuals with different skin tones, physical and mental capabilities, accents, clothing, and personalities are often judged before they are accepted. Perhaps, she suggests, we revert to exclusion because we do not want to accept the diversity of the world simply because we cannot control it. Instead, societies often push for homogenization to make them more legible, predictable, and manageable.

Perhaps this fear of difference explains why Trump focuses so much on banning people from Mexico and the Middle East. There could be a desire to maintain a white national identity, which is further proven by the disparaging and racist comments he has made about many people. The focus of this book looks specifically at Mexican migrants because for decades they were the largest group of migrants in the United States, and they arguably receive the most negative attention from immigration discourse and narratives in the United States. Along with other populations with roots in Latin America and the Caribbean, they and their descendants constitute the largest ethnoracial minority in the country, surpassing African-Americans.

This book focuses on several aspects of existing stereotypes and interactions between Mexican migrants, Latin citizens, and other Americans. One of the goals of this project is to allow audiences to understand the viewpoints of the different actors involved in the immigration debates in the United States. The chapters cover a range of topics and perspectives pertaining to the topic of Mexican immigrants in the United States. This book provides opportunities to engage with this topic from different perspectives including discussions with migrants themselves, students interacting with the physical border fence, macro-level analyses, theories on boundary-making, historical precedents, and more.

The overall argument is that boundary formation occurs at three levels, each a part of the book:

1. the abstract level of theory, normative arguments, and categorical thinking;
2. the legal and legislative level, including policy debates, online, and media discussions, and
3. the micro level, as it affects migrants and non-migrants in everyday interactions.

Part I, "Categorical Thinking" includes this introduction and two more chapters. Chapter 2 "Migration and Its Challenges to Political Theory and Nationalism" looks at the theoretical developments of migration and boundaries throughout liberal thought. It traces how liberal theory supports exclusionary policies implemented by the nation-state. Phenomena such as boundary demarcation, migration, alienation, othering, and homogenization will be discussed in order to show how Democratic states face tensions to represent the populations in their territory while also policing boundaries of citizenship and political participation.

Chapter 3, "Boundary Formation: Nationalism, Immigration, and Categorical Inequality between Americans and Mexicans," investigates how and to what extent Mexicans' continued migration into the United States has lessened differences between the two groups. The process of boundary formation is found to exist at three levels: 1) theory and normative arguments; 2) the legal and legislative arena where policy decisions are made, and the popular discourses used to justify exclusionary policies; and 3) the micro in everyday interactions. Ultimately, the chapter discovers that Mexican migrants are still excluded from being considered "American," even if they legally reside here. This chapter makes the theoretical argument for the book as a whole.

Part II, "Anti-Immigrant Speech" shows the extent of anti-immigrant discourses and strategies. Chapter 4, "Border Vigilantes at the University: Anti-immigrant Discourse and Ideological Campaigns," discusses the Minutemen border patrol group speaking at Columbia University and the interruption of their speech by protestors to illustrate a larger ideological struggle in the United States. The student protests show resistance to anti-immigration groups across the country. Tensions between the protestors and the Minutemen at Columbia are connected to events in the 1960s and 1970s. It argues that an anti-immigration policy stance is often also a proxy, a part of the ideological struggle within the United States. Diatribes on the campaign trail against Mexico and undocumented migrants are a whistle blown for nativists, a litmus test for social conservatives, but also a proxy for anxieties around the future of the nation and personal financial insecurities. This chapter documents an early example of conservative figures speaking on a college campus with the hope of facing opposition and creating polemics in the national media.

Chapter 5, "Fronting the White Storm," presents a qualitative analysis of the white nationalist website Stormfront. Researching the website and its members' views provides insight into white nationalists' beliefs. We choose to include many direct quotes from the site in order to allow readers to observe the group's ideology and how white nationalists justify it. It is important to understand the origins of these racist, xenophobic, and anti-Semitic beliefs and acknowledge that they exist.

Chapter 6 also uses qualitative discourse analysis to analyze online comments on news articles pertaining to immigration topics. "Anti-Immigrant Online Comment Sections in the Aftermath of Trump's Election" compares how Western European immigrants' experiences in the United States are drastically different from Mexican immigrants' experiences. The marginalization and isolation that the latter group faces in America are analyzed through the comments on news articles. Racism and xenophobia, paired with disdain for immigrants and welfare recipients, are present throughout these comments. The aim is not to represent the public opinion of the majority of the U.S. population, but rather to show that anonymous online anti-immigrant discourses have attained a new level of xenophobia and increasing calls for the use of violence against undocumented immigrants.

Part III, "Immigration as an Experience," discusses immigration from the point of view of individuals at the border and in New York City to show how on the ground things are different from the scripts about immigrants' actions and to show how different geographic locations in the United States offer different contexts of reception to immigrants. Chapter 7, "Different Understandings of the Border Wall: The Social Meanings of the Wall for Border Residents," features statements from a group of students at the University of Texas, El Paso carrying out group ethnographic research on the U.S.-Mexico border. Because El Paso is located along the border, the students were able to engage with the physical border directly. The chapter shows, in an example of intersectionality, how and why individuals have different social understandings of the border, which is frequently due to people's social position and lived experience. This chapter allows readers to grasp how people who live right next to the U.S.-Mexico border view immigration and Mexican migrants.

Chapter 8, "Fear of Deportation among Mexicans Fleeing Violence," focuses on undocumented Mexican migrants' mental and emotional well-being while living in the United States. Survey and interview data with 35 Mexicans who fled violence in their home cities reveal how the fear of deportation prevented the migrants from reaching out to others in the community and seeking assistance from medical services. Many of the migrants developed mental health problems from the forced isolation. The findings emphasize that despite the Mexican migrants experiencing similar feelings and struggles, they are unable to empathize and support one another for fear of having their undocumented status be made public and lead to deportation. This chapter discusses a hard-to-reach population that receives little attention, Mexicans who are escaping concrete threats were not provided protection by Mexican authorities very rarely received legal asylum in the United States.

Chapter 9, "Invisible New Yorkers: Boundaries, Interethnic Networks, Immigrant Integration, and Social Invisibility," explores how Mexican migrants develop ties with Mexicans and other populations in New York City. Surveys, participant observation, and a decade of fieldwork offer insight on how Mexicans in New York create a home, even if others do not completely accept their belonging. It argues that although these migrant groups exist in large numbers in the city, they are still treated by the media and the majority population as if they do not exist, resulting in what I call "social invisibility."

Chapter 10, "Why Walls Won't Work: Interactions between Latin Immigrants and Americans," describes why building a border wall would be costly and futile, and why real-life interactions between Latin immigrants and settled individuals get sorted out in worksites, public places, and within families as they discover that the similarities between people are larger than the differences.

Quotas, concrete border walls, forced detention, and deportation may lower the actual number of Mexican migrants in America, but these actions will not actually solve existing social issues. Rhetoric fueled by xenophobia and exclusion will continue. The desire for a homogenous society that Hannah Arendt talks about will also remain and possibly increase through anti-immigration policies. Hearing from the perspectives of migrants, their families, allies, and nationalist groups like the Minutemen themselves provides insights that go beyond what the state and media sources normally say about the issue.

Regardless of political party, ideology, or lived experience, all individuals should continue to participate in the conversation surrounding immigration in America. The U.S.-Mexico border is a hotbed of debate and action. Reports of Immigration and Customs Enforcement (ICE) agents separating mothers from their children, former Attorney General Jeff Sessions stating that asylum will no longer be granted to migrants experiencing gang violence or domestic abuse in their home country, and legal citizens being arrested by ICE all happened in one week in mid-June 2018. Americans may have different reactions to reading headlines pertaining to events like these, but regardless, they almost always have something to say. It is important that these conversations happen in a measured way among people who hold drastically different viewpoints on the subject. We need to talk about immigration realities and their challenges and not use views and debates about immigration as proxies for different approaches to taxes, the role of government, or cultural superiority. After reading this book, hopefully, you will be encouraged to share with others new insights that you gathered from your engagement with these pages.

Chapter 2

Migration and Its Challenges to Political Theory and Nationalism

Large-scale social changes took place in the late 1700s among them the American and French revolutions. Not only did these revolutions change the political regimes in those areas, but they were accompanied by radical shifts in the way to think about social organization. They gave rise to liberal regimes, which are understood here as governments that attempted to embody the ideas of the Enlightenment, representative democracy, and enforce negotiated citizens' rights. Consequently, this called into question who qualifies as a citizen. These historical events still shape the way we think today about government, representation, territories, peoples, and sovereignty (Tilly 1992, 1984, Strayer 2016).

French historian Gérard Noiriel (2000) points to the French Revolution and the idea of popular sovereignty as a source of division between "citizens" (members of the nation) and "foreigners" (members of other nations). But what about cultural, ethnic, or religious "foreigners" living within the borders or the nation-state? As Noriel and fellow French scholar Patrick Weil (2005) show, the concept of "the foreigner" has been conceptualized legally in many ways throughout French history. Debates have included how place of birth, civic contracts, marriage, and length of residence affect citizenship. Laws about these issues have changed through time. For example, at one point when a French woman married a foreign man, she would automatically lose her citizenship (Weil 2008, 2005).

This chapter discusses the constraints that the idea of a nation and the international system of states imposes on the admission of immigrants in contemporary democracies. It analyzes the implications that the consolidation of the nation-state and classical liberal political theory have for the treatment of mobile individuals. Theories of political regimes representing supposedly homogenous populations create exclusionary processes. The theory of popular sovereignty, nation-building around the project of the nation-state, has had a "performative" effect in creating the phenomenon of nationalism. As Craig Calhoun (1997, 5) explains, the concept of the "nation" is more prescriptive than descriptive. The idea of the nation is "a way of speaking that shapes our consciousness, but also is problematic enough that it keeps generating more issues and questions, keeps propelling us into further talk, keeps producing debates over how to think about it" (Calhoun 1997, 3). Shaping the world into neat and separate nation-states is a never-ending project.

I will touch briefly on some of the academic literature on nationalism to explain the popular contemporary anti-immigration discourse that I have not only heard in the United States, France, Spain, Switzerland, Germany, and the United Kingdom, but also in Algeria, Morocco, and Mexico. Some people in these countries, despite their local particularities, adopt the same rhetoric about national identity and the need to protect the autochthonous culture from external influences. During my fieldwork in North America and Europe (Castañeda 2018b), I observed how people internalize nationalism and reproduce the nation-state in their everyday interactions by building symbolic walls with foreigners, migrants, expats, and even tourists. While it is hard to disentangle the portions that nationalism owes to 1) new immigration flows, 2) political opportunism, or 3) modern political theory itself, I focus on the theory aspect here.

THE CHANGE THAT WASN'T

Migrants' work and ingenuity lead to economic growth in their host economies (Castañeda 2018a), so why do they face such strong opposition in public discourses? What are the juridical, theoretical, and practical challenges to multiculturalism? Why is it that despite the rise of international discourse in favor of universal human rights, the liberalization of markets, and economic globalization in the last decades we did not see a decrease in national identifications or an opening of borders besides the European Union? How is it that economic and political liberalism approach national borders and migration differently?

The last two decades of the twentieth century saw a rebirth of the belief in free markets, the reduction of tariffs, and an increase of international trade, like what we saw in the nineteenth century. The return of this ideology in the 1980s gained such force and quasi-religious zealotry by the late 1990s that many authors call the dogmatic belief in the power of free markets "market fundamentalism" (Block and Somers 2014, Stiglitz 2003). Subscribers to the neo-liberal ideology asked governments to refrain from intervening with market forces. Industrial and financial capital moves freely through national boundaries but many still clamor to regulate labor mobility.

After the fall of the Berlin Wall in 1989, the demise of the USSR, and China's incremental opening to international trade, President Bill Clinton celebrated "The New Economy." The roaring 1990s saw campaigns around "globalization," sold as an unstoppable and inevitable natural force. The Internet brought with it the potential to connect people all over the world, allowing them to trade goods and ideas faster than before. Thomas Friedman celebrated that people around the world were eating at McDonald's, drinking Pepsi, wearing jeans, and listening to rock 'n roll (Friedman 1999), and naively claimed that "the world is flat" (Friedman 2005). Globalization as an ideology had won and become hegemonic.

Maybe not since the writings of philosopher Immanuel Kant (1724–1804) had the advocates of multilateralism, international law, and a global community had such great influence in policy circles as they did in the 1990s. This decade saw a quick rise in international non-governmental organizations and in the legitimization of multilateral institutions among cosmopolitan elites, middle classes, and the disenfranchised. Yet, despite all the speeches, advertisements, promises, dreams, and utopias about building a Global Village—where the concept of the nation-state would disappear—there are few indications that the different nation-states are ready to give up their sense of autonomy. Some theorists were too quick in predicting the decline of the importance of the nation-state and the convergence of humanity into one economic system and global culture. The nation-states still matter. Our studies are incomplete if we do not include internalized nationalisms into intergroup relations between immigrants and "natives."

While global trade has increased in relation to the interwar and postwar periods, it was probably proportionately higher at the end of the nineteenth century (Chatterjee 2004, 84). Capital and goods move freely across the world, but there is one area where movement has been deliberately controlled: labor migration. With the exceptions of Europeans traveling within the European Union or the Schengen area, most countries still have relatively closed borders. Despite outcries about migration and refugee crises, global migration is lower now than it was in the nineteenth century (Chatterjee 2004, 85).

We should neither assume a teleological approach that claims a natural, historical progression or evolution into a world without borders nor should we take a world organized in clearly delineated nation-states as the only option for the future. Instead of taking for granted the right of a national government to dictate migration and population policies, we should probe these assumptions to understand why national identity and borders have kept their strength. To do this, we must look at the ontology and epistemology of the political, legal, and spatial borders. In doing so, it is helpful to keep a critical distance from the traditional concepts used to study the nation-state. As Bourdieu writes,

> To endeavor to think the state is to take the risk of . . . applying to the state categories of thought produced and guaranteed by the state and hence to [forget that] . . . one of the major powers of the state is to produce and impose (especially through the school system) categories of thought that we spontaneously apply to all things of the social world—including the state itself. (Bourdieu 1998, 35)

It is the state that often defines the terms of debate, determines which are valid political demands, and what are the national problems. What is the national community and who speaks for it? Joining groups and preferring members' of one's own family and tribe is an old phenomenon, but believing in a national community is a relatively recent phenomenon.

The Territory of One People

Migration has occurred for thousands of years because human groups have always naturally tended to move from place to place in search of new resources and better living conditions (Massey 2018). People and ideas move through contiguous spaces, yet with the advent of the nation-state, the nature of these flows has changed. There are many hypotheses for why this is. Max Weber pointed toward the creation of a legal-rational system of centralized power in national bureaucracies; others point toward the new art of governing a population as a task of the rulers. James C. Scott argues that

> the state has always seemed to be the enemy of "people who move around," to put it crudely. . . . Nomads, pastoralists . . . hunter gatherers, Gypsies, vagrants, homeless people, itinerants, runaway slaves, and serfs have always been a thorn in the side of states. Efforts to permanently settle these mobile peoples (sedentarization) seemed to be a perennial state project—perennial, in part, because it so seldom succeeded. . . . These efforts of sedentarization [are] a state's attempt to make society legible, to arrange the population in ways that simplified the classic state functions of taxation, conscription, and prevention of rebellion. Having begun to think in these terms, I began to see legibility as a central problem in statecraft. (Scott 1998, 1)

Wandering people are harder to keep track of, regulate, and tax. In this way, for the state to carry out its basic functions—such as tax collection, contract enforcement, ensuring security, and guaranteeing rights (Castañeda and Schneider 2017)—it needs to organize its population and tie it to particular places.

The state presents itself as the legitimate representative and protector of a "race" or group of people who, through collective myths, claim to have a common origin and to share a culture, language, and practices (Tilly 1996a, 2005, 2002). In national myths, a group aspires to form a nation of homogenous people represented by its own government. Contemporary secessionist and independence movements in Quebec and Catalonia, among others, make these kinds of claims (Tilly, Castañeda, and Wood 2019). But historically, the causation arrow seems to have gone the other way. A warlord would create an area of influence with territorial boundaries delineated through war, conquest, and threats of violence, and then would attempt to administer the territory and engage in the process of nation-building (Castañeda and Schneider 2017). This power of the state in creating the nation is clear:

> In the period of movement from tribute to tax, from direct rule to indirect rule, from subordination to assimilation, Charles Tilly remarks, "states generally worked to homogenize their populations and break down their segmentation by imposing common languages, religions, currencies, and legal systems of trade, transportation and communication." (Tilly 1990, quoted in Scott 1998)

The modern state has a self-serving interest to create the view of one nation and one common origin that must be preserved, including through the use of violence. Nation-states are founded on the idea of the homogenous citizen. The nationals constitute the "us" in opposition to those who reside outside the borders claimed by the nation. The modern nation-state is founded on the claim of a homogenous set of citizens whose duty is to protect their common welfare; this necessarily requires the exclusion of others despite liberalism's claims of universalism and equality (Castañeda and Schneider 2017). As influential German conservative political theorist Carl Schmitt writes,

> Every actual democracy rests on the principle that not only are equals equal but unequals will not be treated equally [citing Aristotle]. Democracy requires, therefore, first homogeneity and second—if need arises—elimination or eradication of heterogeneity. To illustrate this principle [we have] . . . Turkey with its radical expulsion of the Greeks and its reckless Turkish nationalization of the country, and the Australian commonwealth, which restricts unwanted entrants through its immigration laws, and like other dominions only takes emigrants who conform to the notion of a "right type of settler." A democracy demonstrates its political power by knowing how to refuse or keep at bay something foreign and unequal that threatens its homogeneity. (Schmitt 1988, 11)

It is common for liberal presidential and parliamentarian democracies to claim that their legitimacy comes from the sovereignty of the people they represent. This idea assumes a homogenous group of families, who gathered together in a mythical event to sign a social contract to create a nation and a government representing it.

As Bourdieu, Tilly, and Scott discuss, the idea of natural homogeneity is misleading. A closer look through historiography or genealogy muddles the concept of "the French," "the German," "the American," "the Italian," "the Indian," "the Pakistani," "the Turkish," "the Mexican," or any other such categorical grouping, as a particular set of people. These are not primordial identities but relatively recent constructs, which were forged through forced conquest and ideological homogenization directed by the state, starting with national educational institutions (Bourdieu 1998, 1996 [1989], Vaughan 1997). James Scott documents how the state initiated some practices such as

> The creation of permanent last names, the standardization of weights and measures, the establishment of cadastral surveys and population registers, the invention of freehold tenure, the standardization of language and legal discourse, the design of cities, and the organization of transportation seemed comprehensible as attempts at legibility and simplification. In each case, officials took exceptionally complex, illegible, and local social practices, such as land tenure customs or naming customs, and created a standard grid whereby it could be centrally recorded and monitored. (Scott 1998, 2)

Scott argues that this simplification of the natural and social world depended not only on the adoption of the metric system but also

> that other revolutionary political simplification of the modern era: the concept of a uniform, homogenous citizenship. As long as each estate operated within a separate legal sphere, as long as different categories of people were unequal in law, it followed that they might also have unequal rights with respect to measures. The idea of equal citizenship, the abstraction of the "unmarked" citizen, can be traced to the Enlightenment. . . . The Encyclopedists . . . envisioned a series of centralizing and rationalizing reforms that would transform France into a national community where the same codified laws, measures, customs and beliefs would everywhere prevail. It is worth noting that this project promotes the concept of *national* citizenship—a national French perambulating the kingdom and encountering exactly the same fair, equal conditions as the rest of his compatriots. In place of a welter of incommensurable small communities, familiar to their inhabitants but mystifying to outsiders, there would rise a single national society perfectly legible from the center. The proponents of this vision well understood that what was at stake was not merely administrative convenience but also the transformation of a people. . . . The abstract grid of equal citizenship would create a new reality: the French citizen. (Scott 1998, 32)

However, "the French citizen" could only appear at the expense of the Norman, the Breton, and other previous local identities, and in competition with the Anglo, the German, and so on. Nowadays "the French" are defined in contrast to the Arab, the African, and the Asian.

> The aspiration to such uniformity and order alerts us to the fact that modern statecraft is largely a project of internal colonization, often glossed, as it is an imperial rhetoric, as a "civilizing mission." The builders of the modern nation-state do not merely describe, observe, and map; they strive to shape a people and landscape that will fit their techniques of observation. (Scott 1998, 82)

It is important to stress how successful many states have been in this quest. According to Benedict Anderson (2006), through censuses, maps, museums, and the national press, governments have been able to construct national identities that people embrace. In the French case, the abstract promise of national citizenship in the name of universal values translated in practice through the hegemonic expansion of elite Parisian ideas and practices (Bourdieu 1998, Elias 2000 [1939]).

To social scientists, nations are sometimes nothing more than "imagined communities," meaning they are socially constructed by those who feel they are part of them (Anderson 2006). Nonetheless, the idea of open borders is vehemently opposed by many because they dearly hold on to their imagined homogeneity, their everyday practices, categorizations, and common socialization with neighbors and co-nationals. In the same way, national governments are not likely to call into question the idea of citizenship based on belonging to a nation, because this could result in the weakening of their power. People and governments believe in their nation, and an important number of people are ready to defend their collective identity, even with their lives.

It is also important to note that nationalism has its positive side too; it may give people something to believe in, increase altruism and solidarity. It should also be understood in the light of struggles of independence and self-determination in Latin America, Southeast Asia, and Africa (Chatterjee 1986, Lomnitz 2001, Fanon 2007 [1963], Anderson 2006). In these cases, nationalism proved very successful in fighting and culturally counterbalancing imperial powers and it created unique, rich, and vibrant modern non-European cultures.

Liberal political theory and classical historiography point to the rise of the modern nation-state after the American and French revolutions as an embodiment of the Enlightenment's ideas of the Encyclopedists, including Rousseau; and as a victory of popular sovereignty, equality, and democracy à la de Tocqueville. These times saw the rise of the individual as a circumscribed actor for the first time, and popular revolts as the result of a collective embracement of democratic ideas. While the role of these ideas was crucial in the fall of absolutist monarchies, it is still unclear whether these were truly popular general movements or takeovers by the bourgeoisie or maybe the successful manipulation by a few leaders and political entrepreneurs.

Undoubtedly, the ideas of freedom, democracy, and popular well-being are a crucial part of liberal political theory, discourse, ideology, and practice. However, we do not have to take these concepts at face value in our analyses. These values could persist even when decoupled from the national sphere, for example, the universal human rights discourse. However, because these liberal beliefs are held by many and acted upon along ideas of national sovereignty, we should look at the consequences of the prevalence of these concepts and values.

In his lectures from January 1976, Michel Foucault proposed that war is intrinsic in society, although the enemies change. One form of warfare, related to migration, is his theory of racial struggle, which many times results in the splitting of a "race" into many races and sometimes in their aggregation into one. Foucault claims that

> the discourse of race struggle . . . will become the discourse of power itself. It will become the discourse of a centered, centralized, and centralizing power. It will become the discourse of a battle that has to be waged not between races, but by a race that is portrayed as the true race, the race that holds power and is entitled to define the norm, against those who deviate from that norm, against those who pose a threat to the biological heritage. (Foucault 2003, 61)

Foucault (2003) speaks of "biopower" as the state's control over people's bodies to maintain control and order. Race is one of the classifications the state may use in asserting power over certain peoples. There is no scientific truth behind the concept of human race (Castañeda 2018a). The concept of race may appear to be scientific in a social context that has naturalized its use as a demarcation of differences between people. A discourse of racial struggle is likely to evoke strong emotions from racialized minorities and the majority group (Bonilla-Silva 2006); this may be used by opportunistic politicians in times of economic instability.

The Migration "Problem"

Migration presents a problem for states advocating for cultural homogeneity, enclosed sovereignties, and mutually exclusive nationalities. To some, migrants threaten the social fabric, the local traditions, and racial purity, putting the host society at the risk of changing or even disappearing. People believe they must defend their culture from guests, silent invaders, and outsiders. Helmut Schmidt, former German chancellor, declared that Germany should never have employed Turkish guest workers in the 1950s and 1960s because, he said, "Multiculturalism can work only in an authoritarian society" (Bernstein 2004). According to Schmitt, in an authoritarian society there are no pretensions of democracy and therefore no claims of representing the popular sovereignty, so social homogeneity is not required. This argument is often mentioned when discussing Yugoslavia under the dictatorship of Josip Broz Tito, whose death in 1980 may have opened the door for ethnic genocide and religious cleansing. Yet, there are many historical and contemporary examples of peaceful democratic states demonstrating that diversity and multiculturalism is feasible in democratic regimes.

Assimilation versus Multiculturalism

Both cosmopolitan elites and transnational laborers move from one place to another following economic and professional opportunities. The literature on transnationalism refers to a temporal migration that allows for individuals to live in both the host society and at home by keeping strong ties with their society of origin and replicating some of its features in the host society (Levitt 2001, Appadurai 1996, Smith 2006, Sassen 1996). Nonetheless, these ethnic enclaves may seem like immigrant colonies and cause discomfort to the host society, which may frame them as a cultural threat. For example, Germans criticize the existence of Turkish migrants in their midst:

> The Turks in general constitute what is being called a "parallel society." And so the political discourse generally rejects multiculturalism and diversity, emphasizing instead the duty to adopt the leitkultur, to learn German, to accept Germany's Judeo-Christian heritage as well as its Constitution, with its guarantees of equality for women. . . . Many political figures and commentators have been saying that immigrants should accept what the Germans call the leitkultur, the dominant culture, as their own, or they should leave. "We cannot allow foreigners to destroy this common basis," warned Jörg Schönbohm, the interior minister of the state of Brandenburg. (Bernstein 2004)

Similarly, conservative political scientist Samuel Huntington summarizes this polemical argument for the United States:

> The persistent inflow of Hispanic immigrants threatens to divide the United States into two peoples, two cultures, and two languages. Unlike past immigrant groups, Mexicans and other Latinos have not assimilated into mainstream U.S. culture, forming instead their own political and linguistic enclaves—from Los Angeles to Miami—and rejecting the Anglo-Protestant values that built the American dream. The United States ignores this challenge at its peril. (Huntington 2004a)

While Huntington presents a popular view, it is albeit a misinformed one because it dismisses previous immigrant waves, and the ability of people to adapt to a new country. While these critics favor a homogenous society, proponents of multiculturalism argue that racial and cultural diversity is healthy and contributes to the strength of the local society by bringing new and useful ideas, foods, practices, and worldviews that may fecundate and enrich the host society.

The Limits of Transnationalism

Some authors have theorized new forms of sovereignty that go across borders, one of them being migrant transnationalism. The concept of transnationalism does not offer a real alternative to national categorizations. Despite the first impressions from walking the streets of any global city, or the well-meant hopes for the potential benefits that "transnationalism from below" could bring, it is important to highlight the realities and limits of transnationalism for migrants by explicating the mechanisms that produce transnational life. Labor migrants often come from disadvantaged backgrounds, and, for the most part, they can only move up socially by accessing secondary labor markets outside of their community. They do this while keeping an active social life in their former social circle. In a certain variation of "the tragedy of the commons," the paradox of collective transnational life is that temporal migration and remittances can only benefit those engaged in it as long as most others keep the same social relations and economic status at home. But when migration is widespread in a community, this is no longer the case.

Some authors discuss the appearance of a new transnational sphere. A state of limbo is the logical third place that, for example, is neither "American" nor "Mexican." Yet, a truly transnational sphere can only exist if the national spheres involved are otherwise kept separate and different. This is indeed what we see empirically: individuals who can interact with two cultures and political systems, but who can only engage with one at a time. These people often do so by spreading their already limited resources across boundaries. Migrant workers' remittances constitute a major source of foreign currency for their countries of origin, but this does not necessarily mean the remitters are wealthy. Remittances and other aspects of transnational life underline a very interesting feature: people often migrate to improve and preserve their communities of origin (Castañeda 2013a).

It is the opposite for some international students, professionals, and international elites, who may migrate to become embedded in a "preferred" external dominant culture. Nonetheless, the nationalizing processes may either reinforce national identities or allow "internationalization" at the expense of severing many ties with the culture of origin, or by the compartmentalization of life along geographical and temporal locations.

The State of Exception: The Case of Amnesty and Naturalization

To define citizenship as limited to the people born in a country and their descendants precludes foreigners from becoming local citizens. Nonetheless, reality is not as straightforward as the liberal theory. Even if outside of the framework of modern liberal democracies, the cases of people with multiple nationalities, as well as political and economic refugees, are pervasive. There are people migrating either temporarily or permanently and a considerable amount of people becoming citizens in new countries in their lifetime or having children who do. But it is only through legal exceptions that the host state can make these new members citizens of the polity. Therefore, these prerogatives depend on initiatives by the people, the executive, or the promulgation of new laws by the legislative power.

Important policy questions include the following: How should states allocate visas or work permits to foreigners? Which rationales should be used to grant citizenship to people born in other states? When is it right to grant amnesty to migrants? These issues have been dominated by normative constructions that label undocumented migrants as illegal, therefore normalizing birth or blood (*jus sanguinis*) as the only legal ways to become a national citizen (Weil 2008, Brubaker 1992).

Often just by being born in a territory, citizenship is guaranteed by law without the person having to claim or make any conscious confirmation of that nationality at a later age. This allegiance to a certain sovereign state is inherited and not chosen. Only when children of nationals are born abroad can they have various citizenships, and when they reach adulthood, they may choose their nationality. In these rare instances, we see that what is supposed to be natural is not so.

The nation-state sees people who migrate into the country without the mediation of the state as *illegal*. But when these populations ask for permission to stay, making legal or political claims on the state, they enter the field of the political (Chatterjee 2004). Following Foucault's concept of governmentality, we could say that it is in the interest of the state to offer amnesty to some *illegal* migrants in order to bring them inside the law and the state. An administration can do so by guaranteeing local citizenship to foreign "aliens" who follow certain bureaucratic and symbolic processes. A performative act brings them inside the local law and the state. Political theorist Partha Chatterjee explains how refugees, landless people, day laborers, homestead, below the poverty line—are all demographics categories of governmentality. That is the ground on which they define their claims. . . . The categories of governmentality were being invested with the imaginative possibilities of community, including its capacity to invent relations of kinship, to produce a new, even if somewhat hesitant, rhetoric of political claims. . . . These claims are irreducibly political. They could only be made on a political terrain, where the rules may be bent or stretched. (Chatterjee 2004, 59–60)

Therefore, the issue of ethnic citizenship is indeed a political issue and one that can be obtained by making claims on the state. Yet engaging in contentious politics recognizes implicitly the legitimacy of the state and the possibility that the next group will be called illegal until it approaches the state and symbolically promises to abide by the state's laws. These conflicts and victories are only temporary; thus, the struggle continues to get rid of categorical inequality while expanding the process of democratization beyond a narrow idea of who can be a citizen (Castañeda 2018a, Tilly 2007, 1996b, a).

For Italian philosopher Giorgio Agamben, detention centers and concentration camps during times of war are the best examples of the state of exception (albeit one that is increasingly being normalized) (Agamben 2017, 2005). Agamben writes that a crucial characteristic of state sovereignty is to allow itself to rewrite the law or keep the old laws while establishing exceptional cases. By the act of legislation or "naturalization," the state can regain its hegemony and monopoly over the whole population under its territory. This does not mean that the state does not de jure or de facto choose to exercise violence and surveillance over foreigners in its land, but this is a question of policy and strategy.

It is the nation-state, its claims to sovereignty, and its exercise of biopower that proclaims locals and foreigners, and which sometimes is forced to declare *others* as citizens. This is where the word naturalization becomes crucial, since it means that through legal, discursive, cultural, and performative actions like citizenship exams, proclamations, swearing, and pleads, the state can transform aliens and make them "natural," that is, localized, *native*, deserving, worthy, and equal to other citizens.

So, by its assumed sovereign powers, the Democratic Representative State can add citizens to the polity, often after these people make claims on that very state through lobbying, organizing, and participating in social movements. This could be understood as a case of exception, as expansion into new territories, or as internal colonization to govern immigrants who are already living inside the territory. This also occurs in instances of colonialism, for example, the colonized people who were automatically given Roman citizenship, or the case of England and its Commonwealth (Castles and Davidson

2000). Unfortunately, the historical Greek, French, and American democratic regimes only gave citizenship to certain privileged inhabitants of the polity.

By using the excuse of the law to determine who is a citizen and who is not a citizen, the state can penalize certain populations. The policing state and the penal-juridical system define who is inside and outside "the law." How expansive or limited this definition is depends on the ability and wisdom of politicians, as well as on the tolerance of the local people and the legal precedents. Thus, some people call individuals with an irregular immigration status illegal or clandestine, while others focus on their lack of papers and call them undocumented, *sans papiers, sin papeles.*

Europeans seemed to have moved away from the exclusionary national model by reshaping their institutions to create the European Union. While the movement within Europe is rather open, it is also closed to those from outside the European Union through the creation of so-called Fortress Europe. Legal immigration into Europe is discouraged for people from outside European Union member states. Significant migration from Arab countries is bothersome to many people in European societies (Schult 2017). From the moment it was proposed, some local populations saw the idea of the European Union as a threat to local sovereignty and cultures. With the challenge of constructing a new identity that justifies the (white) European project, some politicians often identify "the Muslim" as the other. This affected the prospects for Turkey entering the European Union (Ash 2004).

On the other side, the United Kingdom has been more reluctant to join the European project, shown early on by its rejection of the Euro currency. In 2016 a referendum started the process for the United Kingdom to formally leave the European Union, "the Brexit," which resulted largely from a distancing from open borders especially to immigrants and foreigners.

Country of Immigrants

The United States of America is often described as a country of immigrants, as symbolized by the Statue of Liberty and Ellis Island National Museum of Immigration. There were Spanish-speaking colonizers in the Southwest 75 years before the English landed at Jamestown (Foley 2014, 2–3). Herman Melville, the author of *Moby Dick*, wrote, "Settled by the people of all nations . . . We are not a nation, so much as a world" (Melville 1849). Walt Whitman called the United States "not merely a nation but a teeming nation of nations" (1855, preface). The motto "*E Pluribus Unum,*" out of many, one, talks about this civic union of different peoples in one territory.

But as the Chinese Exclusion Act of 1882, the Japanese internment camps during World War II, Governor Pete Wilson of California, and Samuel Huntington, among many others show, this view is neither uncontested nor agreed upon by all in the United States. Why do people look down on foreigners? Is this because they are racists or is it because they have been brought up to embrace the idea of one people and one nationality to which they belong? While it may be in the interest of the state or a political party to include foreigners under their spheres of influence, the local population may oppose this and see it as a betrayal.

Agamben gives us another possible genealogy for sovereignty, which would be based on the *patria potestas*, the right of the father to dispose of his son's life. Like the case where Brutus, by killing his sons, "'had adopted the Roman people in their place'; it is the same power of death that is now transferred, through the image of adoption, to the entire people" (Agamben 1998, 88). The sovereign becomes the father of the people.

According to this mythology, naturalization and amnesty can be seen then as the adoption of a child (*enfant de la nation* in French) by the motherland (*madre patria* in Spanish) or the fatherland (*patria*), linguistic anthropomorphisms of the political institution observable in many languages. Nevertheless, this legal and moral act could bring issues of competition over the resources and attention of the paternal state for the "legitimate" older sons and daughters.

Another case of opposition faced by legislators or executives trying to bring about amnesty to illegal migrants is the argument that people who previously broke the law are easily forgiven or even rewarded. An additional critique is that since these amnesties are temporary and specific, they discriminate against past or future groups, or against the people who do not fit the criteria of the amnesty but who would also like to be legalized, brought back into the realm of law.

Bernard B. Kerik had to decline his nomination as director of the Department of Homeland Security in 2004 because he had employed an undocumented worker, breaking the very immigration laws he would have had to oversee. Kerik, along with millions of other Americans, consciously hire undocumented workers, which, although a common practice, is at odds with current laws. A change in this legislation would not be possible until local governments and voters accept the benefits they personally obtain from migrant workers, the overall positive effect this group has on the economy and general well-being, as well as recognizing immigrants' entitlement to rights as people.

A solution to provide cheap labor to advanced economies is for labor to move to labor-scarce regions. Another way is for industrial capital to move to places rich with cheap labor. There is a balance between outsourcing versus migration: each one has a different effect on the workers, producers, and consumers in advanced countries. In the case of textile import tariff elimination, this will, in principle, benefit the American consumers and it will change the balance of who produces and where production occurs (*New York Times* 2014).

According to Agamben, the ultimate test of sovereignty is passed when the state can put its citizens to death. Yet can it put foreigners on death row? By bringing a case to the International Court of Justice at The Hague, the Mexican government questioned the legitimacy of "the convictions and sentences of the inmate, José Ernesto Medellín, and 50 other Mexicans under death sentences in nine US states. The court, usually known as the World Court, ruled that all 51 had been deprived of their right under the Vienna Convention on Consular Relations to meet with Mexican government representatives" (Greenhouse 2014). According to liberal political theory on popular sovereignty, as well as international law, in times of peace, the state has the privilege of punishing and killing only its citizens. After losing the case, the U.S. Supreme Court took this case to analyze whether the Texas penal system was overextending its power over the life of civilian non-citizens, specifically undocumented individuals from Latin America. The implications of the case are very important. According to Agamben, the killing of undocumented migrants in U.S. prisons negates the argument of the persons' not belonging to American society.

There is also an argument that when undocumented immigrants commit crimes they are legally recognized by the state. This paradox is discussed in Hannah Arendt's *Origins of Totalitarianism*, in which she wrestles with the mass exodus and migration of persecuted groups and refugees, especially during and after World War II. She discusses that

> the best criterion by which to decide whether someone has been forced outside the pale of the law is to ask if he would benefit by committing a crime. . . . As a criminal even a stateless person will not be treated worse than another criminal, that is, he will be treated like everyone else. . . . The same man who was in jail yesterday because of his mere presence in this world, who had no rights whatever and lived under threat of deportation, or who was dispatched without sentence and without trial to some kind of internment because he had tried to work and make a living, may become almost a full-fledged citizen because of a little theft. (Arendt 1958, 301)

Because the "right to have rights" is dependent on formally belonging to a polity, refugees and migrants who lack designation as citizens are not seen as deserving of rights. Migrants may need to break the law to be recognized by the state in which they reside (Arendt 1958, 296–97). Arendt notes that what is so shameful is "not the loss of specific rights, then, but the loss of a community willing and able to guarantee any rights whatsoever, [which] has been the calamity which has befallen ever-increasing numbers of people" (Arendt 1958, 297). Because it is the state that provides rights, the stateless also become rightless and thus subhuman.

CONCLUSION

As political philosopher Thomas Nail writes, "Political theory has tended to privilege citizens and states over migrants and their circulations" (Nail 2018, 15). Nail notices a few noteworthy exceptions. Marx saw the mobility of labor as critical to the growth of capitalism. Nietzsche saw migrants, himself included, as heroic figures: "'We homeless' migrants are too 'well travelled' and too 'racially mixed' to fall prey to 'the European system of a lot of petty states'" (Nietzsche 1974, 340, cited in Nail 2018, 17–18). He used the German term for homeless, *Heimatlosen,* which literarily means without Fatherlands, without a homeland.

Contrary to some misreading of his work by white nationalists, Nietzsche directly rejects German nationalism:

> The word "German" is constantly being used nowadays, to advocate nationalism and race hatred and to be able to take pleasure in the national scabies of the heart and blood poisoning that now leads the nations of Europe to delimit and barricade themselves against each other as if it were a matter of quarantine. . . . [We] do not feel tempted to participate in the mendacious racial self-admiration and racial indecency that parades in Germany today as a sign of a German way of thinking and that is doubly false and obscene among the people of the "historical sense." We are, in one word—and let this be our word of honor—*good Europeans,* the heirs of Europe, the rich, oversupplied, but also overly obligated heirs of thousands of years of European spirit. As such, we have also outgrown Christianity. (Nietzsche 1974 [1882], 377–78)

In this text from 1882, not only does Nietzsche reject racist German nationalism but he prefers for himself a European identity. Furthermore, by downplaying the European Christian heritage, he goes beyond the primacy of the European and is open to the world, to a cosmopolitan identity. Thus, migrants are truly citizens of the world and carry the promise to overcome nationalism and race wars.

Rousseau, Marx, Nietzsche, and Arendt experienced migration and exile. As Nail writes on Arendt,

"Only with a completely organized humanity," she writes, "could the loss of home and political status become identical with expulsion from humanity altogether" (Arendt 1951, 297). Only when the entire world has been divided into nation-states that define the rights of man as the rights of the citizen, do we see the truly exclusionary nature of nation-states. Political rights exist only when protected by a political community. It is thus with the emergence of stateless migrants, a people who are truly in-between places, without a legal origin or destination, that the universal pretensions of the supposedly "inalienable" human rights show themselves to be false. (Nail 2018, 18–9)

Migration is at odds with political theory. This results from a modern project producing a rigorous categorization of human beings, not into individuals of equal status but into qualified members of a national group and assigned to a land. As Arendt discusses,

The reason why highly developed political communities, such as the ancient city-states or modern nation-states, so often insist on ethnic homogeneity is that they hope to eliminate as far as possible those natural and always present differences and differentiations which by themselves arouse dumb hatred, mistrust, and discrimination because they indicate all too clearly those spheres where men cannot act and change at will. The "alien" is a frightening symbol of the fact of difference as such, of individuality as such, and indicates those realms in which man cannot change and cannot act and in which, therefore, he has a distinct tendency to destroy. (Arendt 1958, 301)

Such a focus on homogenization not only threatens stateless refugees, migrants, and displaced persons, but it also harms the stability of nation-states themselves. This fear of difference that Arendt and other scholars discuss must be analyzed further. The current trend of "othering" those who are not born within the nation-state is part of a long history. The permeability of borders will continue to exist, no matter how much security or how many restrictions are put in place. Therefore, we may be forced to reckon with the actual desirability of nation-states, which in turn raises the question of who is deserving of rights, and who can guarantee these rights.

Nationalism remains strong in real life and public discourses. Academic research is often plagued by methodological nationalism, because even attempts to transcend the logic of the national may be forced to start by using nation-states as the units of analysis (Wimmer and Glick Schiller 2002). In the next chapters, we will engage in implicit parallel comparisons of normative liberal theory and processes of "boundary formation" in practices and narrative accounts that reify and reinforce existing nationalisms and exclusion of Latin people in the historical and contemporary United States.

Chapter 3

Boundary Formation

Nationalism, Immigration, and Categorical Inequality between Americans and Mexicans

Is large migration from Mexico into the United States diminishing the distinctions between Mexicans and Americans or is it reproducing and magnifying cultural differences? What are the mechanisms that reaffirm or erase these exclusive national categorizations? I argue that boundary formation occurs at three levels: 1) the level of theory and normative arguments; 2) the legal and legislative level, including policy debates and discussion in the public sphere; and 3) the micro level, as it affects migrants and non-migrants in everyday interactions. There are feedback loops between these three levels so a change in one area affects the others. This chapter explores the process that serves to keep Mexican immigrants outside of the category of "the American," most significantly through the creation and use of the label of "illegal immigrant."

Geographic borderlands are spaces where distinct political bodies and identities lie next to one another. Historically, borderlands have tended to be places full of cultural and commercial exchange, frequent crossings, and hybridization—where new understandings are continuously constructed (Anzaldúa 1987, Brubaker et al. 2006). Borders are not natural; they are historically contingent, a product of previous wars, political claims, and power relations (Eyal 2006, Calhoun 1997, Sassen 2006, Tilly 1984). For example, the borders between the former 13 English colonies and Mexico were greatly redrawn in 1845 (Texas Annexation), 1848 (Guadalupe-Hidalgo Treaty), and 1853 (Gadsden Purchase) (Gómez 2007).

Cultural exchanges between members belonging to different groups do not occur exclusively in the borderlands. Migration, work, international education, and tourism all bring different people into contact. In these encounters, groups redefine themselves in relation to each other, creating the opportunity for the fading or reinforcement of previously existing categories. In addition to challenging immigrants to adapt to a new environment, migration may cause locals to contrast themselves with the recently arrived groups. Boundary-making categorizations are contingent, historically grounded, and socially constructed (Brubaker 2004, Ignatiev 1996). The challenge is to discover just how this social construction occurs (Tilly 1998c).

One way to study nationalism is from a top-down perspective, by giving priority to laws, policies, wars, and international relations. Another is through a bottom-up perspective, emphasizing the mechanisms that reinforce and reproduce categorical conceptions of otherness. Highlighting the similarities and differences ascribed to a group defined as "Other" may allow people to reinforce their own group identity, including their own cultural practices and self-understandings. Interactions between members of different categorical groups may have possible implications for group identity, policymaking, and the construction of new social theories and normative views.

This chapter sketches how nationalistic views arise in the interactions between people from different origins and the discourse that surrounds these interactions. It discusses boundary formation between social groups and the reproduction of political borders through actions that re-create differences among people living in the same spaces, as well as the continuous work of governments, social groups, and individuals to reinforce the differences between Mexicans and Americans. This chapter discusses implications and ends with a general framework of analysis for the contradictory demands around migration policies.

SYMBOLIC AND SOCIAL BOUNDARIES

Boundaries provide a general theory to explain the continued reification of nationalism and categorical inequality produced by group differentiations. Michèle Lamont and Virág Molnár define symbolic boundaries as "conceptual distinctions made by social actors to categorize objects, people, practices, and even time and space" (2002, 168). Group boundaries result from a process of relational identifications and feedback loops. For example, group X defines itself in relation to group Y. This is likely to cause a response from group Y, which could, in turn, further affect group X's self-conception. This process repeats itself continuously. Boundary work refers to the practices reinforcing the belief that group X is naturally different from group Y. This often results in moral distinctions and differences on how they view the world that reproduce these divisions and turns them into durable inequalities (Tilly 1998b, Castañeda 2018a).

Different mechanisms guarantee that X remains different from Y (Thorne 1993, Roy 1994, Massey 2007). According to sociologist Andreas Wimmer,

A boundary displays both a categorical and a social or behavioral dimension. The former refers to acts of social classification and collective representation; the latter to everyday networks of relationships that result from individual acts of connecting and distancing. On the individual level, the categorical and the behavioral aspects appear as two cognitive schemes. One divides the social world into social groups—into "us" and "them"—and the other offers scripts of action—how to relate to individuals classified as "us" and "them" under given circumstances. Only when the two schemes coincide, when ways of seeing the world correspond to ways of acting in the world, shall I speak of a social boundary. (Wimmer 2008, 975)

Wimmer (2008) uses the concept of boundaries to study ethnic groups in multicultural societies. Boundary work reinforces perceived differences, even those seen as natural. Racialization is a subset of boundary-making (Massey 2007, 146). We see this boundary work in the United States used to maintain differences between blacks and whites. Similarly, as we will discuss further, many historical and contemporary processes create social boundaries between Mexicans and Americans.

Boundaries, Ties, and Identities

Boundary work is necessary to maintain separation between groups. Below is a heuristic diagram explaining basic boundary processes:

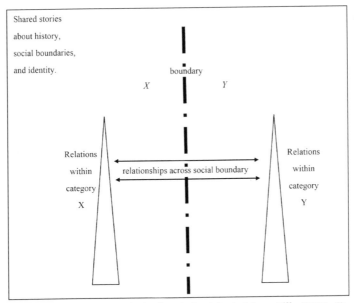

Figure 3.1.   Social boundaries heuristic. Adapted from Tilly (2005, 8).

As seen in the diagram (Tilly 2005), we have two groups, group X and group Y. A "shared story" (national myths, official history, stereotypes, and "common sense") presents X as naturally different from Y. The boundary between X and Y reinforces this distinction. Boundary work is necessary to maintain this separation as members of group X and Y interact. Furthermore, the differences between X and Y are underlined and assigned more importance than the differences that are likely to exist within individual members in each group. For example, in the United States, slaves and slave owners were in continuous contact, yet behavioral patterns ensured that social distance and thus categorical inequalities embodied by certain groups were maintained over time (Tilly 1998b). The slaves who worked inside the master's mansion had a higher social status than those working on the plantations. Those working inside could have been of lighter skin or offspring of the masters, yet they were not considered fully white. In a similar way, not all white Americans were in the economic position to own slaves. In summary, more boundary work is employed in establishing the difference between group X and group Y, for example, slaves and slave owners, while slowing the creation of possible alternative identities such as landowners and non-landowners, rich and poor, etc.

Once a certain social boundary is legislated and institutionalized, there is a feedback loop where learned attitudes and predispositions shape perceptions and interactions that affect the distribution of resources. This resource allocation, in turn, creates a self-fulfilling prophecy where underserved groups receive fewer material resources, which appears to justify the negative conceptions that others have of them. Thus, symbolic boundaries become social boundaries with material consequences (Lamont and Molnár 2002).

A compatible theory, the Stereotype Content Model (SCM), "posits that stereotypes reflect the perceiver's knowledge of power relations in society" (Lee and Fiske 2006, 755). If a disadvantaged group is seen as unworthy, this may result in further exclusion and subordination. The SCM proposes the categorization of social groups based on two variables: warmth (likeability or the ability to produce empathy) and competence (the degree to which a group is seen as intelligent, deserving, and worthy). A two-by-two table of these characteristics produces four categories: the esteemed in-group (high in warmth and competence), the envied out-group (high in competence, but low in warmth), the pitied out-group (low in competence but high in warmth), and the despised out-group (perceived as low in both warmth and competence). Surveys indicate that homeless people and undocumented migrants are seen as despised out-groups (Lee and Fiske 2006). Undocumented Mexican immigrants, as a categorical group, are seen as potentially dangerous, stealing jobs, and deserving of the worst pay and working conditions. This view shows their low position in society, the relative little power, and reinforces it.

Illegality is produced by immigration laws but it is perpetuated by social perceptions and stereotypes that conflate low class, Mexican or Latin American national origin, perceived criminality, and limited English proficiency with "social illegality" regardless of actual documentation (Flores and Schachter 2018).

The Use of Illegality

Besides openly racist discourse, the American/Mexican boundary has been constructed through the twentieth-century category of the "illegal immigrant." Undocumented immigrants have been scapegoated for many social problems including rising public budgets, economic crises, declining wages, and the dissemination of diseases (Kraut 1995). As Tilly reminds us, "The act of giving credit or (especially) assigning blame draws us-them boundaries: We are the worthy people, they the unworthy" (Tilly 2008). Once these beliefs are internalized, it is difficult to erase them and humanize "the Other."

Material interests can foster boundary-making that results in exploitation, social closure, and opportunity hoarding (Tilly 1998b), the accumulation of resources by a small group. Categorical inequality between Americans and Mexicans has served to create a "better underclass" of disposable labor that lacks civil and political rights (Massey 2007, 113–57). While Mexican-Americans have lived in America since 1848 (Gómez 2007, 13), in recent years Mexicans have been disenfranchised by a number of legal actions and the stigmatized label of "illegal" that accompanies unsanctioned immigration and that is often applied to citizens of Latin American origin (Flores and Schachter 2018). While fulfilling a demand in the United States' contingent workforce, many migrant workers are simultaneously denied access to community resources and are considered pariahs by the greater community (Verea 2008).

U.S. laws regarding immigration have changed greatly throughout the decades. For many centuries, having sufficient funds for the travel was the main requirement to immigrate to the United States. The federal government's first attempt to control immigration, due to the racist perception that the Chinese threatened the social order, was the Chinese Exclusion Act of 1882, which reads,

> Whereas in the opinion of the Government of the United States the coming of Chinese laborers to this country endangers the good order of certain localities within the territory thereof: Be it enacted by the Senate and House of Representatives of the United States of America in Congress assembled, That . . . the coming of Chinese laborers to the United States be . . . suspended; and during such suspension it shall not be lawful for any Chinese laborer to come, or having so come after the expiration of said ninety days to remain within the United States. (CEA 1882)

We can see boundary work in the repeated use of the categories "the United States" and "Chinese laborers," and in the call to end any Chinese immigration and asking for the departure of those already in the United States, who otherwise would be deported or worse (Ngai 2004).

To avoid the same denigration, the Japanese government signed the Gentlemen's Agreement with the United States in 1907 promising to curtail emigration from Japan. The West was still sparsely populated by Europeans, which meant that the agricultural, mining, and railroad construction labor previously done by Chinese and Japanese in the West had to be done by another group. Employers in these industries looked south for a convenient form of temporal labor.

As George Hinman reported in his 1926 "Report of the Commission on International and Interracial Factors in the Problem of Mexicans in the United States,"

> Two years ago California came before this committee [of the U.S. House of Representatives] and stated herself in opposition to Chinese and Japanese immigrants and in favor of Chinese and Japanese exclusion; stated that they wanted to develop a great big white state in California, a white man's country; and now you come before us and want unlimited Mexican immigration. I cannot see the consistency. (Hinman 1926, 24)

In contrast to New Mexico—which was kept as a U.S. territory for a while partly because it had a majority population of Mexicans and Native Americans (Gómez 2007)—California became a federal state soon after the U.S.-Mexico war because after the gold rush it had a Euro-American majority population. Even though California was a Mexican state before 1848, Mexican laborers were imported from farther south as workers without any political rights, and thus could be easily repatriated.

Between 1892 and 1954, Ellis Island served as one of the dominant entryways into the United States. It is now celebrated as a *lieu de memoire* with a museum in place of what used to be an immigrant processing center, a hospital, and a detention center for those under quarantine or about to be deported. Immigrants who were deemed "unworthy" (often following eugenic conceptions) were sent back to their countries of origin on the boats they came in—though with an alleged rejection rate of less than 2 percent (Daniels 2004). Despite humiliating medical revisions and quarantines, most Europeans reaching the United States were granted admittance. While many immigrants often decided to return to their countries of origin, there is a false but common narrative today that says that immigrants who came in previous waves came here to stay and broke ties with their hometowns. In contrast, Mexicans—who only immigrated in noticeable numbers in the last

100 years—have been viewed more as seasonal workers than as welcomed settlers, and they have always faced the threat of deportation (Daniels 2004).

Unlike European immigrants, Mexican immigrants entered the United States through a land border as opposed to the sea, meaning that some passed through immigrant control stations and others did not. In the last two decades, crossing has become increasingly difficult (Massey 2007). After the militarization and surveillance of large portions of the borderlands, the threat of death has increased drastically in the last 10 years with over 500 people dying annually while trying to cross the U.S.-Mexico border (Castañeda 2007, 58; De León 2015, 35–36).

Undocumented migrants live in a state of continuous fear (see Chapter 8). The clandestine labels they are given delay assimilation, reduce their commitments to their host society, and put them in an ambivalent position that facilitates a hesitation in their decision to choose their permanent residence. This uncertain status figuratively keeps them closer to home since their stay in the United States is contingent upon the changing enforcement of immigration laws. This uncertainty is one of the main reasons for the strengthening of transnational life (Castañeda 2013a).

Mexican workers are sometimes labeled as "illegal" because many do not pass through designated customs posts and therefore lack government documents authorizing their presence in the United States. While this has been the case for decades, there was de facto amnesty because deportation and the imposition of fines for people who employed undocumented immigrants were not implemented for years. Nonetheless, defining these workers as "illegal aliens" has its own advantages, as it allows further labor exploitation by employers since the workers are dependent on their employers and have less legal recourse than citizens.

The practice of informal seasonal migration gave Mexican laborers the flexibility to avoid paperwork and visa queues. They were also able to leave and rejoin family members and social networks at their own schedule and in tandem with upticks of U.S. labor demand. The tightening of the borders has since reduced temporal migration and increased labor availability in the United States (Massey, Durand, and Malone 2002), an important change from previous seasonal migration (transhumance) that was mainly tied to seasonal agriculture and only later transformed into longer stays, as the border closed and as workers moved into service and construction sectors and stayed in the United States for longer periods of time without visiting their families, resulting in prolonged separations between parents and children (Castañeda and Buck 2014, 2011).

A conceptualization of migration as "economic," "temporal," or "illegal" allows migrants to escape the attacks accusing them of treason and betrayal of their homeland by non-migrating co-nationals. At the same time, their treatment as "illegal" and the accompanying victimization portrayed in the media creates feelings of empathy among the co-nationals staying at home. To some academics, the many ordeals migrants must endure crossing the border, river, or sea also transforms these undocumented immigrants into heroes who defy the nation-state and its repressive apparatus. However, at the end of the day, the continued labeling of many Mexicans in the United States as "illegal" solidifies the social boundaries between Mexicans and Americans. This is further fueled by nativist discourse which conceals xenophobia by arguing for the use of the term "illegal" while saying that they are only "asking for the law to be respected," going to the point of supporting armed border vigilantes (see Chapter 4).

Another unintended consequence of labeling some immigrants as "illegal" is that one can de facto live and work in the United States without having to be de jure part of the nation, thus leaving the door open for the "myth of return" (Castañeda, Morales, and Ochoa 2014), which allows immigrants to differentiate between their national identity and their place of employment. For example, I have interviewed dozens of Mexican migrants in California and New York and found that most workers see themselves as Mexicans working abroad. They feel part of the Mexican political community and think that, therefore, they should be allowed to participate in Mexican elections and affairs. Although, after years they also see themselves as New Yorkers (see Chapter 9).

National Boundaries

Writings about the distinctions between Mexico and the United States have a long lineage. Influential Mexican writers such as Carlos Fuentes, Octavio Paz, and Adolfo Aguilar Zinser have written about the differences between the two countries: British colonies versus Spanish ones, Caucasian versus Indigenous, Protestant versus Catholic, Industriousness versus Sloth, Democracy versus Dictatorship, Industrialization versus Backwardness. These many exaggerated contrasts, stereotypes, and caricatures have become mental categories feeding into symbolic boundaries.

There are cultural differences between Mexicans and Americans, but it is important to look at specific ways in which migration reactivates these categories and solidifies national self-identifications. Instead of taking these national categorizations as stable social constructions or widely agreed-upon "imagined communities" (Anderson 2006), one should instead analyze how the experiences of migration and cohabitation are changing these self-identifications, what many theorists call "identity" (Brubaker 2004, Chapter 2).

What are the mechanisms that reaffirm these exclusive national categorizations? Is massive migration from Mexico into certain areas of the United States diluting the distinctions between these two groups, or is it reproducing and magnifying cultural differences, national myths, and traditions? These questions ask how categorizations become conceptualized over time in the public discourse and will undoubtedly play a major role in the future self-understanding of both Mexican and American citizens.

Among others, Samuel Huntington (2004b) discussed the effects that Mexican immigration could have on "American Identity." Analysts remain attached to the idea of "the Mexican" and "the American" and have, for the most part, refused to acknowledge, understand, and much less value the daily culture of millions of Mexican-Americans and other Latin people. The acknowledgment of the successes, particularities, and contributions of this group would aid in bridging the boundary between Mexicans and Americans. Unfortunately, most pundits and conservative politicians do not recognize Mexicans as one of the *traditional* stocks of the current American populace along with the English, Dutch, Germans, Swedes, Polish, Irish, Italians, etc.

Ethnographic studies show how local cultural understandings change with transnational migration (Smith 2006). Emigration has also changed the "Mexican character" in Mexico (Fitzgerald 2009). During most of the twentieth century, the Mexican government, official history, foreign policy, and national self-conceptions denied the migrant experience of many of their co-nationals. Stories of migration did not form part of the national collective consciousness until the PRI (Partido Revolucionario Institucional) lost the presidency in 2000 after decades in power. The government of Vicente Fox (Partido Acción Nacional [PAN]) recognized the reality and importance of the Mexican diaspora and put migration issues at the forefront of the bilateral relationship with the United States. A new understanding of this reality has had important implications on how Mexico views itself and its relationship with the United States, as well as how consulates interact with Mexicans living in the United States (Delano 2018).

I will now briefly discuss the three levels in which the exclusion of Mexicans and Latin people in the United States takes place.

Boundary-Making at the Relational Level

For Mexican temporal labor migrants, nationalism and collective self-conceptions both play an important role. In fact, when migrants explain their migration experience, they typically express a strong desire to return home someday (Sayad 2004). These individuals emphasize that they came to the United States for economic reasons, not because they preferred "American culture." The lack of opportunities at home catalyzed their migration, even though they might also prefer to live in the United States and wish to follow the American dream.

Although many Mexicans who recently arrived in the United States may report wanting to return home after saving money, Mexican workers continue to immigrate to the United States. These workers often mention that it is difficult to adapt to life in the United States and they long for their homeland. In the first years, their ability to communicate in English is limited. They are often segregated from their host communities in geographic, cultural, economic, and political terms. This concentration leads to a reproduction of some cultural practices they engaged in at home in ethnic enclaves and the creation of a thriving market for nostalgic Mexican products and brands (Portes and Manning 1986, Akhtar 1999a).

Many Americans feel threatened by these ethnic enclaves and displays that they view as "Otherness." Because of this, they oppose Mexican influx into the country, fearing the *Hispanization* of America, the United States becoming more like Latin American. This folk theory has a few spokespeople in academia (Huntington 2004b). Some Americans say that the unlimited growth of a group with a different language, religion, genome, etc. will change who they themselves are. We can observe the same discourse in Europe. Immigrants do contribute to the host culture, and established residents have to negotiate while interacting with newcomers (Jiménez 2017b), but this does not change historical trends, forms of government, or power relations.

In contrast to political refugees escaping state persecution (Akhtar 1999b), many labor migrants wish to return home, and their hosts want them to leave, yet, many times, these migrants end up staying permanently. Why does immigration continue to occur despite these contradictory feelings? It is often posed that the "migration problem" would be solved if people stayed on their ascribed side of the border. But this is just a reification of national borders and a homogenous national society, a pernicious postulate to avoid (Tilly 1984).

Stereotyping a Labor Force

Some pundits claim that Mexicans do not assimilate completely into American culture due to their devotion toward their home culture. Dating back to 1926, George Hinman stated in an official report,

> One can hardly avoid the conclusion that the Mexicans in the United States appear to the majority of Americans a peculiarly unassimilable element, purposely avoiding cultural assimilation, and concerned merely for their own economic advantage, though this is probably due to the fact that they are not considered by Americans generally except as an attractive labor supply, and have on the other hand a rather unique idealism toward their native land. (Hinman 1926, 20)

During this time, Americans considered Mexicans mainly as laborers, and Mexican agricultural workers primarily interacted with one another and their employers. This purely economic relationship did little to improve mutual understanding. Misconceptions persisted despite these interactions in labor markets like agriculture. As that report noted, pre-migration prejudice prevailed after migration: "Mexico knows America by its whiskey and divorce; America knows Mexico by its filth and ignorance" (Hinman 1926, 20).

The Department of Industrial Relations conducted a series of surveys related to Mexican labor. The results were published in the report of the Mexican Fact-Finding Committee of 1930 to Governor Young of California. It states, "Of the 312 firms which employed Mexican and non-Mexican labor, 216 commented upon their [Mexican workers'] relative desirability. One hundred and nineteen firms said in effect that the Mexicans were satisfactory laborers and are fitted for the work at which employed" (Fact-Finding Committee 1930). The following are a few typical comments made by the firm representatives:

"All Mexicans kept steady are good workers."
"Desirable and efficient in our estimation as relating to our type of work."
"We have found Mexican labor entirely satisfactory. We find that they are as efficient as any other nationality in the capacities in which they are employed."
"Not quarrelsome or 'agitating.'" (Fact-Finding Committee 1930)

These opinions show the employers' satisfaction with their Mexican workers, but they depend on generalizations and stereotyping. Other opinions denote an openly negative view of Mexican workers,

"Mexican labor satisfactory when placed in occupations fitted for. They apparently fit well on jobs not requiring any great degree of mentality, and they do not object to dirt. In certain parts of our plant, particularly the dirtier jobs, Mexican are the only kind of labor that we have found in the west that will stay with us."
"In general laundry work they are more reliable, but not as efficient. We seldom hire them in important positions, such as distributing or heads of departments."
"Slow to learn, but more dependable. Mexican women work harder than Americans because more necessitous. Their work is also cleaner."
"They are slow to learn, but become efficient and thorough."
"Lazy, ignorant, not dependable-not wanted." (Fact-Finding Committee 1930)

In addition, Hinman's survey results from "Report of the Commission on International and Interracial Factors in the Problem of Mexicans in the United States" (1926, 166) bring forth several categorical characterizations:

Advantages of Mexicans as farmhands:	Objections to Mexicans as farmhands:
Dependable, steady, and reliable	Lazy
Good workers and willing to work	Dirty
Move off when not needed	Slow
Cheaper	Unreliable
Less trouble	Limited intelligence
Board and house themselves	Thieving
Experienced	Untrustworthy and tricky
Tractable and cheerful	Dishonest
Easily satisfied	Require herding, driving, and constant
Will follow instructions	watching
Can stand heat	
Require less watching	
Will do work by contract	

Again, we see conflicting images of Mexicans. The pros and the cons contradict each other, yet the employers seem fine with this cognitive dissonance that frames Mexicans as both hard workers and as generally lazy. In the objections, we found the employers thought Mexican laborers lacked intelligence and work ethic. Some employer comments show their cynicism and aim at exploitation: "easily satisfied," "can stand the heat," "cheaper," and "move off when not needed," which partly explains the extended use of Mexican laborers in the Southwest.

As we have seen, many employers had very bad opinions of Mexicans despite the great profits they obtained from their work. However, while not all these American employers made racist remarks, we cannot deny that some openly made racist statements toward Mexicans. Phrases such as "those dirty Mexicans" and the denigrating term greasers were frequently used (Hinman 1926, 20). With American employers' use of the terms like wetback and illegal, Latino migrant workers are imagined as the antithesis of their values and become de facto racialized as different from the employer.

The quotes from these early reports show the opinion of Californian employers regarding Mexican labor in the early twentieth century. Some of these workers remained in the United States, became citizens, and had American children. Mexican-Americans suffered from categorical inequality and had lower access to political representation as concluded in the report of the California State Advisory Committee to the United States Commission on Civil Rights of 1971:

While it is not a generally accepted public belief that the Mexican-American community is victimized by racist attitudes to the degree that other minorities are, the Committee found that racism has been a major factor in denying the Mexican-American access to our political and governmental institution in California today. (California Commission on Civil Rights 1971, 14)

While Mexican-Americans are not as openly disenfranchised as African-Americans, they still lack appropriate representation and full inclusion into the United States, despite legally being part of the country since at least 1848. For example, in 1985, Border Patrol agents profiled Mexican immigrants near a schoolyard in San Diego. Border Patrol Chief Gene Smithburg claimed that "a new type of crime is being perpetrated by undocumented aliens: extorting lunch money from school-children" (Eisenstadt and Thorup 1994, 2). This absurd charge can only be understood in the context of the criminalization against undocumented migrants.

Mexican immigrants have faced racism especially in periods of economic insecurity, as demonstrated through California's Proposition 187 in 1994, spearheaded by Governor Pete Wilson, which denied access to emergency care for undocumented migrants. Brenda Payton explains how "Wilson, who had the lowest rating of any governor in the history of poll-taking, was able to reverse the slide and win reelection by blaming illegal immigrants for the state's multiple and complex economic problems" (Payton 1997, 214). After Wilson attacked Mexican immigrants, the public found a scapegoat for the economic depression; his popularity went up, and he was reelected.

Wilson's election neither ended the demographic change toward a majority-minority state nor curtailed the existence of undocumented workers in the labor force. Inequalities between migrants, residents, and employers are not only rooted in history and codified in immigration laws, but are also reinforced in everyday interactions. In a chapter on *jornaleros* (day laborers), Kevin Beck and I offer examples of how social boundary-making works in hiring practices, worker-employer relationships, the allocation of community resources, and the built environment (Castañeda and Beck 2018). Through ethnographic work, we outline the intersections between migration and labor regimes, racial stratification systems, spatial dynamics, and stigmatization. Seeing *jornaleros* as "illegal" facilitates and rationalizes their exploitation. Immigrant day laborers are employed only under the *worst* working conditions for the *lowest* salaries in the local labor market (Castañeda and Beck 2018).

The stigma of being "illegal" marginalizes *jornaleros* in the communities where they work (De Genova 2004). For those holding negative stereotypes about immigrants, being "illegal" implies more than an unauthorized immigration status; it suggests a propensity toward criminality, a lack of skill, and being unworthy of sympathy (Lee and Fiske 2006). The category of the "illegal" has become commonplace and it brings stigma and shame to those to whom it is applied. The continuous drawing of these social boundaries marks migrants as outsiders and facilitates their exploitation (Holmes 2013, Tilly 1998b).

Being "illegal" refers to a particular type of vulnerable participation in the informal workforce (Alberti 2014). It is not simply the willingness to perform jobs that natives are unwilling to take, but also an explicit willingness to live while being dominated by employers and larger socio-spatial power structures (Nevins 2010, Thompson 2010). Migrants do not work as equal participants. Rather, they submit to working conditions imposed by legislators, employers, and established residents.

The imposed illegality on *jornaleros* is a symptom of larger historical processes. Migrant labor has benefited the United States both economically by externalizing the costs of labor reproduction to migrant-sending countries (Burawoy 1976), and in the process of defining American citizenship by contrast between newcomers and established descendants of immigrants. Stigmatizing migrants is part and parcel of the construction of national citizenship. Following the end of slavery and Asian exclusion acts, Latino workers have become "subjects" against which American citizenship and identity are redefined (Ngai 2004). The process of defining citizenship is a political one, and so, too, is the process of defining "legality" (Zolberg 2006). Indeed, local forms of boundary work are founded on "restrictionist" legislation. Whereas the 1920s quota laws were used to determine who was allowed in, today's laws such as Arizona's Senate Bill 1070 also favor profiling and deportation by defining who is visibly alien within the United States.

The category of the "illegal" has been used as a justification for discriminatory and exploitive practices that are otherwise prohibited by law. Identifying people as illegal allows employers to break verbal work agreements. Implicit in the word illegal is the idea that the people should not participate in local communities beyond their role as workers, thus normalizing a separation between labor participation and civic participation. As deportation becomes a routine mechanism to enforce political borders (Hernandez 2010, Golash-Boza 2015), illegality serves as an instrument of attrition that dissuades undocumented migrants from asserting their rights.

Boundary-Making at the Theoretical Level

Why do some Mexicans continue to work and live inside the United States despite the presence of strong national and cultural allegiances from both groups? Implied in this question are the mutually exclusive categories of "Mexican" and "American." These are national memberships that actors, politicians, media, and social scientists use, reifying them as representing homogenous or cohesive groups (Brubaker 2004, 16, 58). When examining boundary-making, one must include the previous concepts and debates set forth by experts and social scientists, including issues of citizenship, membership, exclusion, and the persistence of collective categories. These concepts deal with the legal, theoretical, and embodied conception of "nationalism."

As modern nation-states, the United States and Mexico have clearly demarcated borders, as well as different official languages, national histories, governments, and collective self-understandings. Legally, membership into modern nation-states is based on the concept of citizenship—a legalistic way to define membership in a political community that sets the normative framework for the practice and application of laws and policies regarding formal political participation and the distribution of welfare services (Rosenberg 2006). Citizenship is a central concept for political systems since it defines who is represented and protected by the government. Thus, citizenship is tied to reciprocal rights and obligations. Citizenship is historically specific and has worked in varied ways through time. In classic Greece, citizenship was reserved to city residents who had similar cultural and class standing as those in the elite, while the Roman Empire gave citizenship to all living inside its empire despite linguistic, class, and religious differences (Castles and Davidson 2000). The notion of who is defined as a citizen results from political acts (decrees, amnesties, and legislative changes) occurring within a historical context, and larger economic and political regimes.

According to social theorist Craig Calhoun (1997, 30), there are three main views of nationalism from a theoretical perspective: primordialist, instrumentalist, and constructionist.

Primordialists tend to assume a logical correspondence between nationality, common ancestry, and common cultural practices. Immigration and ethnic minorities question the assumed correlation between cultural homogeneity and citizenship.

Instrumentalists conceive the modern nation-state and its deriving membership as social artifacts constructed by skillful leaders and political figures whose national legacies have been maintained for generations, for example, the Founding Fathers in the United States, Bismarck in Germany, or Cavour in Italy.

Constructionists debunk conceptions of nationality, citizenship, and identity by explaining them as social constructions. While this contributes to social science, the historical understanding of the formation of present categories by academics does not do away with their effects or their allure for large parts of a population. Social analysis must still account for the appeal of nationalism.

Yet, in the long run, academic understandings may affect popular perception. Following Bourdieu and paralleling Michel Callon, Brubaker (2004) suggests that by providing categorizations, labels, and frameworks for others to use, social scientists create a *performative effect* on the society they study by shaping understandings, which, within a representative democracy, may shape public debates and policies. Therefore, social scientists' conceptualizations can be included as part of an "interest group" in democratic politics. Studies that start and stop at political boundaries are examples of methodological nationalism, and they serve to reify nationalism (Wimmer and Glick Schiller 2002). Thus, studies limited to one given nation-state (e.g., race in America) are methodologically nationalistic. Tilly (1984) warns us to avoid theories and research methods that assume that there are autonomous, homogenous societies separated by clear territorial and moral boundaries. The world's communities are far too interconnected to use national borders as containing independent units of analysis (Babones 2014).

The Permanence of the Nation-State despite Globalization

Besides the *constructionist* and *instrumentalist* critiques of the concept of the nation-state, a different critique arose during the 1990s when a neo-Kantian belief in international law, universal human rights, and multilateral institutions peaked. This coincided with the height of the discourse about "globalization," the "new economy," and the "global village." Bill Clinton's tenure in Washington, D.C. embraced Robert Keohane and Joseph Nye's concepts of "global governance" and "soft power" following the fall of the USSR in what Fukuyama called "the end of history." Keohane and Nye believed in "complex interdependence," which is "a situation among a number of countries in which multiple channels of contact connect societies" (Keohane and Nye 1987). We see Clinton's support for globalization and neoliberalism in treaties like the North American Free Trade Agreement (NAFTA). But the belief in an imminent cosmopolitanism declined with the responses and interpretations that the Bush administration made after September 11, 2001. Additionally, the promises of shared economic wealth by proponents of neoliberal international trade have not only failed to materialize, but have created unemployment, cuts in social problems and growing inequality, and the economic crisis of 2008.

The signing of NAFTA did not result in one "North American identity." Despite Huntington's fears of the Hispanization of the United States and its potential impacts, Hispanic cultural influence is not bound to overtake the entirety of American popular culture. Furthermore, Hispanics or Latinos are not a cohesive group. National origin and immigrant generation matter in degrees and feelings of assimilation (Loza, Castañeda, and Diedrich 2016; Castañeda, Morales, and Ochoa 2014).

The idea of open borders is far from materializing, due to the fact that many populations still hold dear their real and imagined homogeneity, everyday practices, and a common socialization and culture. In the same way, governments are not likely to call into question the idea of national citizenship, as this would immediately result in a decrease in their own legitimacy and a weakening of state power. People believe in their nation-state, and some are ready to defend it with their lives. Historical descriptions of the social construction of the nation-state constitute interesting social and historical analysis, but they do not explain or do away with the resilience of nationalism. Global governance is far from becoming a reality, and the benefits of cosmopolitanism are largely enjoyed only by the elites (Calhoun 2003, 2007). Economic globalization has not led to the overall demise of the nation-state. As discussed in the previous chapter, according to liberal political theory and historical legacies, each nation-state claims jurisdiction over a certain fraction of the world's population, which subscribes to, benefits from, and is invested in the belief of a national community.

Despite alluring theoretical claims about the diminishing power of the nation-state, national identities and citizenship are still relevant. Even majorities of many countries in the European Union, the most integrationist region in the world, were reluctant to vote in favor of a European Constitution. Brexit (Britain's 2016 vote to leave the European Union) exemplifies this reluctance to give up claims about national sovereignty, control over economic forces, and a national identity.

Boundary-Making at the Policy and Rhetorical Levels

The Politics of Migration

What drives migration is as much political as it is economic. Labor migration may be caused by economic reasons, but such flows are more than simple economic transactions between workers and employers in a liberalized labor market. International migration becomes politicized since it has implications for the modern welfare state regarding membership, and cultural and civil self-understandings. Concepts such as "international migration" or "immigration policies" can only make complete sense in a world made up of mutually exclusive nation-states.

Migration is a political event at both the national and personal levels since it touches on issues of membership, resource distribution, categorizations, boundary-making, and self-identification. Though it is greatly driven by economic, cultural, and social forces, immigration is deeply political in how host and sending nation-states address, portray, study, and perceive it. Migration policy has to do with the political and ideological constructions of the nation-state, and the way in which representative democracies solve contradictory demands from different economic and civil sectors. These national constructions are embedded in legal documents and history books, and they are also embodied in the taste and language of national subjects (Bourdieu 1984 [1979], 1994, 1998, 1991).

The framing of migration as a bi-national relationship has deep political implications. This is another example of the performative effects that theories and analyses have on thought and practice. Thus, public intellectuals and the media put forward knowledge claims about the state that influence the ways students, policy makers, and the public think about migration. The framing of migration may lead to the personal and national redefinitions of self-understanding, which may, in turn, create further demands for policies to cease, ease, or leave international labor arrangements as they are (Hollifield 2000, 146).

Changes in immigration studies show how scientific framing also has political implications. For decades, sociologists studied the assimilation of new immigrants into the United States with the ideal "melting pot" as referent. But after the civil rights movement, multiculturalism became preferred over assimilationism. Defendants of the multicultural thesis were respectful and conducive to the creation of ethnic self-identifications.

In early debates about multiculturalism, some pointed to the benefits of cultural exchange and cross-fertilization, while "nativists" and "primordialists" preferred independence and isolationism. Turning multiculturalism and rights-based liberalism on its head, conservative activists such as Ward Connelly used the language of non-discrimination to write a proposition against affirmative action and another that prohibited the state of California from gathering categorical racial or ethnic information. Now, nationalists are using the language of collective identity to defend the American way and attack affirmative action as an anti-white discriminatory practice, especially in the newly reinvigorated open discourse on white nationalism following Trump's election.

Contradictory Demands and Strange Bedfellows

If the policy demands were unidirectional, and the state's commitment to them complete, one could imagine a case where illegal migration would be driven close to zero, despite large territorial and maritime borders. For example, East Germany and the USSR were, to a large extent, successful in controlling the mobility of citizens and non-citizens alike among and within their borders. Totalitarian governments like that of North Korea are necessary if the explicit goal is to limit migration. Minorities already living in a country pose a greater challenge. Totalitarian regimes such as in Nazi Germany, Guatemala, Yugoslavia, and Rwanda have dealt with demonized groups through eugenic and genocidal campaigns. Despite these negative precedents, one could imagine a country using and justifying aggressive deportation campaigns to repatriate illegal aliens to their countries of birth.

Massive deportations of whole categorical groups are an exception in liberal states. One hypothesis is that this occurs because these states are Democratic, do not constantly surveil their populations, and are ideologically in support of tolerance, privacy, and free movement. However, recent developments in the United States and France point to a de-democratization of liberal regimes (Tilly 2007). In France, President Nicolas Sarkozy assigned quotas to public servants to deport 25,000 people before the end of 2007. Between January 2009 and December 2015, Barack Obama's administration deported over 2,749,854 people and returned over 2 million individuals, the majority of whom are of Mexican and Latin American descent (Golash-Boza 2015). The official definition of immigrant "removals" show a circular reasoning in their justification:

> Removals are the compulsory and confirmed movement of an inadmissible or deportable alien out of the United States based on an order of removal. An alien who is removed has administrative or criminal consequences placed on subsequent reentry owing to the fact of the removal. Returns are the confirmed movement of an inadmissible or deportable alien out of the United States not based on an order of removal. (DHS 2016, Table 39)

Another claim is that, by their very nature, democracies and parliamentary systems face multiple complex demands from different interests. Therefore, strict monolithic policies like the one mentioned above are increasingly difficult to maintain. According to James Hollifield (1992) and Christian Joppke (1998), the more open a political system is, the more probable it is that its leaders will discuss migration as an issue and indeed receive "unwanted migration" because "rights-based liberalism" has undermined effective immigration controls (Joppke 1998). If this is true, a tighter immigration control would go hand in hand with the deterioration of civil liberties and rights for citizens and foreigners alike.

Pro-Migration and Anti-Migration Dialectics

The Bracero program was a guest worker program that recruited workers in Mexico to work in the United States. While workers were initially reluctant, through the years the program became part of the life of certain Mexican towns and the recruitment became easier and self-propelled. After decades, some guest workers decided to stay in the United States and bring their families. Something similar happened with guest worker programs in Europe following World War II. A Swiss writer famously reflected, "We asked for workers and they sent us humans" (cited in Hollifield 2000, 149). Policy makers focused on increasing the labor force, yet the workers were whole humans with families and culture. So, employers like immigrants because they grow businesses and the economy but some dislike immigrants because of their foreign culture.

On the pro-immigration side, we find many immigrants themselves, some recently naturalized citizens from the same places of origin, and immigrant rights groups interceding in the name of human rights and peaceful cohabitation. Some studies have shown that in the United States, there is a direct correlation between higher education and tolerance for immigrants; the more educated the person, the more pro-immigration he or she will tend to be (Mayda 2004). Wealthier individuals also tend to be more cosmopolitan. Other pro-immigration interests are specific to certain industries: big agrobusiness, construction, restaurants and hospitality, multi-nationals, universities, hospitals, and high-tech companies, and any industry that benefits from employing foreign workers. Economic dynamics and labor trends move skilled workers to highly paid positions, which in turn increases the demand for low-skilled, low-educated, flexible, and cheap labor to perform basic functions in service industries. This happens without requiring expenses legally owed to citizens by the welfare state, or employer-sponsored compensations for workforce reduction, paid vacations, health insurance, and retirement funds.

Immigrants bring economic benefits to the host economy by accepting lower wages or by meeting a demand for high technical skills. They also increase profits for the businesses they work in and reduce prices for the local consumers. This produces an overall positive effect on the host economy (Chavez 2001). By allowing businesses in practice to hire undocumented workers under worse conditions than under which they could hire citizens, the state provides an indirect subsidy to these businesses in a manner that goes beyond the scope of free trade agreements and the World Trade Organization fair trade laws.

Undocumented migrants are flexible workers detached from the protection of labor laws. They fit nicely into a post-Fordist flexible economy where cheap labor in and from other countries continues to be a driving force for the expansion of capitalism (Heyman 2018). Nonetheless, employers have no interest in recognizing this fact because they profit from it; they lobby to keep cheap labor available only when the supply is largely threatened.

Policies versus Results

Hollifield (2000) makes a distinction between *policy outputs*—ceremonies, speeches, or bills—and *policy outcomes*—the effect that these policies and their implementation have on actual demographic changes. In this model, the production of satisfactory-appearing anti-immigrant policies obtains a functional character when combined with a partial implementation that guarantees a steady immigrant inflow. Decrying immigration without real systemic solutions represents a form of compromise, since it presents anti-immigration legislation and discourses, while simultaneously providing cheap, docile labor to entrepreneurs and employers, as well as money for migrants to remit home. This makes it difficult, costly, and counterproductive to change and implement policies drastically, which is another case of invested interests and reproduction of the status quo.

Nonetheless, incremental policy changes can build up once the precedent has been established. For example, Operation Hold the Line, which policed the borderline in El Paso, TX, and Operation Gatekeeper, which constructed a fence/wall between San Diego and Tijuana. Both have been expanded year by year (see Chapter 7). Similar projects in other U.S.-Mexico border states were in place prior to George W. Bush's approval of the construction of a wall along most of the U.S.-Mexico border. This is a symbolic and physical manifestation of boundary-making. Unsurprisingly, the Mexican public felt deeply offended by this project, and it has thus hardened the social boundary between Americans and Mexicans. This sentiment has only been exponentially revived and publicly broadcasted since Trump's 2016 presidential campaign and his continuous call to "build the wall."

In this way, symbolic boundaries are physically materialized. Nevertheless, what started as a limited bill to fence cities while displaying a policy output has not stopped the unwanted outcome of irregular migrants (Nevins 2010). By increasing the difficulty for immigrants to cross into the United

States through border cities, a higher percentage of immigrants tend to cross through more desolate desert areas, which, in turn, creates a demand for Congress to approve bills and assign budgets to extend the construction of the fence on the U.S.-Mexico border.

Consequences

Not surprisingly, many Mexicans with and without proper documentation who live and work in the United States feel attacked and unwelcomed in their place of residence, which reinforces Mexican/American boundaries and makes the integration of new migrants harder. Yet, the new category of Latino in media discourse represents a hope for integration into American society that stands in strong contrast to the simultaneous discourse against illegal migration. It is not uncommon to have parallel processes of inclusion and exclusion, for example, the "Latin" category, which opens a mode of incorporation in American society, and the "illegal immigrant" discourse, which closes it.

It is important to remember that there are many boundary-blurring mechanisms, such as intermarriage. Yet, this chapter has concentrated on boundary-making mechanisms. In order to know if we are facing a social boundary, we would have to answer in the affirmative to most of the following questions in our Boundary-Making Test:

- Is there a name, label, or word to designate this group of people?
- Is there a behavioral script to treat these people?
- Is there a clear boundary between groups?
- Is there a popular story or negative stereotype about these people?
- Is there a popular history of differences and conflicts?
- Are there real socio-economic differences resulting from belonging to this categorical group?
- Do we see low levels of intermarriage, education, and upward mobility?
- Do these processes lead to durable inequality through the institutionalization of opportunity hoarding and exploitation (Tilly 1998b)?
- Do we see the construction of an underclass?

When thinking about undocumented Mexicans in the United States today, the answer is affirmative for most of these questions. Thus, we can speak of a social boundary between Mexicans and Americans that results in categorical inequality and health disparities.

CONCLUSION

International borders are an intrinsic subject of wars, national interests, and international diplomatic relations (see figure 3.2). Migration policy deals with sealing and opening borders and the intermingling of non-citizens. Thus, migration policies should also be a major topic for those studying international relations. But as Hollifield (2000) points out, "Migration is the product and expression of a historical relation of international domination, at once material and symbolic," Immigration is a "'relation from state to state' but one that is 'denied as such in everyday reality'" (Sayad 1991, 267, quoted in Bourdieu and Wacquant 2000). In this form, states tend to forget the multinational dimension of migration and deal with it as a "domestic" issue using the locally available laws and institutions (Bourdieu 2000).

The perception of a "foreign civil invasion" or of "barbarians at the gate" may drive some to demand action from their government. In contrast, those who Tilly (1998a) calls political entrepreneurs may create or reinforce a boundary in order to gain salience and profit from the support of one group at the expense of another. Politicians, incumbents facing challenges, or challengers looking for issues to embrace (such as Le Pen in France or Wilson in California); ideologues; and provocateurs rallying against migration create anti-immigrant rhetoric. As a result, the government is pushed to react to popular demand and to limit illegal migration, enforce the official language, monitor tax payments, maintain minimum wage laws, etc. If the policy outputs are insufficient to reach the desired outcome, then nationalist civil groups may organize direct action such as civil arrests, intimidation acts, or patrolling border areas. These policies, discourses, and actions may produce, in a dialectical manner, a pro-immigration reaction, restarting the cycle.

Migration is, in the end, a political phenomenon. The policy outputs and outcomes respond to complex coalition formations. The state is the ultimate actor determining citizenship since it can include new members in its polity or keep it bounded through declarative acts of exception (Agamben 1998). The way in which these inclusions or exclusions get framed will have profound implications for new categorizations, group self-understandings, and for the weakening or strengthening of group boundaries with specific consequences for cohabitation, exploitation, and inequality.

The inclusion of Mexican migrants into the public discourse within Mexico in political speeches, media, popular culture, and bi-national meetings is enlarging what it means to be Mexican. This recognition was institutionally

Chapter 3

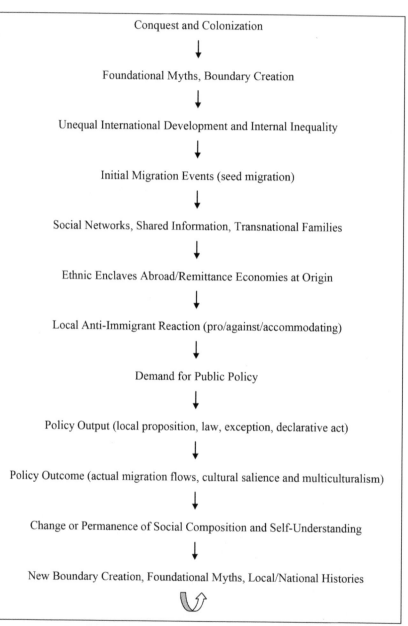

Figure 3.2.   Cycles of nation building and boundary-making. Created by the author.

locked in with the recent grant of voting rights to Mexicans living abroad for the Mexican presidential elections as well as the local elections in certain states. Even though the first attempts at creating a system of voting from abroad has had a plethora of problems, it has established a precedent for the future. Mexico must expand its conception of society to include the many Mexicans living abroad as well as the many immigrants arriving in Mexico from Guatemala, El Salvador, Argentina, Colombia, Venezuela, Lebanon, Israel, the United States, Korea, China, etc. Politicians and public figures in the United States can continue the current immigration debates and ensure future confrontations, like those seen in France, or avoid them by realizing its mythical self-image as a land of immigrants, democracy, and freedom. The political leaders on either side of the boundary are the ones who must decide between two challenging choices: a country can either try to keep its self-conception and population composition the same and risk confrontations while also forgoing economic growth, or adopt the only self-image that solves the liberal conundrum we have discussed—the idea of a nation of immigrants that believes in freedom and democracy while respecting the differences among its population.

Part II

ANTI-IMMIGRANT SPEECH

Chapter 4

Border Vigilantes at the University

Anti-immigrant Discourse
and Ideological Campaigns

In 2006 I attended a talk at Columbia University by the Minutemen, a group that boasted about patrolling the U.S.-Mexican border. A group of undergraduate students interrupted this talk. This chapter explains the implications of this event for the present immigration debate. It shows how immigration debates are largely about U.S. politics and have antecedents from the 1960s and 70s. The Minutemen and similar groups are part of the ideological struggles within the United States that go beyond migration policy. This case is presented as an example of dialectical boundary-making through discourse and political strategy. It argues that often immigrants are scapegoats for existing social problems and are used as proxies by national political parties to advance their own agendas. Nonetheless, militias and self-appointed vigilantes can have deadly consequences for the groups targeted by this exclusionary discourse.

BACKGROUND

Chris Simcox—a former kindergarten teacher at a private school in Brentwood, California—began a group known as the Civil Homeland Defense Group in 2002. James Gilchrist—a retired accountant and Vietnam veteran from Orange County, California—formed the Minuteman Project in October 2004. Both groups staged a border watch in Arizona in April 2005, which received widespread media coverage (Kelly 2005). Later Simcox and Gilchrist parted ways due to personality conflicts. Yet, as Leo Chavez writes, "In the final analysis, the success of Minuteman Project was not in numbers of border crossers found and detained, but in the attention the project received and the disciplining it achieved, that is, the ability to force governmental reaction aligned with its cause" (Chavez 2008b, 27–28). Thus, the incident below is as important, if not more, than their patrolling of the border.

Action

On the evening of Wednesday, October 4, 2006, a Republican student group at Columbia University sponsored a talk by the anti-immigrant organization called the "Minuteman Project." After finding out about the invitation that was extended, various other student groups—among them the Chicano Caucus, a Latin American student group, and an international socialist group—along with independent students came together to demonstrate their moral repudiation of the Minutemen, which they qualified as a group of armed nativists. Even then-President George W. Bush had branded them as "vigilantes" and "a militia." On the day of the event, a large contingent came together in a peaceful and organized protest outside the auditorium where the conference was being held without incident.

Inside the auditorium, the opposing group's original idea was to let the speakers talk, and at the end, challenge the Minutemen with arguments, facts, and civil debate. But the discourse of the first speaker, an African-American, Republican minister, was seen by activists interviewed as lacking logic, excessively offensive, dogmatic, demagogic, incongruent, and presenting inaccurate information as facts. Half of the audience was composed of protestors who showed their disagreement. Protestors became increasingly agitated at the xenophobic and provocative statements. Every pause during the minister's oration was filled with disagreeing commentary from members of the audience. Later, someone began to heckle him, which was followed by applause from the crowd. After this, some students stood up holding small protest signs. Then many in the audience turned their backs on the speaker, who could not convince much of the audience with his statements.

When the Minutemen co-founder Jim Gilchrist took the podium, a group of activists stood up in front of the stage holding a sign that said, in various languages, "No human being is illegal." A few Minutemen and Republican students literally tried to kick them out as they tried to get onto the stage, but the protestors peacefully got on the stage and unfurled the banner. Gilchrist left the stage, and the event ended. I interviewed many of the protestors afterward. They said they acted because they felt the need to express their disapproval of this xenophobic group that further damaged the relationship between immigrants and Americans. They said they refused to listen to the offensive discourse of such an exclusionary and racist organization that claimed to be a group of heroes and patriots.

Reaction

However, as many had anticipated, the Minutemen's main goal for their campus visit was to provoke and to promote themselves by attracting media coverage. They released a tendentiously edited video on Fox News and other outlets depicting the taking of the stage to show how they were victims of the "extreme radical left" and of liberal universities, which, according to Bill O'Reilly, then of Fox News, were "training internal terrorists."

After various media outlets harshly criticized Columbia, Lee Bollinger, the university president, who is a judicial expert in freedom of expression, apologized for the interruption of the talk and said that protestors had curtailed Gilchrist's freedom of expression. In the same way, many centrist student groups took the same position to not appear intolerant. Right-wing groups also used the argument of freedom of expression to problematize the protest, conveniently denying the offensive speech of the Minutemen at the university as well as their actions at the U.S.-Mexico border. As a result, the student protestors' intention to demonstrate "the absurdity of the anti-immigration rhetoric of the Minutemen" and the travails of undocumented immigrants receded into the background.

Since the "taking of the stage," groups from the right and from the left of the political spectrum used this incident to defend their causes. The Minutemen used this contentious event for media exposure and to further their position against Mexican immigration, as well as to condemn those who disagreed with them as uncivil. This incident most likely helped the Minutemen obtain more donations. Additionally, the fact that the protest took place in an Ivy League university served as an opportunity for the right to ridicule liberals and intellectuals as cut off from the working class and rural America and oblivious to their needs (Brooks 2000, Hochschild 2016). Such criticisms are similar to those used against John Kerry and the Democrats during the presidential campaign of 2004 (Frank 2004), and against Hillary Clinton in 2016.

At the same time, many groups joined in defending the rights of immigrants and critiquing the Minutemen to show opposition to Republicans, the war in Iraq, the state of Israel, and capitalism. These causes are only indirectly linked to the needs of undocumented immigrants, who largely observed the protest that took place at Broadway and West 114th Street from their respective restaurant and retail jobs across the street from the university; they later told me that they did what they could to stay clear of the area.

Polarization

Unfortunately, Latin immigrants often are not given the chance to participate in debates in the public sphere (Habermas 1989). Frequently, the people who speak for the migrants are sometimes dominated by their passion in the face of injustice and do not prioritize the demands that the immigrants themselves seek. Despite their good intentions, these allies may strengthen partisanship, the nativists' stereotypes, and their demonization of migrants.

The protest in the street and the dynamic between the different groups inside the auditorium reinforced the images, ideas, and stereotypes that each group had of the other, brightening symbolic boundaries. For example, the nativists complain that the Spanish language is going to replace English. During Gilchrist's time at the podium, a sarcastic Chicano in the audience shouted at him, "In Spanish, please!" Often, Chicanos are framed as violent and criminal; thus, the taking of the stage, justified or not, turned into a self-fulfilling prophecy.

After these kinds of events, the groups from both sides tend to become more extreme. This event did not lead to a rational debate where both opposing parties were able to come to an agreement or a solution (Habermas 1989). It was unlikely that this could occur in an event dominated by groups with such strong ideological stances. As Stanley Fish (2006) argues, this was not an academic event, but a spectacle for an audience beyond the university, the purpose of which was provocation and political positioning.

Anti-immigrant Discourse as a Proxy for Other Problems

In the last years, we have seen an increase in media disputes between American isolationist and pro-immigrant groups. These debates often equate contemporary immigrants with Latin people and most often Mexicans. Other groups of immigrants have been stigmatized and used as scapegoats in the past. The federal government terrorizes Mexican immigrants with occasional raids led by armed officers and militias like they did in the 1920s and '30s. In the nineties California Governor Pete Wilson launched a strong xenophobic campaign with short-term electoral victories. But his anti-Mexican tactics resulted in increased naturalization rates and higher political participation by immigrants and minorites to the point that in 2019, California is a majority Democrat state with good minority representation and a progressive stance towards immigrantion. So, in the long-term the Latin people that were able to remain in California won the political battle. We also have had examples of this scapegoating and pro-immigrant pushback in Arizona (Romero 2011). Targeting immigrants has served as a distraction from national problems. Various U.S. Congressional candidates running in the midterm elections of 2006 approved nativist spots on the radio and television. These xenophobic campaigns appealed to the heightened fear and patriotism after 9/11, adding to the anguish generated by the increased cost of living, with stagnant wages and increased job insecurity. Trump campaigned on these fears, yet the 2018 midterms may have shown the limited appeal of the worn strategy.

Despite paying taxes, working arduously, living decently, and contributing to the economy through their businesses and purchasing power, undocumented immigrants still walk through the streets fearing that at any moment they can be deported and separated from their jobs, family, and friends. Migrants live and work in the United States in part due to circumstances beyond their control, in a system where immigrants are quickly hired but poorly paid. They often have to risk their lives crossing through the desert in order for the government to pretend that the border is controlled (De León 2015). This is the *status quo* where American society benefits from the system while the families of the immigrants suffer daily.

The Minutemen

The term Minutemen refers to a small militia in colonial Massachusetts in the seventeenth and eighteenth centuries, whose members were ready to enter battle in "a minute." American history tends to glorify their role as patriots in the War of Independence. The Minutemen of the twenty-first century are groups of volunteers that patrol the border to stop the "human tsunami" of illegal immigrants who appears to be "over flooding" the United States. The Minutemen demand that the American government implement current immigration laws; at the same time, they demand to take charge of the law and guard the border themselves to prevent more Mexicans from crossing into the United States. They are often armed, yet legally they cannot do anything else but notify the immigration officers when they see migrants crossing the border.

In 2005, the Minutemen asked the federal government to declare a state of emergency on the southern border of the United States, to send the National Guard, and to construct a wall along the border with Mexico to stop undocumented migration. Regardless of these demands being considered extreme at the time, these proposals were publicly echoed by politicians, pundits, authors, and academics such as Pat Buchanan, Lou Dobbs, Ann Coulter, and Samuel Huntington. These individuals influenced the public debate in some sectors of the American electorate and, thus, encouraged enterprising politicians to exploit this fear of immigrants. Even President George W. Bush —who had supported an integral comprehensive immigration reform with paths to citizenship for the undocumented—ceded to the pressure and sent the National Guard to the border. Bush also supported an increased budget for immigration enforcement, the Border Patrol, and the construction of a series of walls and fences along the border.

Jim Gilchrist, one of the founders of the Minuteman Project, has been on tour for years, first in California and Arizona and then across the nation. He makes many public appearances with the supposed objective of "informing" the public about the imminent *Reconquista* of the western territories that were part of Mexico before 1848. The call to reconquer the southwest from Anglos is unrealistic and is only made by a few Chicano activists. Yet, it gives fodder to nativists to anchor their arguments about cultural and military threats (Bebout 2016). Gilchrist boasted in 2016 on his website that he and the Minuteman Project had over 1,000 media appearances in the last 12 months. The leader of these groups ran aggressive media campaigns on the Internet and on television in programs such as Fox News' *The O'Reilly Factor* and CNN's *Lou Dobbs Tonight*. The Minutemen used these platforms to speak passionately against "illegal" immigration and to inflame the public against this fictional threat. As part of their campaign to obtain support and influence public opinion regarding immigration, the Minutemen organized protests in front of Mexican consulates in cities such as New York.

The Minutemen, the Universities, and the 1960s

The Minutemen visited several universities in the United States, even though Gilchrist is not a scholar, has held no elected position, and represents a small organization based in the Southwest. Invitations do not often come from faculty or administrators, but from chapters of the College Republicans and similar student clubs sponsored by national conservative organizations (Binder and Wood 2014).

Maybe to generate publicity, justify his visits to universities, or to appear more academic, Gilchrist co-wrote the book *Minutemen: The Battle to Secure America's Borders,* published in July 2006 by the small, right-wing publishing company World Ahead Publishing. This press publishes titles that openly mock famous Democrats, guide people on how to "take back" America, disparage abortion, and advocate many other conservative themes. Gilchrist did not write this book on his own; the coauthor is Jerome Corsi, who has published various polemic books. Corsi was also the coauthor of *Unfit for Command,* which argued that 2004 Democratic presidential candidate John

Kerry was not fit to become commander in chief given his supposedly questionable actions in a swift boat in Vietnam, and because of his activism against the war after he returned to the United States. The book's publishing was clearly a partisan act linked to a series of television spots that damaged Kerry's campaign and helped George W. Bush's reelection.

After analyzing Gilchrist's and Corsi's biographies, one can see how their concerns go beyond the issue of Mexican migration. As in the biographies of other neoconservatives, their actions relate to ideological debates of the '60s and '70s. Gilchrist and Corsi became active proselytizers of conservative causes after what they saw as the cultural victories of hippies and the left.

Corsi obtained his doctorate in political science at Harvard during the '70s. In 1968, Corsi published a study about African-American military men and their confrontation with the police. In his doctorate thesis, *Prior Restraint, Prior Punishment, and Political Dissent: A Moral and Legal Evaluation* (1972), he criticizes the protests against the war in Vietnam especially by Vietnam Veterans Against the War (VVAW), a group that publicly demonstrated against war. John Kerry joined this group as he returned from Vietnam in 1970, making regular media appearances and testifying to Congress against the war. During Kerry's presidential campaign in 2004, Corsi again framed Kerry's activism as unpatriotic. Corsi published *The Obama Nation: Leftist Politics and the Cult of Personality* in 2008, full with unbacked statements, and *Where's the Birth Certificate? The Case that Barack Obama Is Not Eligible to Be President* in 2011, where Corsi claimed that Obama was not born in the United States.

Gilchrist served in the Vietnam War between 1968 and 1969. He was injured in combat and received a Purple Heart. But like many veterans from Vietnam, after his return, he felt mistreated, demonized, and not appreciated enough for his service. Indeed, most of the Minutemen are Vietnam veterans. In an interview for the *New York Times*, one veteran that now patrols an area of the U.S.-Mexico border describes how despite losing an eye in the war and being awarded a Purple Heart, most of his fellow Americans treated him with animosity after his return and questioned his actions in Vietnam. Now defending his country from invisible enemies who cross the border at night, this veteran, unemployed and living on a pension, signals that his participation as a lone patrolman with the Minutemen has once again given purpose to his life. He feels that the organization provided him with a mission that permitted him to feel patriotic and useful (LeDuff 2006, Shapira 2013b, Cepeda 2013).

The biographies and public statements before Corsi and Gilchrist published their Minutemen book demonstrated animosity toward the social causes supported by the Democratic Party. So, it could be said that they were using immigration to fight a cultural war against the left and to stoke a patriotism that would push for their causes. Like many of the neo-conservatives that led George W. Bush into the presidency, Gilchrist and Corsi sought "revenge" against the liberals of the 1960s and 1970s who had a great influence in popular culture, the media, and the public life for the following decades (Brooks 2000, Frank 2004, Hartman 2019, Robin 2017). Gilchrist and Corsi were not satisfied with Bush's attempts at reverting the social agenda from those years and used the immigration theme to push public opinion and the government farther to the right.

Ideological Currents in the American Universities

During the '60s and the '70s in the United States, progressive groups dominated the public arena in colleges and they confronted the universities' administrations in a symbolic attack against the system as a whole. In 1968 university students in the United States, like many in Paris, Mexico City, and elsewhere, desired social change. Students at Columbia University; the University of California, Berkeley; Kent State University; and others became a symbol of a generational repudiation of Nixon and the Vietnam War. The "Free Speech Movement" began among pacifist groups of students at the University of California, Berkeley that wanted to justify the right to speak against the Vietnam War, and the ongoing discrimination of racial and ethnic minorities. This movement was part of the civil rights movement, and demanded equality for African-Americans, Mexican-Americans, Filipinos, women, and other excluded groups. The movement became institutionalized through the Civil Rights Act of 1964 and strongly influenced American culture. What once was seen as radical turned into a norm, and now it is "the conservatives" who present themselves as radical outsiders willing to challenge the mainstream and the liberal elites (Robin 2017).

Inspired by contemporary conservative university groups, the Minutemen took advantage of the classical liberal ideal of "freedom of expression" to justify presenting their conservative agenda in a privileged way. Like other neo-conservative groups, the Minutemen justify their proselytism in universities and public places using academic, religious, or juridical arguments, depending on the issue and audience. They ridicule dissenting liberals by calling them totalitarians, intolerant, and incongruent, including those who argue that freedom of expression, while fundamental, should be limited when it puts someone in danger or when it instigates violence, exclusion, and hate.

Paradoxically, the Minutemen use old tactics and even phrases from the left to avoid being labeled as "politically incorrect" or racists. As in the case of the Columbia talk, and in some of the YouTube videos of their rallies, the Minutemen systematically gave the microphone to their few African-American members during public talks and press conferences to give an appearance of inclusion and to show that they were not racist because they had members of color, including some Mexican-Americans. This tactic was used to try to show that their actions were not motivated by xenophobia or white nationalism, but by the concern for the rule of law and states' rights.

The Murder of Brisenia Flores

While Minutemen are not legally allowed to shoot immigrants during their patrols, many members have used excessive violence publicly and faced criminal charges. Shawna Forde, 43, was convicted on February 14, 2011, for the first-degree murder of Brisenia Flores, 9, and her father Raul Flores, 29 (Hing 2011, AP 2011). Prosecutors believe Forde besieged the Flores's home in Arivaca, Arizona, because of a suspicion that Raul Flores was a drug smuggler and would have cash in the house. Forde was looking for money to fund her border protection group, Minutemen American Defense (MAD). During the trial, Gina Gonzales, the victims' wife and mother, testified that two men and a woman barged their way into her home claiming to be law enforcement. She also said one man shot her as well as her husband, killing him, while the 9-year-old Brisenia Flores begged not to be hurt. The child was then shot twice. Forde was also convicted of aggravated assault, robbery charges, and attempted first-degree murder for shooting Gina Gonzales. The other two men involved in the murders were Jason Eugene Bush and Albert Robert Gaxiola; both were associated with MAD (Hing 2011).

Forde is linked to many right-wing groups, including the Tea Party, the MAD, and FAIR, an anti-immigration group that assisted in the design of Arizona's controversial SB 1070, which allows police officers to profile and detain individuals "suspected" of illegally being in the United States. Since the 1970s the Arizona border has been a prime place for racist activity. More anti-immigration hate groups are created every year, like Forde's MAD.

In response to the crime, Sheriff Clarence Dupnick of Pima County, Arizona, said, "This was a planned home invasion where the plan was to kill all the people inside this trailer so there would be no witnesses. To just kill a nine-year-old girl because she might be a potential witness to me is just one of the most despicable acts that I have heard of" (Smith 2009). Writing about Shawna Forde's crimes, Chuck Stonex, a member of the Minutemen, said, "This is not what Minutemen do; Minutemen observe, document and report. This is nothing more than a cold-hearted criminal act, and that is all we want to say" (Smith 2009).

Mainstream media did not cover the story and trial until days after it occurred. The media was criticized for the oversight (Belew 2011). Bloggers argued that the reasons for the lack of media attention was that the victims were Latin individuals and the murderer was a conservative activist (Sterling 2011). The Brisenia Flores case is not an isolated event, though, with increasing rates of anti-immigrant crimes showing up across the nation.

Update

The Minutemen were largely a spectacle which got out of control. In 2004 Jim Gilchrist

> emailed a few dozen friends and family suggesting that concerned civilians personally combat illegal immigration by traveling to the Arizona border with him. Gilchrist lives in Orange County, Calif., but the Arizona border was the most heavily trafficked and sparsely patrolled. That email reached thousands of people and touched a nerve. Hundreds showed up in April 2005 to patrol the border. Some of them brought floppy hats, lawn chairs, binoculars and American flags. Others toted guns and protest signs. The group banned neo-Nazis from attending, though some came anyway (Holthouse 2005). A movement was born. Gilchrist estimates he did 4,000 radio and TV interviews over the next five years as his group's membership swelled and the media attention exploded. "It was just literally overwhelming," he said. (Goodwin 2012)

The border patrolling and talks at universities were part of a spectacle to draw members and donors. As Gilchrist himself states,

> That first border event was a dog-and-pony show. It was political activism. I organized it to draw attention to the failure of the government to secure our borders, and it did that in spades. Patrolling the border is only about 5 or 10 percent of what the Minuteman Project is about. The other 90 to 95 is driving this issue up through city councils, mayors, state legislatures, and governors into the halls of Congress to force change. (Thomas 2008, 124)

This goal was largely accomplished with the passing of numerous bills, and the construction of a 344-mile-long fence along the U.S.-Mexico border during the George W. Bush administration. Mitt Romney and later Donald Trump borrowed the idea to wall the border for their presidential campaigns.

Gilchrist says that "it was a popular movement and then it more or less got co-opted by the politicians and it seemed to dissolve throughout the country" (Goodwin 2012), though Gilchrist was part of this trend. He became a member of the Tea Party (Goodwin 2012). Gilchrist still maintains his Minutemen website, and regularly updates it with articles related to the border, immigrant policy issues, and statements by Trump. However, his personal impact has declined since he unsuccessfully ran for Congress in 2005. In 2011, some Minutemen alleged that Gilchrist "was using the group's funds inappropriately" (Thomas 2008, Goodwin 2012).

The Minutemen phenomenon spread beyond Gilchrist's project: "The Minutemen is a name contested by several volunteer groups" (Gaynor 2009, 246). As such it is sometimes difficult to determine the true nature of these groups. What they all do have in common is a certain kind of vigilante Wild West conception of justice. They gather at the border to watch for individuals crossing the border in order to inform the U.S. Border Patrol (Gaynor 2009, Shapira 2013b). Most carry weapons in self-defense, and most are white middle-class individuals, which serves to exacerbate accusations of racism and bigotry against them (Krieger 2008). Other groups separate from the Minuteman Project have adopted the name and taken up the task of defending the border. These include the Minutemen cofounder Chris Simcox's splinter group, the Minuteman Civil Defense Corps; Andy Ramirez's Friends of the Border Patrol; and Jim Chase's California Minutemen (Gaynor 2009).

A number of splinter groups developed around the Minutemen. Yet membership often petered down. The number of Minuteman groups dropped from 115 in 2010 to only 53 in 2011, and Gilchrist claims that these groups range in membership from 1 individual to 20 (Goodwin 2012). There are dozens of websites for various groups throughout the nation, and even a few on the Canadian border, but how active these groups are is a different question. Gilchrist mentions that the economic downturn starting in 2007 took a toll on the movement (Krieger 2008, Goodwin 2012). Simcox's Minuteman Civil Defense Corps disbanded in 2010. In June 2016, he was convicted of child molestation (Hauser 2016).

Xenophobia and Panic Beyond the Border

In the beginning of May 2018, nearly two dozen people came together in Jamul, California, to organize and "report unauthorized entries into the United States." The *Los Angeles Times* reports that many of the members of the group belong to the Minutemen. Tim Donnelly, a leader of the Minutemen and a congressional candidate, was also present at the meeting (Fikes 2018). This occurrence shows that the Minutemen and related groups are not only patrolling the U.S.-Mexico border but still engage in local and national party politics.

In Iowa, a bill was passed on April 10, 2018, that bans sanctuary jurisdictions from being designated in the state (Hatewatch 2018). Sanctuary cities offer undocumented migrants protection from being deported or detained because of their status. Unsurprisingly, "the Minutemen were one of only two groups to register in support of the bill" (Hatewatch 2018). The passage of bills barring sanctuary cities like the one in Iowa reveals that there is still anti-immigrant sentiment throughout the United States. However, the Minutemen group was declining in size and presence (Hatewatch 2018). This may be due to the fact that policies that were once advanced from the fringe by the Minutemen became the official "zero tolerance" policy of the Trump administration.

There are still groups across the country who feel it is their right to maintain security around the U.S.-Mexico border through their own means. While the Minutemen have declined in membership, former members have created their own border patrol groups. Formed in 2011, Arizona Border Recon is a group that was inspired by the Minutemen. The mission of the group on its website reads, "Our focus on obtaining intelligence through reconnaissance operations sets us apart from many other groups. We take on the challenge of locating and documenting the smuggling activities and players within our borders" (AZBR 2016). The group claims to

> take the law very seriously, and to that end we ensure our members are knowledgeable in the applicable areas of law that govern civil rights, use of force, citizens arrest and many more. This ensures our members are acting appropriately, are safe, and provides for the individuals we come into contact with by affording them the same humane and civil treatment. (AZBR 2016)

However, the Forde case above reveals the potential consequences of allowing armed groups who do not want Latin people in the country. While the Minutemen may be declining in number, the relationship between the ongoing immigration policy debates and the social movements from the 1960s and 1970s reminds us that attacks on immigrants often work as proxies to attack the welfare state and political enemies. Nonetheless, this is another way in which immigrants are collateral victims and through which social boundaries between "Mexicans" and "Americans" are perpetuated. Furthermore, the polemic methods of Gilchrist visiting Columbia University to generate media coverage have been replicated by Milo Yiannopoulos and white nationalist Richard B. Spencer. In doing so, their arguments get some legitimation, are covered by naïve journalists wanting to show "both sides of the story," and therefore enter mainstream discussions (Corbett 2018, Miller-Idriss 2017).

Chapter 5

Fronting the White Storm

Dennis West and Ernesto Castañeda

Stormfront.net was founded in 1995 as the first website geared toward people who self-identify as white nationalists (WNs) (Dentice 2018). The anger and anxiety in the white nationalist community is often blamed on the "other" (Hirvonen 2017, 251), including Jews and those who do not have white skin. A popular book for WNs is the 1978 novel *The Turner Diaries,* in which a small group of elites start a global race war (Hawley 2017). The anti-Semitism embedded in modern white nationalism was not part of its origin. As had happened previously, "The Whites instead found that anti-Semitic slogans were much more effective in mobilizing the semi-literate and illiterate masses" (Budnitskii 2012, 174). Thus, an enemy was found and there was something to unify against.

The Southern Poverty Law Center classifies WN forums and organizations as hate groups. Hate groups have a long historical lineage; "ultimately, two historical lines produced the current hate group scene in America: the domestic line of nineteenth-century white Protestant supremacy groups and the influential line of German Nazism in the first part of the twentieth century" (Roy 2002, 115–16). Current WNs and the Alt-Right have roots in these previous exclusionary movements but try to differentiate themselves from the KKK, white supremacists, and white skins, and try to show a modern, professional, sophisticated, anti-racist façade.

Sociologist Arlie Hochschild (2016) writes in her book *Strangers in Their Own Land* that Tea Party members and other conservatives believe in a "deep story" in which minorities and immigrants are cutting ahead of them in the line to the American Dream. In this distorted vision, the government is seen as preferring everyone but whites when providing benefits and support. WNs believe this theory and now argue that this is done at the behest of a Jewish conspiracy to brown America.

METHODS

The material from Stormfront.net was taken without interacting directly with the community. No attempts were made to contact any individual posters and no posts were made in attempts at furthering or inducing communication. All the material used below was obtained through open forums on Stormfront, called specifically the forum archive, "Opposing Views Forum," which is open to non-members as well as members. This portion of the forum was not behind a password or registration wall and was accessible to the public. This information was in the public domain and there was no assumption of privacy. All comments used are from the thread "Testing a strategy to attract white liberals to the cause of White Nationalism—white liberal opinions needed!" Posters were both registered and non-registered members of the Stormfront community. Most posters used a username but were not required to do so. We do not reproduce usernames to provide privacy. The goal is not to analyze or critique what an individual thinks but how rationales for a WN movement arise through these collective discussions. The time frame of these posts ranges from August 21, 2012 to April 21, 2013. This decision to limit the scope of the data to analyze was made based on the overwhelming amount of data available. At the time of this writing over 3,100 posts had been made. The site has been through numerous domain hosts so the data from the forum was downloaded as PDF files in February 2018. PDFs of the first 500 comments were imported into NVivo software for coding and qualitative analysis. Word frequency tests were not conducted because large portions of other posts were frequently quoted and embedded in later posts.

The material was reviewed numerous times before an inductive understanding could be gained from it to elucidate major concepts and tropes. Coding began with many emergent themes. The discussion was centered around justification for being or becoming a WN and the beliefs that they adhere to or demand from their alleged members. While Stormfront is an American-based organization, there were numerous comments from self-identified Europeans and people who mentioned being born or living in Europe.

The iterative process revolved around the common themes and tropes used by the WN members on Stormfront to understand the sentiments put forth by members who believed and agreed with the movement at large. Intragroup arguments were key to the analysis, but obvious trolling was discounted. The term anti is used by the community to identify users or commenters who are against their cause. Obvious "anti" comments were avoided, but all other opinions including ones going against the prevailing consensus were included. No editing of posts for spelling, grammar, or punctuation was done. While it may be possible that some commenters were lying about their beliefs or were not speaking in good faith, their comments were taken at face value. The quotes used below represent ideas commonly expressed in these posts around 10 self-reinforcing themes that appeared from the discussion aimed to create a coherent ideology and a set of arguments to recruit members. This forum explicitly aimed to convince and convert liberals into white nationalists. They use the term liberal in the American sense to refer to Democratic voters, center left, or progressive individuals. Thus, the arguments here are not some of the most racist and derogatory ones found in the forums for those openly identifying as white nationalists talking to other believers. They show the process of identity and racial formations where a few political entrepreneurs are trying to construct a new collective identity with particular economic and political outcomes to guarantee that white people as a category stay on top in Europe and in settler colonial societies like the United States.

Pro-White Ideology

While the ability to trace White lineage through European descent and having white skin are additional qualifiers, the most important thing required for acceptance in the group is getting things "right" on race. A "pro-white" ideology is the most important part of being a WN. As someone writes,

> I find it a little odd that some people consider themselves pro-White, and can speak of Race as being the essential building block of a nation, yet spend so much time disregarding another pro-White view, simply because they've taken a social issue and placed it above the core of Race.

WNs can disagree on social issues and policies as long as they fall in line with the main underlying issue of race. One of the most frequent posters addresses this concern to hopefuls:

> Please note that our people espouse all kinds of economic beliefs. Some of them advocate socialist ideas. We have many members who are passionate believers in closely related national-socialist economic concepts. Even if you thought that money grows on trees, that should not prevent you from becoming a member of WN community in good standing as long as you got the race issue right.

The poster may be wrongly identifying German national socialism with a socialist economic agenda, yet the point is that WNs can have different views on politics and economic policy and still should give primacy to the WN identity they are building collectively through these fora. Different lifestyles and aesthetics are allowed, but the people participating in this online forum as representatives of white nationalism emphasize that the main agenda is protecting the white race:

Speaking of non-comformity - Many of us WN's are quite different - some of us
are skinheads, some us have tattoos all over their bodies, some of us dress casually, some of us are clean-cut and straight, some of us smoke, some of us drink,
etc. What we have in common - we all agree white race is in danger of being
genocided in many subtle ways and feel left-out by our government/business as
such entities pay more attention to non-whites.

WNs are afraid of being "replaced" by non-whites. For WNs, being "right" on
the main issue requires one to believe that whites deserve to have the freedom
to be separate from other races. The central tenet of white nationalism is the
desire for a white homeland where whites can live and prosper as one people
without influence from non-white actors. Despite a long historical record
to the contrary, a WN ideologist explains what happens when "others" are
allowed to enter a white society: "Unfortunately, when you introduce alien
races, both economic systems collapse and formerly prosperous white nations
become third world cesspools." Even in rewriting history, the exclusion of
non-whites is the overwhelming factor that holds the WN community together.
    One of the areas where pushback is initially introduced is the idea of white
supremacy. For a large portion of members, the white race is superior in
numerous ways:

Dear white liberals, as you can see, the white race is intellectually, culturally, es-
thetically and physically superior to all alien races combined, many times over!

But a subset of WN individuals would be willing to bypass that argument by
calling it irrelevant. While many WNs would debate the vast superiority of
the white race, the point is that whites should be with whites regardless of
merit. Whiteness is the strongest bond that should hold their people together
and be celebrated. They try to make an argument parallel to black pride:

Just as blacks from Africa, Caribbean countries and North America consider
themselves black, first and foremost, whites from Europe, North and South
America, Asia, Australia and South Africa should proudly celebrate their joint
white identity.

Outsiders would correctly argue in the forum that race is not a biological factor and cannot be used to separate people. However, most WNs would argue
against these points. Others would claim that whites are not the superior race
according to one test score or another. The next post sums up the debate about
superiority succinctly:

I think that the focus of white nationalists should be on the preservation of white culture. You should argue for a homogenous white state, as opposed to focusing on proving non whites are genetically inferior. It is contentious to argue that whites are genetically superior, but more importantly, it side tracks the discussion and inflames people of a liberal mindset. Besides, if it were proven to you tomorrow that non white people are not genetically inferior, would you stop clamoring for a fully white state? Of course not. You should focus on the point that a white state deserves to exist, and that it would be a shame if white culture and people were to disappear.

In this way, these online ideologues were creating a dogma and a way to rationalize criticisms.

Even if they are indeed wrong empirically, characteristically this WN writes that it doesn't matter:

The point I was trying to get across, and which non-nationalists are stuck on, is that it doesn't matter if we are 'correct' or not on the race issue. It doesn't matter whether or not there is scientific substance to what we want. It doesn't matter whether racial nationalism is progressive or enlightened. What matters is that a group of people are being oppressed and denied a homeland, and socially assimilated, thus leading to their gradual extinction from our planet. That part is biologically real; it's not fantasy.

While minorities draw attention to health disparities and white privilege, in the WN's eyes, the embodiment of white culture is only possible through the protection and propagation of the white race, which is supposedly at the risk of extinction. This renaissance of white culture can only happen if whites have a distinct homeland that is theirs. In this new incarnation of racism, the paramount issue is not white power and supremacy but the desire for "a white homeland."

Whites for Whites

Despite their white privilege and living in the economic wealth of the global north, White Nationalists argue that there are real threats against white culture. One of their goals is to create a political identity around the misleading belief that whites are a homogenous group that shares a common struggle for survival:

We are a homogeneous group of people who want to be left alone, while the anti-white coalition is a hodgepodge of folks who dislike each other. . . . In my opinion, all of us whites including white liberals, these cynical lying hypocrites, are in this struggle together. We'll either win as a race or all disappear, their descendents as well as ours.

Despite the emphasis on genes and descendants, white culture is the common phrase used to describe the shared values and tradition that bond whites together and to talk in code about the WN agenda: "True, conventional WN wisdom says that we should avoid the expression 'white race' and instead talk about 'our people,' 'our culture' etc." The upholding of this white culture is seen as another common goal of WNs, and an argument that can be used to bring others into the fold. This white culture is most commonly exalted in this online forum through tropes like scientific achievements. Lists of great white inventors and their discoveries are laid out over numerous pages to show the fruits of white culture. Posters frequently compare this list to the non-existent advances made by those other than white, falsely claiming on numerous occasions that non-whites have done nothing worthwhile in the scientific community. In some instances, the trophy counts of "white nations" during the Olympics are given as examples of its bounties. In addition to physical feats, acting white is another part of this white culture. Non-whites rarely if ever possess this ability.

> I would be 100% Ok with black people if they acted white. I see it like this, there are Black people who are normal, then there are subhuman apes, just like we have with white people, there are normal rational white people, then there are trailer trash who can't spell their names. The only difference is that with whites, morons are the minority, and with blacks, 99% of them are retarded.

This racist statement tries to give a sense that hypothetically a non-white person could "pass" and be accepted. Yet, like in racist thinking there are exceptional individuals of color but that does not disprove the superiority of white culture. While white culture is to them the superior one, they practice creating new racist scientific-sounding theories (Kendi 2016). A female poster gives her descriptions of racial traits without hints of any awareness of her reliance on large generalizations and false stereotypes:

> Whites are on average extremely creative, and extremely relatively willing to incur costs to bring the social "game" more into line with basic justice and liberty. Blacks have very little mental machinery for operating in systems for anything except immediate, socially-mediated acquisition of sexual opportunities and basic material benefits. Asians have a higher ability to delay gratification for complex ends within a social system than whites, but less of a sense of when to incur costs in order to shift the overall social system away from one of oppres-

sion. They are highly creative for a form of life but not so much as Whites, by a significant margin.

These types of arguments justify a sort of racial hierarchy. Yet for WNs this ranking is largely arbitrary and irrelevant in the larger picture since different groups of non-whites may be better or worse than others, but they are still not white and thus seen only as a burden. In this new WN ideology, whites are painted as just another ethnoracial minority claiming for cultural and civil rights. They are fighting but for the maintenance of symbolic and racial boundaries and for the reification of whiteness as a real thing.

Race-Mixing

WNs believe that many people hold a desire to be white and use this as an example of why their race is superior. Some participants in the forum wrote that Hispanics value white identity:

> Whiteness is correctly viewed as the most desirable trait, the mythical shinning city on the hill that everyone should strive to reach. Naturally, mestizos are very particular in terms of their mating behavior.

Mestizos are the mixed-blood children of indigenous people and Europeans. While their "race" is deemed inferior, their aspirations appear reasonable to WNs:

> Please take a look at mestizos. They are very proud of their white ancestry that made their skin whiter. They want to race mix with us so that some day they can pass for whites. Again, the idea is to improve their genetic fortune.

WNs see Hispanics as accepting "their inferiority" and plan to improve that status in life by race-mixing. Their goal is for the descendants to pass for whites:

> What about other races? Mestizos value whiter shades as well. Unlike blacks, they don't seem to be as angry about their color and overall racial inferiority. Instead, they view their miserable race as work in progress. All they want in life is to race-mix with white people in order for their children to become whiter, smarter and more successful.

WNs go into detail about "The Fundamental Law of Miscegenation":

> In other words, a person may only race mix up, but never down. Nowhere can this dynamic be observed better than among mestizos who, albeit inferior, are among the more racially astute groups in the U.S. Let's first evaluate the racial

background of this peculiar sub-race. As we know, mestizos are a mix of Spanish, Amerindians and black slaves. In the Caribbean blacks were so numerous that they swamped the natives, who died of exposure to diseases that blacks brought with them from Africa.

Along with a rewriting of who brought deadly pathogens to the Native Americans, WNs see Hispanics as unique and think they see the race problem in the same way they do. Their desire to improve their children's lives by "whitening" them is thought of as the right thing to do. While WNs do not want this to happen to their community, that action is exactly what they believe an inferior race should do. They agree with the positive aspects of race-mixing, even using the Spanish term mestizos. WNs understand this tactic but disapprove of it happening at the expense of the white race. They worry that this would contribute to the browning of America. Given their fixation with race purity, mestizo is a label often used to describe all Latin people:

> For example, let's look at mestizos. Among this fairly 'diverse' population we have Guatemalans, Mexicans, Puerto Ricans, Colombians, democrats, republicans, old Texan families, illegals who arrived 3 months ago, rich, poor, Catholics, evangelicals, etc.

The race-mixing is easily identifiable in the Hispanic community as evidenced by the variety of skin tones. WNs do not care too much about the individual differences between populations, just where the balance of power lies. While America is racially diverse, the leadership must stay white, like in Latin America:

> True, Latin American ruling elites are always white. I think that about 20-25% Mexicans are white also, but those who come here are overwhelmingly mestizo.

They have an obvious solution to the problem, Latin exclusion:

> Latin Americans of course celebrate whiteness, but in reality whites are a small minority, other than in the far south. After all, if Latin American immigrants were white, we wouldn't be having all these problems.

This statement clearly explains the anti-immigration position as a racist move to exclude people from Latin America from entering the United States. The biggest problem that WNs have with Hispanics is immigration. By infiltrating the country, they are deemed as a threat:

> That giant mistake led to massive importation of alien races that has irreversibly turned the most advanced civilization in the history of mankind into a third

world cesspool of dirty, violent, and profoundly inferior beings. That is why we have ghettos and barrios, why you are worried about crime and why the public school system in your community is collapsing despite investment of massive amounts of your tax dollars.

They argue that white liberals are too brainwashed to understand why immigration is a problem. Only after they move into the community does the problem become clear:

I became more racially aware shortly after graduation. It simply took me many years (20) of reading thru a trickle of books & alternate press . . . here and there about hints of race issues to fully understand the problem. I became more aware of race issues when I was seeing many more mestizos in my area - they just literally invaded in a matter of short time. Hence it wasn't too long after that I joined here.

Once the community is "overrun with non-whites" is when the appeal of white nationalism starts for some. Procreation is seen as the primary focus of immigrant groups; White genocide commences.

Mestizos do not value studying either, as it interferes with their lifelong preoccupation with keeping señoritas pregnant around the clock.

There is paranoia over their race being replaced by people of Latin and Asian descent in the future. This fear is not helped by progressive phrases such as "demographics is destiny."

The Multiculturalism Lie

WNs argue that most races want to be around their own people and continue their shared ancestry. The international system of ethno-states is the most logical to them (Chapter 2). The promotion of multi-culturalism is the result of a Jewish conspiracy. According to WNs, the rise of immigration in "white" countries and the idea of multiculturalism are lies propagated by Jews to perpetuate white genocide. Non-whites may be the agents that destroy the white race but they are only fulfilling a "Jewish agenda":

History and common sense tell us that ethnically homogenous, nationalistic nations are least likely to tolerate Jewish subversion. That is why Jews view these nations as their worst enemies and try to make them less ethnically homogenous and more multi-racial. In the course of that transformation, the Jews seek to destroy traditional nationalism (which caused them so much grief throughout history) and replace it with globalism they are promoting today.

In their view, Zionism and the push to have Jews return to Israel show that an ethno-state is a worthwhile idea but is only available to Jews. Any other group of people would be stopped from having such a place. There is the belief that Jews are only interested in themselves:

> Cunning and connected, the Jews always dominate the disparate, multiracial groups of individuals who have nothing in common apart from their elitism and snobbery. Jews are the glue that keeps liberal enterprise together and drive their anti-white agenda.

The stereotypical argument that the Jews control the media is also used as reasoning for the alleged conspiracy:

> That's why the most important thing we can do to convert white liberals to our side is to shatter the myth of racial equality that Jewish-run media implanted in their heads.

Not only is racism a constant in Stormfront, but so is anti-Semitism. White anti-racism is seen as a Jewish ploy causing complacency with the supposed white genocide:

> Then Jews introduced the laughable, patently absurd, yet devious concept of racial equality in order to facilitate race mixing. They clearly understood that as long as we viewed nonwhites as lesser beings, we would not want them around, let alone at the kitchen table.

For WNs multiculturalism is an unnatural imposition:

> The misguided belief in racial equality, basically a license to race mix, along with Jewish machinations, is the root of all our problems.

They disregard any mention of other societies having members of cultures living side-by-side. Any goal of diversity or overcoming differences among people is labeled as a lie:

> It exposes "diversity" and its supposed benefits as the sickest fraud in the history of mankind, To them, living in a multiracial society is a normal state of affairs, diversity is a virtue and white solidarity is a very bad thing. Their misguided views were shaped by nonstop, cradle-to-grave brainwashing that takes place in schools, media, workplace, churches, civic organizations and, sadly, at the kitchen table.

The theory of white genocide does not stop there. Taking this Jewish conspiracy to an extreme, one member even suggests that part of the plan is to poison the DNA of white people through the advice of doctors:

> I think Whites need to think of sex and healthy sex for soon the Jewish doctors (and their nonWhite ilk for White men can no longer pass the advanced math and science tests like the other races and are discriminated against for blacks and browns don't have to pass yet can become doctors. Wouldn't want one of them to work on me!) but soon the Jewish doctors are going to create babies thru 'sperm banks.' And once Whites have degenerated from overuse of drugs, alcohol, cigarettes, junk food, intentionally put on us to destroy us, the doctors won't want our sperm for it is 'damaged.' We are at a crossroads and it is time Whites make decisions for Whites. We know the path of genocide and degeneration which is going to be a horrible last 100 years of are existence is in front of us.

This conspiracy insists upon a multifaceted approach to the browning of society by intermixing whites. Race mixing would be the result of immigration of non-whites into typically white countries:

> Importing masses of antagonistic, radical black Muslims is clearly the most effective way to destroy white Christian countries.

In the end, they state that the goal of Jewish people is to abolish the white race to maintain power and control of the world. They misinterpret the words of scholars:

> Noel Ignatiev, Harvard professor and Jew declares that, "Abolishing the social construct known as the White race is so desirable that no one but a committed White supremacist could object to it." His supporters have also said that nothing should be rejected beforehand for achieving that goal. In other words, if Whites won't go quietly into that good night it's OK to exterminate them.

Ignatiev writes about how the Irish became white at the expense of black people, showing how whiteness is a social construct meaning an idea, a collective myth more than a scientific reality (Ignatiev 1996). Ignatiev is not "anti-White." In the quote, Ignatiev is talking about the toxic idea of whiteness as an excuse for dehumanization, exclusion, and exploitation. WNs want to keep the status quo. So, this comment showcases the conflation of criticism of race as a social construct into a bigoted effort by enemies to eliminate the white race. This post furthers their goal by quoting a well-known academic to give legitimacy to their conception that there is a conspiracy set out to destroy the white race. Their defense of racism becomes an attack on anti-racists, who are labeled as anti-white racists with their own racial agendas in mind. In this ideological remix, the racists have become the victims of racism.

Brainwashed White Liberals

For WNs, white liberals are the enemy: "IMO the white liberal is second only to the Jew as the greatest enemy of the white race." They are traitors to their own race and have turned against their kin:

> Probably the most painful aspect of our struggle for survival is dealing with white liberals, who are often our worst enemies. Blinded by vicious anti-white ideology invented and promoted by an alien race, these whites express open hatred toward their own people and attempt to destroy White Nationalism altogether.

Liberals are seen as one of the greatest threats because they thwart the attempts of WNs to unite the white race. They strive for equality and justice for all and do not tend to fight for people of their own kin first. WNs say liberals love to help the disadvantaged because it makes them feel better about themselves. WNs look down on white liberals:

> To me they are just genetically less intelligent then other whites and it would be good for eugenics if they were either sterilised or deported into a foreign gene pool. Low IQ liberal whites having lots of children with other liberal whites will do more damage then having those liberal whites breed with coloured races, at least then they will diverge from the European blood line and be "out of the way." . . I've often referred to coloured races (especially blacks) as "genetic garbage" however to me most white liberals are exactly that. Yes there are intelligent white liberals who live in middle-class areas who are liberal simply due to ignorance, but in the UK (for example) most white liberals are liberal despite being spit on by minorities.

Contrary to the call for racial unity and a shared destiny, for many WNs, as shown above, white liberals are a scourge on the white race that needs to be converted or eliminated, and they are a threat because they hate WNs:

> Only white liberals do not view other whites as their own people whom they should support. Instead, they hate us for having the audacity to promote white group identity, something our common ancestors took for granted.

WNs, attribute this to "white self-hatred."

As a rule, White Liberals hate us more than they hate Conservatives and Republicans - and that is saying quite a bit! White Liberals are the ones who brought us "Multiculturalism"! They hate us and everything we stand for. They will always hate us and if they ever say they don't hate us THEY ARE LYING!

Many Stormfront commenters considered liberalism to be the result of lies and brainwashing, while others frame liberalism as a "conditioned response":

People have been conditioned that 'racism' is the ultimate evil. To a well conditioned liberal, being called a 'racist' is even worse than being called a 'fascist,' a 'Hitler' or a 'naziwhowantstokillsixmillionjews.' Liberalism is a conditioned response. Overcoming that response is like trying to keep one of Pavlov's dogs from slobbering when a bell is rung. I don't think that logic or thought processes are involved. I wish that I had a good suggestion for you but I don't.

For WNs, one of the biggest problems with liberals is that they feel as if they are superior to WNs because of their pledge to diversity. They hate white people who are proud of themselves because they see them as lesser peoples:

The dominant, overwhelming sentiment among white liberals is their sense of class superiority. They can't stand us, not so much because we are white nationalists, but because they consider us to be 'unrefined,' 'trailer trash who can't spell their name'—truly unforgivable offenses in the world of intellectual sophistication.

In this worldview, white liberals' hatred of other whites is rooted in their sense of ideological superiority in social issues as well. According to WNs,

White liberals are, first and foremost, self-absorbed elitists who have no tolerance for people whom they view as intellectually inferior, regardless of their race. That is at the core of their antipathy toward blue collar whites and their 'backward' views on guns, God and gays.

Instead of a desire to be with their own kin, liberals are said to prefer to be with others who profess the same love of multiculturalism and cultural acceptance:

Basically, liberals swapped their white tribe for an educated multiracial tribe because of pure snobbery and elitism!

WNs believe that because of this sense of superiority, liberals are going to take pride in taking down their own people. They will be complicit in their own destruction. They are merely puppets of Jews and minorities.

White liberals, please remember that pretending to believe in the odious lie of racial equality doesn't make you noble, it doesn't make you righteous, it doesn't make you civilized, it simply makes you a mindless accomplice in the destruction of your own race! What about you, cowardly punks? Do you enjoy groveling at the feet of your Judeo-African masters who manipulate you like circus animals?

WNs say that even when liberals accept differences between races, liberals do not correctly identify the source of the difference and attribute it to environmental factors:

I can't speak for any liberal, but I think they're big fans of environment influences behavior theory (recall our discussion on 'environment influences education' vs. genetics), rather than genetics influences behavior theory. I'm guessing they think by letting wild Africans into white countries tames the Africans - i.e. white environment tames the blacks.

The quote above shows the attempt, albeit rudimentary, at having a pseudo-academic debate about the WN cause. Rather than presenting themselves as aggressors like the KKK, WNs complain about being the victims. Clearly, white nationalism is unlikely to become a reality in terms of only-white countries given that most so-called whites in the world are not interested in this project. WNs wrongly argue about an equivalent of Marx's "false consciousness," not about class but about race.

Why Can't We Have a Whites Only Group?

WNs complain that whites are not allowed to be proud of their race, and that to have a racial identity is publicly acceptable for everyone but whites. Whenever whiteness is celebrated, it is often met with contempt and shouts of racism. Taking the phrase "race card" to an absurd point, a post argues that

as long as whites, and only whites, are not allowed to think of ourselves as a distinct group with distinct interests, the ultimate result will be white dispossession. Imagine a card game where the whole country is the stake. Each ethnic group has a hand and a stack of chips, but only non-whites get a trump: the "race card." No matter how huge the white pile of chips is at the beginning, as long as we play under those rules, we will eventually be left with nothing in the end.

One of the most common talking points is that other people can be proud of their races, but whites cannot be proud of theirs:

But, if we whites decide to join something as innocuous as White Engineers (or Teachers) Society, liberals and their Jewish friends would probably take us to the court, as they did in other white countries. Do you realistically expect blacks, mestizos, and other non-whites to fight for the rights—of white people????!!? If whites do become a minority, would we whites be allowed to form our own white organizations?

Forgetting that whites are the majority group in the United States, and that whites occupy most powerful positions, WNs complained that whites are not allowed to have their own advocacy groups:

> Whites, on the other hand, are not allowed to have any white organizations, let alone the Congressional White Caucus. We are precluded from organizing along racial lines, period. Yet, our liberal friends, deeply committed to racial equality, applaud this shocking double standard—against their own people!

WNs feel that whites are not only not allowed to be proud of themselves or their accomplishments but are blamed for the world's problems. A former liberal explains,

> I want to think I'm a good person who wants to make the world a better place. After believing that White Nationalists are evil and indeed, that the majority of the worlds problems can be attributed to White people, it was hard for me to completely turn my thinking around and view myself in that category. I truly believed that I was fighting against discrimination and bigotry, and I feel so stupid now. But, what I've seen and learned through my time here can't be unseen.

In his views, this reinforces the need for a forum like this to re-educate white Americans:

> I think the mainstream needs Stormfront to be some big, scary, evil threat. They've made racism one of the worst offenses possible, and now they need to justify themselves. There's an entire industry of fighting racism and discrimination, and it's certainly not going to admit that they created the entire problem that they claim to fight against. Unfortunately, the effects of this run deep. I kid you not, some people would rather be called a murderer than a racist.

Supposedly, because whites cannot be proud of their own race, they have to act subserviently, like a conquered people:

> What kind of people has to surrender everything to others, upon demand? A conquered people. We whites have to behave as a conquered people in our own country. If we persist in this long enough, of course, we will physically cease to exist as a people. We will succumb to miscegenation, demographic collapse, or outright mass murder, as conquered and enslaved peoples often do.

Whites are the majority in both the United States and Europe; their cultural legacy is under no risk. Yet they seem to equate colonization and immigration. While these are two very different processes, WNs see immigration as parallel to historical European colonialism and native genocide. English and European settler colonialism resulted in the repopulation of North America, South Africa, Australia, New Zealand, etc. at the expense of native populations through land expropriation, war, and genocide. But contemporary immigrants into the global north are not engaged in any of these activities, they are in the numerical minority, and they could not fight against the large and sophisticatedly equipped armies of these countries. The comparison is inaccurate and anachronistic.

White Exploitation

In another inversion of empirical reality, WNs think that whites are naturally a hardworking people, but that they do not always bear the fruit of their labor because their hard work is exploited by non-whites through welfare that supposedly goes mainly to minorities. They believe

> governments in white countries take loads of hard earned white people's money to support over breeding of unemployed criminal negroids . . . abusing welfare, that was created for responsible white people.

Non-whites are seen as lazy and undeserving. Additional connotations of people of color being criminals or single parents are attached to their identity to explain why they should not be eligible for hand-outs. This kind of thinking about redistribution is related to the sense of providing for one's own kin and no one else. Since their main issue is race, WNs say others of the same race should be the only ones that benefit from their labor:

> Why wouldn't nonwhites strive to separate from their alleged oppressors, as did every other aggrieved minority in the history of mankind, save for a peculiar tribe of people whose pathology we'll expose in the next section? Because nonwhites have an overwhelming economic interest to feed off of us like parasites.

In this view of the world, whites are seen as hosts while non-whites are parasites living and feasting off their backs:

> In white lands nonwhites become social parasites, living on welfare and engaging in crime. How can we maintain our status as the most advanced country in the history of mankind, the nation that sent a white man to the Moon, if most children under the age of 18 are functionally illiterate nonwhites? We can't.

For that reason, this country is gradually collapsing economically, as we can all attest.

This sense of collapse is also blamed on Jews:

> Can't you understand that we are witnessing the systematic destruction of white people by hordes of inferior beings relentlessly deployed by Jews, these social parasites and despoilers of humanity since times immortal?

In this distorted view non-whites create nothing of value and nothing original that a white person could not come up with. Whites cannot pillage the spoils of other races because they do not have any:

> But wait, it gets worse! As many of these black and brown children are basically borderline retarded, they are destroying educational opportunities for our unfortunate white children as well. In order to accommodate nonwhites, the standards are set so low that intelligent, white children can pass tests without opening any books, so they don't learn much either.

The feeling of despair and decay blamed on non-whites expands into education. The inferiority of non-white lowers the bar for all.

The Silent Liberals

WNs believe that liberals secretly agree with them although they will never admit it. WNs believe liberals do not want to live around non-whites. As much as they talk about racial equality and diversity being great, if white liberals had the choice to live in an all-white neighborhood, they would.

> It has been pointed out many times on this site that liberals usually live in mostly white areas, and there are exceptions to the norm in all races. Black people who exhibit [typical black behavior] live in the ghetto, and liberals rarely encounter them. Black exceptions live in the suburbs, so they are what liberals think are normal black people.

According to WNs, liberals hold the same beliefs about the inferiority of non-whites but have been educated not to express them. Secretly they know that whites are superior and would prefer to be with their own kind. These liberals want to look good to their other liberal friends, so they will lie and reject this notion outright. A poster asks,

> Why am I fighting against my own people who look and behave like me, who share my culture, my history, my ancestry—on behalf of strange, alien races that

we have nothing in common with, all of whom are shamelessly ethnocentric? How does that make any sense?

WNs feel that because of the importance of being "politically correct," liberals believe they cannot express what they really think:

> Liberals are here because they are searching for answers, tired of the nonsense and hypocrisy present in their lives. They want the truth.

This "truth," the one that is openly discussed on forums like Stormfront, is a guilty pleasure for the white liberal according to WNs. It feeds their inner desire and vindicates how they see the world:

> White liberals actually enjoy when we tear blacks down as that validates their deeply held antipathy toward alien races, an antipathy that almost all whites share, regardless of what they say publicly (nonwhites, please always remember that!).

A few WNs used to be liberals in their youth, and now they have finally been exposed to the truth. One such person details his change:

> It's not easy to admit I was wrong. It's hard to admit that not all races are created equal. It wasn't easy to start to think un-PC thoughts and to see myself as something I once hated. It was even harder to admit I was lied to my whole life. I cringe reading some of the stuff I wrote. I don't want to think I could ever be that foolish and irrational. Sometimes, it's easier to make excuses and try to validate the ideology I followed and made a part of my identity. Some people will do anything not to have to admit they are wrong, and I don't want to be that type of person.

While these hate sites are converting former liberals, that is, average white-identifying people, into WNs, there are powerful memoirs of individuals rising out of hate, like the son of the founder of Stormfront, now denouncing the tactics of white nationalists and his previous beliefs (Saslow 2018).

The Government against Whites

Not only are government policies such as affirmative action and welfare set out to turn the tides in favor of non-whites, but WNs feel the actions of our elected leaders harbor ill will toward whites:

> Our own elected representatives apparently consider whites 'lesser' constituents who deserve no compassion.

This feeling of hatred from government tops off when president Barack Obama is mentioned. While in reality whites hold the majority of positions in the federal government and many local governments, it does not feel that way to WNs:

> It's a bit hard when you're the government and media's number one enemy, anyone who speaks up is quickly labeled or attacked. Jewish government has a hand in keeping whites disenfranchised. Whites being in charge was just the norm until recent decades. Everything in the American media and government is based around ruining white people at every turn possible. This is one of the first times in history whites have lost control of their own country or let it slip to other people. Whites have never really been ruled by other people, i dont think it's going to go well.

In this "deep story," when non-whites are in positions of power, whites are blamed for social problems and the solutions that these government officials come up with take power away from whites:

> Most importantly, what do you think is going to happen to our political rights once we lose our majority status, given the fact that the American public (including non-whites) has been bombarded for decades in the schools and the mainstream media with continuous information blaming whites for every single injustice??? Non-whites in positions of power don't always see us whites as good/nice people and will treat us accordingly, as evidenced by anti-white statements by guys like Attorney General Eric Holder.

WNs believe that government officials are also complicit in white genocide by creating incentives for non-whites to come into the country and reward them with opportunities:

> What kind of government would invite and encourage alien invaders to take over American territory, while subsidizing their treacherous activities? Obviously, a government that is anti-American and pro-Mexican!
>
> Political Correctness is not like a religion, it is a religion. One foundation of it's religion is that all members must believe they are free thinkers because they think just like all other cult members.

According to WNs posting in Stormfront in 2012 and 2013, government officials were members of the church of racial equality and worship at the altar of diversity, all to the peril of white people; not coincidently, the president and attorney general at the time were black.

CONCLUSION

President Trump called himself a "nationalist" at a campaign rally in Houston on October 22, 2018. Thus, it is extremely important to understand groups that embrace this label fully. WNs used to be a largely unknown fringe group lying low and rarely making the news. Recently the rise of hate crimes and incidents in Charlottesville and Pittsburgh have brought the views of these individuals into the mainstream. While the comments analyzed are from a few years back, their relevance has only increased. The underlying themes of "white genocide" by immigration and minorities provide fuel to the anxiety of WNs. They feel that "their people" are on the losing side of a race war. Even if this war is not real, their beliefs and corresponding actions are. To understand WNs, one must know their underlying beliefs.

From the outside, the most basic understanding of this group is that they are merely racists. This view is oversimplified and fails to articulate the extent to which the movement views the world and plans to change it. WNs' worldview revolves around the assumption of a plot against whites as an aggrieved minority. They live under constant threat of attack by the "other," orchestrated by a Jewish elite. Many things in their lives are seen through the lens of a plot against them and "their" people. In their view, diversity and immigration are threats to their white way of life.

To a large degree, WNs have internalized the language of the civil rights and the advocacy of African-Americans. Indeed, blacks are not their main targets—in a way they may feel that they have lost that battle. Instead their main targets are Hispanics as the largest ethnic minority, Jews as supposedly overrepresented in the media industry, and Muslim refugee and asylum seekers, all of which they feel the government can keep at bay to protect the white future of America or to Make America Great Again (MAGA) by reverting to a time where whites were clearly on top.

Xenophobia and anti-semitism were widespread in this forum. We did not observe any posts trying to negate or reduce Jewish conspiracies. We did not see any sincere attempts to influence the community to be more open to outsiders and racial others. Clearly, there are demographic and ideological differences among WNs. There is a variance in how much animosity is held on a personal level toward members of other races. There are differences in individuals' willingness to express hostilities toward others in their lives and in the willingness to communicate or socialize with those whom they define as others. Another nuance would be the level of openness about these views that these posters have in their lives off the Internet or even in different online environments. Some members may be completely transparent on these views, as showcased by racist memes or "likes" on Facebook pages, while others may be hiding behind a façade of normalcy or express themselves through aliases. It is exactly the ease of access to people online with confirming viewpoints and ideology that amplifies this racist ideology. Openly hateful, racist, and inaccurate language is only being amplified and legitimized by statements made by Trump, including calling negative press "fake news" and critical journalists the "enemy of the people." When one of the two major political parties in the United States echoes these racist views, we must be wary. Drumming up fear by stigmatizing Latin people and Muslim asylum seekers as invaders is just one example. Political parties around the world have toyed with the politics of white identity. Race baiting can be useful politically in the short term; but if the political agenda of a mainstream party slowly embraces views held by WNs, it could be a very slippery slope to the logical conclusion of apartheid, ethnic cleansing, and genocide. These inaccurate and dangerous views must be addressed and openly denounced.

Chapter 6

Anti-immigrant Online Comment Sections in the Aftermath of Trump's Election

Catherine Harlos and Ernesto Castañeda

My great-grandparents came from Southern Italy and Sicily. At first, they were thought of as non-white in their new home. My mother and her siblings grew up in poor largely Southern Italian-American neighborhoods in New Haven and West Haven, Connecticut. My grandma has told me many stories describing this stigmatized experience growing up first-generation Italian-American in the Great Depression and during WWII, when Italians were feared because of fascism in Italy. Despite changes thereafter, my mother and her siblings faced the lingering effects of xenophobia aimed at Southern Italians, largely due to their Italian last name.

My mother was both bright and fortunate enough to receive a large scholarship to Yale. While she was able to graduate and move up the economic ladder into the middle class, all within the context of the shifting boundaries of whiteness, she felt a great deal of stigmatization and isolation in school due to her socioeconomic background and her last name. In the 1960s and 1970s, my mom and her siblings were also advised to hide their Sicilian (thought of as "less white") heritage when dating other Italian-Americans. Nevertheless, in our white supremacist society, my family was afforded the privilege of being able to assimilate into U.S. whiteness and gain access to the privileges and power that whiteness holds. A couple of generations later, in the 2000s, everyone on my mom's side of the family became solidly middle class, racialized as white, and has very little Italian cultural and linguistic knowledge, despite being fully of Italian ancestry.

The experience of my family could not differ more from that of the migrant or first-generation families of color—whether they be African, Latinx, Asian, Arab, etc.—within the United States. In a time of revitalized white nationalist sentiment and policy catalyzed by the Trump administration, it is important to critically analyze the boundaries constructed between different groups of migrants and their children contextualized by social-historical positioning, race, nationality, class, and gender.

Catherine Harlos

This story is not unique to Italian-Americans; it is faced by visible minorities. Xenophobic national conversations today that blame Latin migrants for "stealing" American jobs and "flooding" cities and towns mirror metaphors stigmatizing "non-white" migrants in the past (Schrag 2011, 10–11). The U.S. migration story is a complicated quilt "woven" together by eugenics, nationalism, expansionists' foreign policies, economic booms and crises, as well as struggles for social justice (Schrag 2011, 16–17). This chapter continues examining racialized social boundaries—held in place by systems of power—between U.S. natives and immigrants using examples from comments in online news sources.

CONTEXT

Racialized exclusion has long been embedded in American history. WASPs (white Anglo-Saxon Protestants) were uncomfortable with immigrants prioritizing communal, familial values over "abstract" WASP values of good governance and efficiency, using these sorts of cultural arguments to justify repression (Schrag 2011, 4). In his book *Not Fit for Our Society: Immigration and Nativism in America*, Peter Schrag describes how some progressives and conservatives united under eugenic campaigns. For example, Stanford University's first president, David Starr Jordan, was part of a "race betterment movement" that aspired to create "human thoroughbreds" and keep the United States "pure" (Schrag 2011, 6).

Therefore, it is unsurprising to see how eugenics bled into policy prohibiting migrants racialized as "non-white" from entering the United States or gaining citizenship (Schrag 2011, 6–7). Eugenicists created ideologies, discourses, and policies claiming that immigrants such as Chinese, Japanese, Turks, Greeks, Jews, and Italians were "intellectually, physically, and morally inferior" (Schrag 2011, 8). Their growing presence in the United States was frequently characterized as a threat to American society. Italian parents were supposedly producing children of lesser intelligence who were then infiltrating and tarnishing American schools (Stoskopf 2002). Black people were marginalized to the highest degree within this discourse; as Columbia University psychologist Henry Garrett wrote in 1954, the only people of lesser intelligence than Southern and Eastern Europeans were people of African descent. Garrett's testimony was used to defend school segregation at the Supreme Court case *Brown v. Board of Education* (Schrag 2011, 8).

Eugenicists in the United States were very influential, and they legitimized and inspired leaders in Nazi Germany. They continued to shape U.S. policy, such as recommending immigration quotas throughout the late nineteenth and twentieth centuries (Schrag 2011, 9). For example, Ellis Island was the United States' first federal immigration detention center when it opened in 1892. Its temporary detentions and inspections (lasting three to five hours) were used to vet Southern and Eastern European immigrants (Rizzo 2015, 40). As Southern and European migrants assimilated into whiteness, more migrants of color began to immigrate into the United States. Migration policy for Europeans was liberalized whereas restrictions were placed upon migrants from all other places in the world.

The racialization of immigration policies can be illustrated by Operation Wetback of 1954, resulting in the deportation of 4,000 Mexican migrants and many of their citizen children and family members (Sen and Mamdouh 2008, 53). White Europeans were never a target of similar policies or practices (Fox 2012). It is worth noting that migrants of color are not only targeted with threats of deportation, but also incarceration. In 1988, Congress passed a law for mandatory detention provisions of undocumented migrants for the first time (Rizzo 2015, 40–41). This law was just the beginning of an era of deepened criminalization and incarceration of immigrant communities (Golash-Boza 2016b).

White supremacists and their ideologies continue to play a key role in the policy crackdowns on black and brown immigrants. For example, the white supremacist Pioneer Fund was started by the Eugenics Record Office superintendent Harry Laughlin. Laughlin contributed over one million dollars to the Federation for American Immigration Reform (FAIR), an immigration restriction organization that has played a major role in resisting the Dream Act and shaping media conversations regarding immigration (Schrag 2011, 9–10).

As Michèle Lamont and Virag Molnár describe, we use symbolic boundaries to conceptually create, maintain, contest, or dissolve socially constructed differences that have stark material consequences (Lamont and Molnár 2002, 168). This culminates in the institutionalization of "principles of classification"—the rooting and weaving of these boundaries into societal structures (Lamont and Molnár 2002, 168), to crystallize power dynamics and hoard resources. Patricia Hill Collins (2015) conceptualizes this as the "matrix of domination"—a system of interlocking political domination that molds social boundaries and inequities including the intersections of race, gender, sexuality, class, ability, nationality, age, religion, and ethnicity (Collins and Bilge 2016).

Upper Mobility

The dominant narrative of immigration to the United States emphasizes upward mobility rooted in meritocracy and "bootstrap ideology," where hard work gets rewarded. But this is not always the case. Some today may want to distinguish between Italian and Latin immigrant experiences because of "whiteness." The largest group of contemporary migrants to the United States is from Mexico, and scholars argue that they face four challenges that their Southern and Eastern European "counterparts" did not face. First, these latest immigrants are largely not seen as white, and the defining borders of whiteness have not shifted to incorporate Mexican and Latin migrants as they did with Italians and other Europeans (Perlmann 2005, 3). Second, the United States has gone through a period of de-industrialization resulting in fewer manufacturing jobs that employed earlier immigrants and paved a way into the middle class (Perlmann 2005, 3). Third, extended educational opportunities of the postwar periods and the GI Bill are largely inaccessible to Mexican migrants. Fourth, many of the institutional patterns of punishment that were created historically to control and subjugate black people are now being applied to Latin youth (Rios 2011, 18).

Irish- and Italian-Americans and other descendants of once discriminated European immigrant groups, today have immense privileges not only attached to whiteness but also the choice of whether to include their European ancestries within their descriptions of their identities, an "optional ethnicity" (Waters 1996). Contemporary Italian-Americans, for example, can celebrate and embrace family history without it affecting their daily lives (Waters 1996). Thus, Italian-Americans are "special" but do not have to face the same obstacles that other ethnic and racial groups do.

Joe Perlmann's research illustrates that while Mexican immigrants and their children are attaining greater opportunities and standards of living, it is happening at a much slower pace than Southern, Central, and Eastern European immigrants did previously due to the different sets of structural constraints that Mexican migrants face (Perlmann 2005, 117). Thus, Mexican-Americans collectively do not have the privilege of being able to choose an "optional ethnicity" when navigating the United States and striving to create better lives for their children and grandchildren.

Methods

This chapter critically examines the online comments sections of several news articles published in the spring of 2017 soon after Trump's inauguration. The stories come from ABC News, *USA Today*, the *Washington Post*, the *Chicago Tribune*, Fox News, AOL, and BuzzFeed News. These are different media sources that span the United States both geographically and politically. Online comment sections give us an insight into the anger, worries, values, and politics of those posting. We include the number of comments, as well as any key observations pertaining to the specific piece's discussion. We select a few comments that capture contemporary narratives about immigration at this historical moment. See Figure 6.1 below.

Figure 6.1. Analyzed comments on online news stories.

Media Source	Date Published 2017	No. of Comments
Fox News	January 25	Thousands
Fox News	February 11	Thousands
Washington Post	February 19	150
BuzzFeed News	March 2	15
Washington Post	March 3	487
USA Today	March 7	3
USA Today	March 15	7
USA Today	March 17	13
AOL–U.S. News	March 18	1,947
ABC News	March 18	73
Chicago Tribune	March 18	18
Fox News	March 18	1,234
AOL–NBC News	March 19	2,481

Analysis

A Fox News online story titled "Trump to Order Construction of US-Mexico Border Wall; Expected to Suspend Refugee Program," January 25, 2017 (DeMarche 2017), had a large volume of comments—in the thousands. Many of the comments expressed wishes for militarized violent responses to migrants at the border. For example, IQ145 presents extreme policy proposals:

> Pass legislation [stating] that attempted infiltration will be met with instant death sentence to be carried out on the spot and the corpses flung back into Mexico with a catapult. . . . Confiscation of property for an individual or business that rents or provides shelter or harbors an illegal alien. . . . Round up and deport all illegal aliens [sic].

Others thank President Trump for "increased security":

> Thank you President Trump . . . the wall . . . increased security . . . YEA! better than opening our borders and passing out cash to all who storm in, Huh Barry????

This comment associates the border wall with safety, implying that porous borders are dangerous and that immigrants were given money by Obama just after coming to the United States. This stems from the false and racist idea that people of color take advantage of social programs (Kendi 2016, Van Hook and Bean 2009), which is used as an argument by conservatives to slash budgets for social programs and safety nets for the poor and the working class (Fox 2004, Katz 1996).

Comments on the article "Trump Notes 'Dangerous' Uptick in Refugees since Courts Ruled against Travel Ban," published on February 11, 2017 (Fox News 2017b), emphasize creating security and safety for "citizens" through the Muslim Ban of 2017 proposing to bar people from Iran, Iraq, Libya, Somalia, Sudan, Syria, and Yemen. Someone comments, "How can someone not see that all President Trump wants to do is to secure the safety and livelihood of American citizens First!" Many comments paint undocumented migrants as violent, criminals, gang members, and unfairly using social programs. These constructions bolster the state's incarceration of undocumented migrants, particularly Latin immigrants.

In comments on the AOL–NBC News article "Federal Government Solicits Design Proposals for Border Wall with Mexico," from March 19 (AOL 2017), we see demands to stop immigration and an open call for the use of violence to achieve so. The arguments in favor of the border wall start with claims about the rule of law, move to welfare abuse, and escalate to the open call for militarized and violent deterrence to one that makes a sadistic spectacle of this "enforcement." Corporate 100 wrote:

> Platinum 1 The Illegal Aliens have no rights in crossing the border from Mexico into The United States. These Illegals once into our Country are assisted with Food Stamps, Housing, Medical Care, Education etc. Who pays for all of the handouts? Of course the Middle-Class Americans who are trying to care for their families and it is totally wrong for our Government to expect all Americans to pay with higher taxes. Enough is Enough!

Kathy wrote,

> We need to work JUST AS HARD to rid the country of the illegals already here, sucking the breath out of our country by getting free medical and welfare monies. Get RID OF THEM!!

Blackbelt Ron wrote:

> I know it [the border wall] is planned to be 30 feet high but it needs to be covered in all sorts of flesh piercing materials and equipped with electrical devices that detect activity and eliminate all intruders. Do It—do it now, protect our country!"

Yep says,

> Electrify that wall and show it on Pay Per View at 9.99 to watch them get shocked, Hysterical . . . now that I would pay for. We could bait it with Tacos! Entertaining and it will pay for the wall!

The discussions of electrification, technological equipment, gun turrets, and weaponry mark an intensified and militarized xenophobia. The comments highlight native citizens' rage at the belief about Mexican immigrants abusing social programs. This is compatible with neoliberalism, which encourages an anti–social program ideology. This ideology was sold to white America to justify slashes to social safety nets in the name of stripping them from low-income people of color. Yet, President Reagan's and Clinton's massive cuts to welfare programs across the country negatively affected both white and non-white Americans. These cuts along with increasing income inequality as the costs of living increased while wages remained stagnant also added to feelings of dissatisfaction and anger against the American political system. In some instances, white Americans assigned blame to non-white citizens and immigrants for contributing to their lack of economic success, which was due to structural neoliberal policies put in place by the government. The assumption that middle-class Americans are the ones who pay for immigrants to survive in the United States is quite flawed, but it is clear that many people choose to assign blame to them.

Carlos Danger wrote:

> I love how the libs call illegals "Undocumented." I guess they would call a Home Invader an "Un invited House Guest."

The metaphor of comparing the "nation" to a "house" was common throughout the comments criminalizing undocumented immigrants by comparing them to a trespasser or intruder entering someone's home. This is a misleading comparison since immigrants enter the economic and housing markets like any new person arriving to a city or town and do not invade any private property.

The BuzzFeed News article "A Mexican Congressman Climbed a US Border Fence to Show Trump How 'Totally Absurd' a Wall Would Be," March 2, 2017 (Hernandez 2017), had a number of comments mentioning barbed/razor wire. Shirley Gordon wrote, "Just needs a little razor wire up there to finish it." Billy Smith wrote, "razor wire. electrified only a bit to make u unconfortable [sic]." The razor wire comments came from individuals in Nacogdoches, Texas; Batesville, Arkansas; Seattle, Washington; and Valatie, New York. In 2019, the National Guard added razor wire atop much of the existing fencing (Hay 2019).

The ABC News article "CBP Issues Requests for Border Wall Proposals: It Will 'Be Physically Imposing in Height,'" March 18, 2017 (Caplan 2017), had 73 comments including one where True Grit proposed a moat:

> A really big moat filled with thousands of gators might do the trick also. A moat with concrete walls so the gators can't get out but keep illegals out of the US.

That individuals conjure up these scenarios of animals killing humans as a form of border protection reveals how strong the animosity is toward immigrants.

The comments posted about the *USA Today* article "Border Wall Materials: Concrete, 'Other,'" March 15, 2017 (Carranza 2017), were mainly concerned with payment for the wall. Warren Weick wrote:

> Since I'm going to have to pay and Mexico is not (despite what Trump says we will never be reimbursed in any way), could you make it cheaper than originally planned? A wall about 2 foot high and made out of adobe bricks would just about be what I would be willing to pay for.

It is interesting that despite many of these commenters' strong desire to have a border wall to feel protected between the United States and Mexico, they are unwilling to pay for the wall. Instead, they want either the Mexican government or Trump to pay for it personally.

In the *Washington Post* article "An 'Abrazo' on the U.S.-Mexico Border Celebrates Unity, but Trump Has Laredo Worried," February 19, 2017 (Milfeld 2017), we see similar rhetoric racializing and criminalizing migrants, as well as more of the anti–social program discourse. As Barry H O Soetoro wrote:

> Mexico loves American Libs, who accept illegals, knowing that the offspring of illegals will vote for more free stuff.

The use of "offspring," a term commonly used for animals, dehumanizes Mexican migrants. The "threat" of babies of color being born on U.S. soil is an ongoing theme among white nationalists.

DRCJR63 interprets Mexican behavior as disrespectful to the United States:

> Mexico screams about disrespect yet it is Mexico and its citizens who have disrespected the US for to long and now face the reality that the US has had enough. No respect for the border and yet feelings of entitlement. Waive [*sic*] your Mexican flag and demand your US benefits. Healthcare, drivers license, education, ability to commit "minor crimes" with no deportation, can't be bothered to learn English, and their government goes around holding meetings on how to stay in the US. Yep, lots of respect there for the US.

CryLosersCry writes about different languages being spoken in the United States:

> Becca, it's not just a border problem anymore. It's embedded into the very core of the US and affects many cities in the core of the US, like Siler City, NC. I was the only person speaking English in McDonalds [*sic*] including the customers and those behind the counters serving the customers. They had to find an English speaking person to service my order? Is this the America we want?

The story also emphasizes the perceived inconvenience this person experienced in a multilingual setting. The comment also suggests a greater fear of losing the perceived "core" of America that once existed in exchange for one full of less white people and English-speakers.

The *Chicago Tribune* article titled "Trump Administration's Rhetoric about Islam Is Key in Travel Ban Rulings," March 18, 2017 (Johnson and Thanawala 2017), had a few comments using the terms terrorists or terrorism. Kasha11 explicitly expresses terror of Muslims, using the loaded word infiltration, which is pervasive across xenophobic discourse. Claiming that Trump is "trying to protect the citizens," Kasha11 constructs Muslim/Arab immigrants to be a threat or safety hazard—the "enemy":

> ISIS has said it is infiltrating suicide bombers and terrorists with immigrants to maim and kill. And they already have done it in San Bernardino, Paris, Nice, Brussels and Frankfurt. And you media types denigrate Trump for doing what a president has as a first priority, trying to protect the citizens? What do you need, the Loop at high noon? Old story: Beware the enemy at your back. But it should not be the media.

Attacks on the media by President Trump himself have been common throughout his presidency. The above comment suggests that these attacks have also encouraged his supporters to defend him. In turn, any media posts that even suggest criticism of Trump's policies are seen as a personal attack.

The AOL–U.S. News article "What's Next for Trump's Travel Ban?" March 18, 2017 (Neuhauser 2017), has 1,947 comments, mostly xenophobic. For example, John wrote:

> Why do liberal[s] want to protect people who would kill them if given the chance? You people are playing politics with our lives.

Clearly, John wrongly thinks that Muslims want to kill him. Such viewpoints are grounded in stereotypes and false generalizations of entire populations of people. Theomegaman72 wrote,

You have to laugh at these self-loathing anti-Americans, so desperate to be liked that they'll welcome their own killers into the country." . . . . "If that ugly pig holding the "no ban" sign is so upset, maybe she should move to the Middle East to be closer to the people she loves" [*sic*].

In this comment, he too quickly labels Middle Easterners "killers," linking Islamophobia to patriotism.

The *Washington Post* article "The Biggest Problem for Trump's Border Wall Isn't Money. It's getting the land," March 3, 2017 (Dickinson 2017), had 487 comments. Steelcreek wrote:

We don't need a wall to stop immigrants. They will voluntarily stop - and self deport - if they can't work, buy or rent lodging, attend school, drive a car or receive benefits once they are here. This can all be done by holding current American citizens accountable for engaging in any of these activities utilizing a comprehensive e verify system that requires every American to have a national photo ID accessible online thru a government site. We need an administrative system that allows drug smugglers caught crossing the border to be executed by firing squad within 3 days of their apprehension. Problem solved with no wall.

These public comments, including talking about firing squads, reveal how violent the discourse has turned. These animosities in the United States began with "othering" those who did not appear as white and were only enforced through border restrictions and the popularization of narratives against migration.

The Fox News article "Dershowitz: If Obama Issued Trump's Travel Ban, It Would've Been Upheld," March 18, 2017 (Fox News 2017a), had 1,234 comments. Steve Demers wrote,

On both sides of the isle [*sic*], we have a continued difference of opinion. Those loyal to the President, want America to come first, just as he does. The Democrats are hell bent on welcoming anyone from anywhere, with open arms. I think it's fair to state, that the mass majority of those mentioned above, know little to nothing, about Muslim men and their regular behavior in their home countries. . . . those that want them here, should house them in their neighborhoods. Maybe then, the anti-gun folks, would understand the importance of being "permitted" to protect their loved ones.

In this comment, he reveals particularly gendered Islamophobia arguing that Democrats do not have adequate knowledge of Muslim men, implying that he does based on his military service. He also speculates that it is unlikely that many American veterans or contractors would approve of Muslim men in the United States. The fact that the comment ends with a push for using weapons against immigrants further illustrates the consequences of social boundary formation.

Overall Findings

There are recognizable patterns across all of these online comments. Most of the xenophobic, racist, and Islamophobic comments overwhelmingly came from posters that presented themselves as white males. When women did reproduce these discourses, they were most often white. This information was only available when the commenter had a profile picture, or when the post linked back to the commenter's Facebook page. However, most of the comments, regardless of political framings, seemed to be from men or from those with masculine names. Also, most of the commenters seemed to be adults—middle-aged and older. Most of the commenters had right-leaning politics. Left-leaning comments were, overall, much less common in these articles. While mainstream outlets did not seem to have more left-leaning comments, they did have fewer comments. Fox News had quite larger volumes of comments beneath their articles, as did AOL. This might imply that older, more xenophobic folks may be more active on these comment sections than others. Indeed, young people do not frequently use AOL. Many of the racist, xenophobic comments came from geographic areas with significantly isolated rural white populations.

The first pervasive narrative throughout the comment sections was violent and militarized xenophobia. These comments would often list off high-tech weapons, describing mass murder with excitement. The second narrative that appeared was racialized, neoliberal, and anti-welfare discourse. Thirdly, commenters spout dubious facts, statistics, and data points with inaccurate citations or no citations at all. These "alternative facts" are deployed to strengthen the discourses made, providing fabricated justifications for mass deportations, detentions, and murders.

The beginning of 2017 was a period of reinvigorated xenophobia, racism, and Islamophobia. Trump had fanned the flames, encouraging the solidification of symbolic, social, and physical boundaries. Already marginalized before the election of Trump, migrants, especially those with Mexican, Latin, and Muslim identities, now face an intensified set of structural obstacles that differ entirely from those of past migrants, such as Italian-Americans, who were able to assimilate into U.S. whiteness and gain the privileges attached to it.

These structural obstacles are rooted in old historical discourses stigmatizing migrants. Understanding, challenging, and dismantling these discourses is just one constructive way to delegitimize these oppressive structures and resist systems of domination. Paired with other forms of resistance, discussing and delegitimizing these discourses is one small step we can take toward decreasing inequities and cultivating a more just future.

Part III

IMMIGRATION AS AN EXPERIENCE

Chapter 7

Different Understandings of the Border Wall

The Social Meanings of the Wall for Border Residents

OUT OF MIND, OUT OF SIGHT—ON THE INVISIBILITY OF THE BORDER FOR BORDER CITY RESIDENTS

National discussions about the United States' border with Mexico focus on rural and sparsely populated areas where groups of undocumented immigrants cross. "The border" is very different in urban areas which have designated crossing sites such as bridges and marked ports of entry. Furthermore, in border cities like El Paso, legal crossings are a daily occurrence, but they are not the only activity that takes place there. As local resident Jessica Duarte writes,

> The border and Ciudad Juárez are right next to us in El Paso, Texas and yet the border is not something we think about in our daily lives. Thousands of individuals come and go through the border every day as part of their daily routine, everyone crossing back and forth having different experiences and different purposes. Unfortunately, crossing the border daily has gotten more difficult each year . . . therefore individuals who cross from Ciudad Juárez to El Paso wait long periods of time in line to cross. Inspection takes longer which means crossing the border takes longer. Individuals are affected by this because most of the people who cross do it for work and school purposes. Personally, I do not cross the border very often. I try to avoid crossing the border due to the long waiting periods. Security in Juárez has improved throughout the years, but it is still something that frightens me. At the end of the day, I only cross to visit my family, and that's about it. I think it is very amazing how the lives of individuals can be so different on each side of the border. I visit Ciudad Juárez, and the building structures, the housing, the colonias, the food, the culture, and even the people are very different. It surprises me what effects a division by one fence

can have, and how can people be so different on one side and the other. Then I come back to El Paso, and I compare and notice the buildings, the people, the food, the government and it simply amazes me how different things can be. . . . On the other hand, I am proud of what the Mexican culture has brought into the United States. It has brought culture, religion, and beliefs that till this day Mexican Americans celebrate and cherish.

In her narrative, Duarte tries to grasp the visible differences on both sides of the border. She also notices the similarities in the natural environment and the influence of Mexican culture. Jessica understands how individuals are shaped differently by the border. Some people cross it every day despite the long lines and bureaucratic demands; in contrast, others very rarely cross, and may even forget that they live in a border city. In the quote below, El Paso resident Gabriel Fontan writes about how the border can become invisible:

As I drove aimlessly towards what I hoped was the border, I couldn't help but become aware of how forced my actions were. This was not something I would have done freely; I had not seen the border in more than ten years. Maybe a little bit of an exaggeration but what I mean is that [given the assignment] I wasn't just passing by it, I had to take notice. The thought that kept coming back to me was of looking back into your blind spot while driving. Though a narrow metaphor, it highlights the behavior in which we are forced to look in a direction that doesn't come naturally. The last time I noticed the border was back when I was 19 and was going to the Juárez strip to go partying and get drunk.

Gabriel Fontan captures the phenomenon of the border line becoming invisible or irrelevant to locals, even for Latin people. He describes the invisibility of the border by comparing it to a blind spot while driving: the border fence is there, but it is "socially invisible" to the local driver unless they make an effort to see it. The border is taken for granted by U.S. border residents, and with the increase in violence in Ciudad Juárez following the militarized war on drugs (Staudt and Mendez 2015, Campbell 2009, Díaz-Cepeda and Castañeda n.d.), many residents in El Paso wished to forget about the other side. The national attention, resources, fence, and heavy policing have ironically caused some border residents to stop thinking about their neighbors in Mexico.

The Borderline as Seen by Local Students

What do people who live in the border region say about the border wall? Do residents of the border region have a different sense of what "the border" entails from those who live far away from it? Data to help us answer these questions come from a project conducted in a sociology class on "methods of research" in the spring of 2013 at the University of Texas at El Paso, where I asked students who lived in the El Paso–Ciudad Juárez border region to engage with these issues. What emerged was a multiplicity of understandings that, theorizing, I call "socially polysemic," which I use to summarize how different meanings of the same object vary by intersectionality or social position. Yet, when pasted together, these different points of view paint a fuller picture of the U.S.-Mexico border fence in the El Paso del Norte Region. This phenomenon is akin to that of the Indian parable of the six blind men and the elephant, where six blind men all touched an elephant in different places. Depending on what part of the elephant the blind men touched (the side, tusk, leg, trunk, or ears), they would provide different descriptions of the animal.

It is important to engage with the border empirically rather than relying on the popular discourse on the topic, even for the El Paso residents. The discourse in popular media often conflates Latin immigration, border crossings, and crime (Chavez 2008a, Dowling and Inda 2013). For example, the numerous TV series such as *The Bridge*, and movies such as Ridley Scott's *The Counselor* or the *Sicario* movies located in border cities, focus on crime, violence, and anarchy. However, as anthropologist Howard Campbell argues, while it is important to study and discuss narco-culture and crime in Ciudad Juárez, this does not represent "Mexican or border culture as a whole" (Campbell 2009). Contrary to what outsiders may imagine, drug trafficking does not have a direct impact on the daily lives of most people in El Paso, Texas. Despite this fact, some college students living in this safe border city share the prejudices of media discourses regarding migration and the U.S.-Mexico border region.

In 2013, I asked El Paso students to rethink the border by doing fieldwork and to encounter the border fence through, for example, personal visits to a part of the borderline, journaling, photography, writing poetry, or creating multimedia projects about this experience. Classroom discussions prior to the assignments revealed that many students had not previously taken the time and effort to study their communities from a larger social, theoretical, or historical perspective. This chapter shows some of the students' work reflecting on the border fence in order to present some of the insights that border residents have about the U.S.-Mexican border. Some residents interpreted their encounters with border walls and fences in diametrically different ways. These reflections illustrate how individuals create different social meanings about the border region and the fence, depending on their own positionality based on age, gender, ethnicity, language, and immigration experience.

Sociologist Pablo Vila elicited common perceptions of people across the border through responses to photographs from the region. Vila presented photos to his interviewees to elicit narratives about the identity, worth, and morality of border residents. He often found common tropes and stereotypes that distorted reality. As follow-ups, he would engage them in dialogues and counter their narratives with additional facts (Vila 2000). He often observed that people would change their narratives about "others" cohabiting in the border region, while at other times, respondents would rely on common plots and preconceptions to justify their original responses.

In the case of this chapter, students took their own photos to show what the border meant to them visually or experientially. This is similar to the photovoice methodology where vulnerable, marginal, or stigmatized populations are given disposable cameras to document their everyday life (De Heer, Moya, and Lacson 2008; Wang and Burris 1997). In this case, most students had access to stand-alone digital cameras or cameras on their smartphones. Yet, the principle is the same as in photovoice to present photographs of symbolic landscapes.

The Border in the Classroom

Because of the many preconceived notions that students have from political discourse, the media, and popular culture dating back decades, teaching about borders in the classroom is not an easy task. Many students believe that international borders are "common sense," natural, and necessary. Instead, borders are historically contingent, the results of war and historical contention. Culture, ideas, and people have rarely been restrained from traveling and spreading by political borders drawn by international treaties. Understanding national societies as self-contained boxes with clear boundaries is a widespread conceptualization that hinders rather than advances social scientific understanding (Tilly 1984). Defining and describing what borders truly are is a difficult task. Historically, the U.S.-Mexico border has been framed in the national imagination as part of "the West," "the frontier," and as a destination for personal wealth and imperial expansion. Contemporarily, the image of the border is defined by the debate surrounding undocumented migrants. Media coverage in the last decades often reproduced the image of a Mexican-born man jumping over the border fence in a deserted area (Chavez 2001). Media campaigns by right-wing groups further gave credence to the fantasy of an immediate need to "secure the border" (Shapira 2013b, Heyman 2013a).

The growing concern about the border paradoxically coincided with a growing discourse about globalization. As sociologist Harel Shapira writes, for border residents,

> Globalization means that you can't go into Mexico to get your teeth cleaned without a passport. It means that every time you want to go to the grocery store you need to pass a checkpoint. It means having to negotiate your relationships to a security and surveillance apparatus. It means that suddenly your identity, as a citizen, as an American, as a community member, becomes organized around the border. . . . We tend to take the border as a given, timeless and permanent. But it is not. The border has a history; it is an ongoing project, and until the government's recent interventions you would be hard-pressed to find something that looked like a border in Adobe, either as a physical object or as an idea organizing social relations. For centuries, the border existed as an abstract political and jurisdictional reality; however, until the past two decades it had neither a prominent physical presence nor a profound effect on the everyday lives of local residents. As a longtime resident recalls: "For as far back as I can remember, people from these parts were going back and forth across the border. Hell, wasn't even a border to really cross. You'd walk into Mexico without knowing it." Ambiguity, however, has given way to rigidity; openness to closure. (Shapira 2013a)

The national border, as a fenced and patrolled area, is a new reality, yet, the image of the border as an empty inhabited desert remains. As anthropologist Josiah Heyman writes,

> While there are broad areas of consensus among border actors, there is not a uniform set of opinions and experiences. . . . [Yet] in US national discourse, the border is generally treated as an uninhabited location of national concerns and policies delineated across abstract geographic space (Nevins 2002). The only relevant persons are transitory crossers who are deemed subject to official examination and enforcement. It is not envisioned as a region with a large, settled population, with interests, opinions, and rights, commensurate with all other people in the United States. Of course, policy makers, public administrators, and specialists recognize the complexity of border flows and the importance of US-Mexico relations, but the dehumanized view of the border captures the essence of how the border is perceived and acted on. Even national actors who should know better are constrained by the political discourse of an "empty border." (Heyman 2013b)

Border residents are often socially invisible in national debates, and their voices are rarely heard. Therefore, in a democracy it is crucial to give them a say in discussions about borders.

Resident Voices

The following excerpts, reproduced with permission, show how students grappled with the assignment to go to a place where the United States' and Mexico's political boundaries touch. The passages show the most common sentiments expressed by different types of students. Most students come from the region. Fifty students were enrolled in the class; 93.9 percent had been in college for three years or more; 20.3 percent were married, in a marriage-like relationship, or divorced; 72.9 percent of them were born in El Paso and 8.3 percent in Ciudad Juárez; 79.6 percent reported speaking Spanish; 81.6 percent self-classified as Hispanic, 8.2 percent as non-Hispanic white, 10.2 percent as other, and none as black. Although a majority were Hispanic, they were very heterogeneous in terms of immigrant generation, with a few born abroad, some immigrating as children, many born in the United States to immigrant parents, as well as some individuals whose families have been in Texas for more than five generations.

Jaime Harris, a thirty-seven-year-old white woman who had lived in El Paso for two years, wrote,

I was surprised when the assignment was given, to realize that we hadn't even considered the fence as another cultural landmark to visit while we were in El Paso. After some thought, I've come to the conclusion that I see the fence in a much different way than almost every other landmark. In my experience, the fence has very negative associations. It's a place to be avoided, an off-limits area. A place associated with those who break the law. Criminals interact with the fence, not law-abiding citizens. So, I'll admit that I was a little nervous about taking my children to the fence since it's a location that is routinely patrolled by law enforcement. However, I realized when the assignment was given, that I had to take my kids. This was a location with a lot of things to teach us, and an opportunity to really test the lessons that I hope I've been teaching my kids all their lives. We drove to a spot on the side of the highway where we could pull over and interact with the fence.

The first thing that I noticed when we arrived was the different reactions from my two children. My youngest [10] seemed curious and a little confused. My oldest [13] was very anxious. In this photo, he is looking back down the highway and insisting that we should leave. At thirteen he seems to have already, the same impression of the fence that I do and is very uncomfortable being there. He is very concerned that the police are going to come and arrest us if we don't leave. And truly, with a large fence, barbed wire, flood lights every 20 feet, and what looks like a moat, it's hard to fault his logic. It is not an inviting atmosphere.

As a member of the military, Jaime's family has lived in and visited over twenty-three countries. She had taken her family to visit a Nazi concentration camp in Auschwitz, Poland, and the Demilitarized Zone between North and

Figure 7.1. Border fence between El Paso, Texas, United States and Ciudad Juárez, Chihuahua, México. Photo by Jaime Harris, 2013.

South Korea; yet, until this assignment, it never occurred to her to set foot next to the border fence between the United States and Mexico because she conceived it as a dangerous and stigmatized place where bad people were. Despite living and studying in El Paso, Jaime acknowledged the negative connotations that she held about the borderline itself. Yet once the assignment was announced, she recognized the opportunity she was presented with for her to teach her children. The visit prompted important questions about the tension between America's self-identity as an open society welcoming of immigrants and one dissuading border-crossing migrants. Jaime writes how, despite her family being white American citizens with military parents, when "a border patrol vehicle drove past us very slowly, it scared [her children] both so we left." They thought they were breaking the law for simply being in this public space. If the presence of the Border Patrol was scary for them, one must imagine how being in this space may feel for Latin citizens not to mention undocumented people. This narrative exemplifies all the fear and negative emotions that the fence creates for both natives and immigrants.

El Paso natives may have strong feelings about the neighboring city, Ciudad Juárez, in the Mexican state of Chihuahua, but most of the time, they

Figure 7.2. Border Patrol vehicle overseeing the border fence in El Paso. Photo by Daniel Delgado.

forget it exists. It is hard to explain to outsiders how naturalized the international border has become for people in the region who often do not think much about it. As the statements below show, for many inhabitants of El Paso, Texas, the border does not refer to their city or their neighborhood, but rather to the actual buffer zone around the river and the international boundary land-posts, including the border fence. For others, it simply means "the other side." As Daniel Delgado writes,

> This image is the El Paso I have come to know my whole life. We are a unique city, not only because we are a majority of Latinos, but because we share a border with Juárez, Mexico. I was asked to write about my experience going to the border. This was something I was never really comfortable with since I had only gone there a handful of times as a child and a couple more as a teenager.

A different view is introduced by Teresa Anchondo:

> I graduated high school in 2002, at this time it was safe to go to Juárez. Of course, my parents would try to fill me with stories of girls getting kidnapped and so on, but I never really paid any heed because I knew this wouldn't happen

to me. I would always attribute a girl getting kidnapped in Juárez with something that she had done wrong on her part. All the same my friends and I would go, and I never really felt a need to worry. We would typically walk over from Downtown and walk back later that night.

I moved to San Jose [California] a couple years later, and that was when there was a war brewing in Mexico, at least that was all I ever heard from the media I was being fed. Yet, one could not deny that Juárez was losing its identity with the constant discovery of mass graves, drugs, and dead bodies. I was worried for my parents and told them to start thinking about moving closer to me or my brother. They, of course, had the same attitude I had as a teenager—they knew nothing would happen to them.

I moved back to El Paso to finish college in 2011, and since then I have never felt the need to venture into Juárez. Before this assignment, the only interaction I had with that side was with the students in the university who still reside there, and with the view I see of Juarez from across I-10.

As I was getting closer and closer to the bridge I found myself becoming nervous. I realized that I felt like this because I was in a place I did not understand. I live in a border city, but never have to deal with the border. The people that I saw, as we got closer and closer to the bridge, all seemed to be a bit rushed, I figured this was because they were either trying to catch the bus or were on their way to some job. When we got to the bridge, I realized that it was much different than I remembered. It looked quite nice, much different than the one I used to cross as an adolescent.

In this narrative Teresa, a Mexican-American woman, also talks about her apprehension about the fence and the international bridges. She accepts her

Figure 7.3.   International bridge. Photo by Teresa Anchondo.

inability to understand what the border means sociologically. After going to this international bridge, she was surprised to find the place was nicer than she imagined. As a college student, she rarely thinks about crossing into Mexico even though her family is from Mexico, she speaks perfect Spanish, and used to visit there as a child. While Teresa has a very different background from Jaime, both share an apprehension and avoidance of the area around the international border. There exists some general shared sentiment of the border when you live in a border city: it is always both present and non-present.

The Border as Arbitrary

Everyday life in a border city is very bicultural, but boundary-making mechanisms are often at work. As Daniela Lizarraga wrote,

> The border is a strange, entirely artificial creation: more of a concept than an actuality. When you think about it, it's almost childish, even; like two children drawing a line down the middle of their room to prevent further bickering. Unless the squabbling children are divided from one another, conflict will inevi-

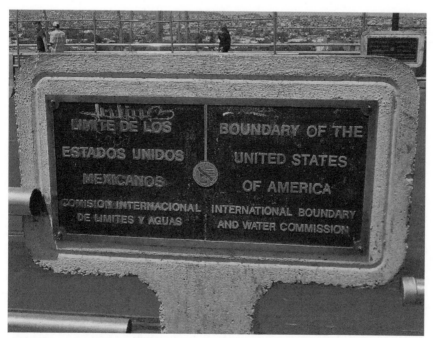

Figure 7.4.   International boundary plaque on a border bridge. Photo by Eric Mateo.

tably follow. . . . The physical space of the border also seems rather arbitrary: at times, it is marked by chain-link fences and barbed wire, while others it is merely the sad trickle of what we call the Rio Grande. The boundary that divides the countries, though, was not forged in such an arbitrary manner. Wars were fought, and an abundance of blood was spilled in pursuit of staking a claim on the expanse of dirt. While some might find the divide peculiar and random, its history belies the idea with a long, convoluted past of violence and death. Like most, if not all borders, ours is one created by men's thirst for power and the sacrifice of human lives.

The disparity in the seriousness with which different people cross the border is striking as well: from a childhood friend who was smuggled over in the trunk of her step-father's car, to the people who can walk confidently over the bridge thanks to a scrap of paper declaring it legal, to the ones who hop, swim, or dash over the border under the shelter of night. It is strange too how much easier it is to cross over into Juárez than it is to come back. For those who seek a livelihood across the border from Mexico to the United States, the border is a real, palpable thing; an adversary of sorts that must be overcome. For some, it has been a pursuit that cost their life savings or even their own lives when the Coyote that promised them everything betrayed them. For most American citizens, it is an annoying inconvenience, a pit stop along the way to partying in Juárez or vacationing on a beach, or perhaps a hindrance to visiting their relatives who remain in Mexico.

Yet, we all take this border for granted, talk about it as if it were a real, physical construct instead of an abstract concept. Of course, there are people who want to make it into a real barrier as well. They perceive the possibility of illegal immigrants coming as one might a plague and wish to build a great wall between our countries or to line the border with armed guards willing to shoot on sight. Others simply accept the border for what it is to their daily lives, which for some means spending hours every day crossing the bridge and back to get to and from work or to visit family. The idea that a border can legitimately separate you from your family, that it can rightfully do so, is bizarre. But is taken as a matter of fact for many.

Daniela Lizarraga takes an ontological and critical view of the border as she discusses the cruel effects it has on the lives of millions of people. While from a theoretical and socio-historical perspective the border is a construct, a "line in the sand" (St. John 2011), it is also a demarcated (Dear 2013) physical reality with real-world consequences, especially for people without immigration papers.

The View from the Mexican Side

The meaning of the border and the border fence are somewhat different for people socialized or living in Ciudad Juárez. As many students wrote, for people in Ciudad Juárez, the border fence is a big "You are not welcome" sign. Yet, many have papers that allow them to cross back and forth. As Eric Mateo describes,

> The ports of entry are full of people doing all kinds of stuff. There are people who want to go to school, people who want to want to get work, people who work on the bridge, people who are going to visit their loved ones, or simply people who want to hang out in a different country. The only trait that could be predicted is that most of the people crossing the bridge are Hispanic. Thousands and thousands of people cross every day, yet I wonder how many people who live in El Paso have never crossed the bridge. I cross every day to attend college. A thought that disturbs me is to comprehend that it only takes me 25 cents to get to El Paso, and to many others, the cost to cross is their life.

Eric Mateo artfully writes about the difficulty to understand how someone like him can cross back and forth and pay twenty-five cents at the international bridge to do so, while others who would gladly pay this toll cannot cross because they lack the appropriate papers. Eric can live a transborder life, accessing the best of both countries, while others have to choose a side because if they cross the border, they may risk their lives, their liberty, their ability to return south with ease, and risk being separated from family members they migrate with, as well as having to leave loved ones behind (Castañeda and Buck 2014, 2011).

However, it should be made clear that the beliefs that everyone has a precarious life in Ciudad Juárez and farther south, and that everyone would like to move into the United States if they could, are false. Eric Mateo photographed a sign in a border mural on the Mexican side that reads in Spanish, "There are also dreams on this side." Many people, including those with papers, visit and go shopping in the United States but prefer to live in Mexico. The testimony of Itzel Rosales speaks to this frequent crossing back and forth:

> I was born in El Paso, but I have lived all my life in Juárez. Since I was about 13 years old, I have studied in El Paso, and although it was a strange experience for me to cross the border bridge every day, I have gotten used to it. When I was younger, I did not know anything about citizenship and the difference between U.S. and Mexican citizens. I did not understand why some people were treated differently. Over the years that I have crossed the border on a daily basis, I have seen the difficulties people endure, such as having to wait in the sun, becoming dehydrated, and even fainting. After the 9/11 attacks on the Twin Towers, the wait time in the lines became ridiculous, but people still had to cross to go to work and school. I don't blame the customs officials for these difficulties because they were just doing their jobs. They had to check every car from the front all the way to the back. During this time many people from Juárez moved

Figure 7.5.   Border fence. Photo by Isabel De La Rosa.

to El Paso, as this was easier than spending more than two hours waiting in line to cross every day. I think this also had an impact on the economy of El Paso, as many people were tired of waiting and stayed home rather than coming here to shop or visit family. We also have family here in El Paso, and my parents used to come every weekend to visit them, but after 9/11 that changed. Now they only come about once a month because they hate waiting in line for so long and dealing with the racism of the U.S. customs agents. Recently, with many rumors of guns being taken into Juárez, even more security has been implemented on the bridges. This has caused changes in how crossing occurs, as now sometimes people that travel from El Paso to Juárez have to wait in line too.

An aerial photograph would show long lines of cars waiting to cross border checkpoints at the U.S. end of the bridge in order to enter the United States, while the cars going to Mexico flow freely into the practically open border into Mexico, where no passports or visas are routinely checked.

Different Words for the Same Object

In 2013, describing the border dividers either as a fence or a wall depended on the background of the person describing it. For some Mexican citizens, it is a symbolic wound in the ground and a painful reminder of the U.S.-Mexico war. For Mexican international students who cross often, the border is a door to a new world. Sometimes these different approaches to the border can only be communicated in Spanish, as in the case of Laura López, who writes about the language used to define the border divide. In El Paso, people talked about border fences rather than walls before Trump's presidential campaign. Laura writes,

I find it interestingly revealing that the word we use to refer to this barrier changes from country to country. "Border fence" has a softer connotation, lighter and less invasive. The translation of the word fence into Spanish is *cerca*, however, in Mexico it is more common to say *muro* (wall) to refer to this physical division between the two countries. The term "wall" contains connotations totally contrary to the term "fence;" a wall is solid, immovable, hard, heavy, made to separate permanently two spaces. While a fence presupposes a transient or temporary action, an object that can be brought down, that is not there to stay. Could it be that the different points of view between Mexicans and Americans about this barrier are so contrary that the words we use reveal our rivalries?

In Ciudad Juárez, I always lived in a house that is located about a block from the Río Bravo [what in the United States is referred to as Rio Grande]. As a

Figure 7.6.   Border fence. Photo by Danny Antunez.

child, I remember going so far on my bicycle that I did not notice that I was no longer in Mexican territory. . . . That huge piece of steel that we call *muro* or fence, is simply a physical object which in itself has no power to dictate laws. However [it] is the most emblematic and powerful element that exists to symbolize the interaction between the two countries and the way that this division is lived differently depending on the social situation in question.[1]

In the paragraphs above, Laura López makes the important point that in 2013, in English, people used the word fence to refer to the divide built between the two neighboring countries, while in Spanish the equivalent of wall is used to describe it. Mexicans referring to the border as a "wall" may also suggest their lack of hope in a future with more open borders and communities. This could be influenced by the stereotypes that many Americans have of Mexicans, increased border patrol, and politicians glorifying the construction of a concrete wall along the border.

In 2018, the structures in El Paso are still closer to a fence than a wall. A "fence" is transparent since one can see across, while the idea of a wall makes references to castles, the Great Wall of China, and the Berlin Wall. As a child playing outdoors in Ciudad Juárez, Laura would sometimes venture into American territory unknowingly. The border was open, and both cities were very safe. Today, the discussions about building a border wall are in and of themselves indicative of an increase in the symbolic boundaries between Mexicans and Americans.

The Passageway

For people living outside of cities on the U.S. southern border, everyday life can sometimes be interrupted by migrants passing by. Manuel Mata offers an insight about how some people used to react to this:

Growing up, I never thought about or even considered the impacts of living so close to another country. I have seen the results of what living so close can bring, and this includes seeing and experiencing a number of times immigrants cross through our house and neighborhood moments after illegally crossing the border. One memory that really stands out to me was on Christmas Eve about ten years ago, my family and I heard some noise outside at night. When we went to go see what it was we were all astonished, it was a family consisting of the mother, father, young son, and daughter. We instantly knew who they were and what they were doing hiding in between tall grass. They immediately insisted for us not to call the police or border patrol; then they explained how they were being chased by the border patrol and that they hadn't eaten or drank anything that whole day. We knew we couldn't do much to help because there are penalties for aiding criminals, but what we did do was give them tamales and something to drink and let them borrow the phone to call the person that was going to pick them up.

Manuel Mata's story exemplifies the ways in which an otherwise tranquil life in the borderlands can sometimes be disrupted by the sudden appearances of undocumented immigrants in transit. In this case, a family appeared on Christmas asking for shelter, and the locals helped the poor and wandering. Manuel writes about how his family was reluctant to help more because they could be punished by the authorities if they were discovered. Still, as good Samaritans, they gave the family food and drink, and let them use their phone. This is an example where empathy outweighed fear. If one stops to think, the immigrant family had much more to be afraid of than the people who lived there. Alejandra Maldonado, who moved to the United States from Juárez as a child, writes,

I had a vague notion of immigration policy as it pertained to the American side, but it was not until I actually saw with my own eyes a piece of the puzzle that made me wonder what was really going on. . . . Driving along the border, I also drove along the fence that is supposed to keep illegal immigrants in their own side of the river. I saw border patrol agents on a daily basis patrolling along, riding their white and green trucks up and down, carefully inspecting the fence. I never actually saw anybody get caught. . . . Then one day . . . I was driving along the border in the morning, almost near downtown El Paso, when I saw three individuals: a girl of about eight, a man well into his forties or fifties, and a younger man of about eighteen years of age. These individuals were running, obviously crossing the border illegally. The three of them hardly seemed dangerous, if anything, they seemed scared. I believe that they were a family by the way they were all holding hands. Then, in their hurry to run away from the fence and deeper into El Paso, the little girl fell down the dirt path where she was running, taking a hard hit and rolling down a couple of feet. The older man, whom I believe to be her dad, hurriedly picked her up by the hand and dragged her along. The little girl, now covered in dirt, limped a little and struggled, but tried to keep up with her companions. The scene broke my heart. I could think of absolutely nothing that would make people feel the need to hurry a hurt child up and run for it. In an ideal world, I thought, they would have been able to stop and check on the girl and tend to her, instead of putting her through that experience of making her run, fall, keep running. I wondered what she felt if she understood what was going on. I felt bad for her and felt ashamed of living in a city where people who stop to help a hurt child would get in trouble for doing so. At that moment, for me, the fence along our border, along a territory that used to belong to Mexico, started signifying shame and unfairness—the failure of human beings to understand and help each other. The images that I see on my way to work every day are very complex: human beings hunting down other human beings (border patrol agents) and a fence that is meant to keep people within a city full of violence and lack of opportunity.

In her text, Alejandra Maldonado, a former legal permanent resident who became a naturalized U.S. citizen in 2008, is quick to empathize with undocumented migrants and feels ashamed for being associated with a system that ruthlessly criminalizes them. As a new American, she sometimes uses linguistic us/them boundaries when talking about documented versus undocumented migrants, and residents of El Paso versus Ciudad Juárez. When talking to her, I could understand how she was internally conflicted because at different times of her life, she has possessed different citizenships. The borderline can indeed create split identities, especially when the dominant

Figure 7.7.   Border fence close-up. Photo by Danny Antunez.

discourse emphasizes difference, and assigns positive attributes to one side of the boundary, and negative ones to the other. As a result, I am not implying that moving from Ciudad Juárez to El Paso creates mental illness but moving across the border is indeed a source of stress and what I would call "identity insecurity"—being unsure about what category one belongs to. As Alejandra elaborated in a reinterview (Vila 2000),

> I consider myself American most of the time, since it makes life easier for me as far as traveling and education here in the US goes. However, when I find myself among certain people, I definitely claim I am Mexican. When I lived in Australia and traveled to London, I could sense the tension against Americans and "pulled out" my Mexican identity. When I was in Germany, however, I was American all the way, I felt more secure that way. However, as I described in my essay, I do feel some shame sometimes when I identify myself as American. I can't help feeling pride in my country (Mexico) these days, when it is progressing, with the economy growing and all; I do get attacked by some fellow Mexican acquaintances, who call me "gringa" and feel I just go with what suits me at the time, like a hypocrite. This is partly true, but as they said in the "Selena" movie, a Mexican-American has to be more American than the Americans and more Mexican than the Mexicans, I feel I deserve a break like this. I literally feel confused between 2 different identities sometimes, and I feel trapped between 2 different judges: my Mexican family and my American expectations. The border is only physical, unfortunately. I wish I could create a border like that in my personality! It would make things less confusing for me, I think.

Alejandra describes how the physical international border and its increased surveillance and stigmatization is something that is internalized by immigrants and border residents.

Danny Antunez, a Mexican-American student, writes about what border crossers meant for him as he was growing up on the northern side of the border:

> Does this huge fence around the border make the border communities feel safer? To some yes it does make them feel safer than when there was no barrier between the two countries. Others like me never felt in danger or feel any safer than before. . . . When I was sitting in my car as close as I could to the border, it brought memories of growing up right near the border community of San Elizario which was a wonderful time for young children as we were. . . . Fields of corn and cotton as far as the eye could see—this was looking out to the backyard. We lived on the last street on our little community, and we were at the time only about 15 minutes walking distance from the Rio Grande. As young boys, my brothers and I would venture off into fields and play games.

Hide and seek was the best as there were endless fields that you could hide in between. Also growing up by the border meant that we could go to the river. At that point in time, there was about neck deep water for us young children and about waist deep water for grown adults. This water was a bit murky but still clear enough that you could spot fish and crawfish while standing by the edge of the water. The barrier that now covers all of the city of El Paso and the southern towns in the county does not let anyone even come within 20 feet of the river where most of our childhood fishing activities occurred. Not only were we able to fish right out of the river itself but also, we were able to go to the Mexican side without any problems with the Border Patrol. I remember the days that we used to cross over and just hang out as kids on the other side. Now if you hang out by the wall, the immigration patrol will surely come and question you as to what you are doing and why.

Another memory I have from when the huge wall was not there was that all the time you would see people that had just come from across the border would be walking around during all hours of the day and night. They never really caused any major trouble. They mostly just passed by, we would not talk to them, and they would not talk to us. In our community, we would just let them be because most of us knew that those had been our parents at some point in their lives. Now with the wall there, I have not seen anyone like that on the streets. It has made a very significant difference. . . . it has stopped many people from entering this country that used to use that method of entry. Now many are coming in through the desert in other states or further south in Texas where there is no barrier up yet. . . . Being a child born in the United States from illegal immigrant parents makes me feel lucky that we had the chance to make it here with some ease as compared to now when it is more difficult with the wall along the border and the heightened security.

In this testimony, Danny Antunez discusses how people felt safe before the building of the fence. People often complained about racial profiling throughout the city and after protests by profiled students in Bowie High School and lawsuits, the Border Patrol was discouraged from detaining people in the streets to check their citizenship papers. In response, Operation Hold the Line was put in place in 1993. It was one of the first attempts to patrol the borderline itself. The "Operation" placed 400 border agents along the Rio Grande as a way of publicly showing the strong surveillance and security in place, which in turn would deter people from illegally entering the United States (Dunn 2009). The militarization of the border and the construction of the fence gained further legitimacy after 9/11, especially in a city like El Paso, which is adjacent to Fort Bliss, a large military base. Even after semi-sealing the border, the dilemma remained of how to deal with people who had already entered without permission.

Security Speech

Contrasting the humanitarian view of immigrants that many students have, some also reproduced the security-oriented discourses about the need for a fence in order to protect America. As a part of their border ethnography, many students engaged in conversations with Border Patrol agents, which, in turn, also humanized the agents. It is also important to note that the opinions in favor of the wall and limiting immigration that were present in the assignments and were very similar to comments one often hears in conservative media (see Chapter 6). Sometimes this anti-immigrant discourse would be reproduced by the same person right before making statements for open borders. People's views over immigration and border security often do not follow a consistent and logical pattern, but follow cultural scripts that elicit strong emotions.

The misconceptions and stereotypes about the U.S.-Mexico border are not only prevalent away from the border, but also among border residents themselves. While there are no rivers of people waiting to flow into the United States, the hysteria of uncontrolled migration haunts residents of border areas. As the vignettes in this chapter show, students who confronted their preconceived notions about the border fence and undocumented migrants decreased their fear. Some of the stigmas regarding the space surrounding the border fence, migrants, Latin people, and border inhabitants were lessened, thus helping to revalue themselves, their ancestors, their neighbors, their city, and region.

The Polysemic Border

The border has different meanings for different people. For some, it is a place of insecurity. For others who are escaping violence or persecution occurring on the other side, it is a place of safety (see next chapter). Some see it as a place of ingrained poverty. But for prospective immigrants, it is a place of wealth and unlimited possibilities. For some border residents, the border fence is a bleeding wound, while others consider it a blind spot. For some, the cities of El Paso and Ciudad Juárez are the same city with a large highway in the middle, while for others they are as if in two different planets. Even the Border Patrol is socially polysemic; it can represent inconveniences for border crossers, panic for undocumented people, but also stable employment and a road to the middle class for veterans, working-class whites, and Latin individuals. The intersectional approach in this chapter shows how these different understandings and social meanings are not based on different ontologies or epistemologies, but on different personal trajectories. The different narratives, descriptions, and definitions of the border are not the result of laziness, half-truths, or intentional cacophony. Rather, they demonstrate what the border is, and how it impacts the lives of individuals depending on their legal status, class, gender, and ethnicity.

NOTE

1. "Me parece interesantemente revelador que la palabra que usamos para referirnos a dicha barrera cambia de país a país. Border fence tiene una connotación más suave, ligera y menos invasiva. La traducción de fence al español es cerca, sin embargo, en México es común decir muro para referirnos a esta división física entre los dos países. La palabra muro contiene tonalidades totalmente contrarias a fence/cerca, un muro es sólido, inamovible, duro, pesado, está hecho para separar permanentemente dos espacios. Mientras una fence/cerca supone una acción pasajera o temporal; un objeto que se puede derribar, que no llegó para quedarse. ¿Será que las diferencias en puntos de vista entre mexicanos y estadounidenses acerca de esta barrera son tan contrarios que las palabras que usamos delatan nuestras rivalidades? En Ciudad Juárez, siempre viví en una casa que se ubica a una calle del Río Bravo. De niña, recuerdo haber ido tan lejos en mi bicicleta que no me dí cuenta que ya no estaba en territorio mexicano. . . . Ese pedazo gigantesco de acero al que llamamos muro o fence, es simplemente un objeto físico que en sí no tiene el poder de dictar leyes. Sin embargo, es el elemento más emblemático y poderoso que existe para simbolizar la interacción entre los dos países y la manera en la que esta división se vive diferente dependiendo de la situación social en cuestión." —Laura López

Chapter 8

Fear of Deportation among Mexicans Fleeing Violence

Ernesto Castañeda, Natali Collazos, Eva M. Moya, and Silvia Chávez-Baray

This chapter discusses the fear of deportation migrants hold, drawing on interviews with 35 individuals who relocated to El Paso, Texas after escaping violence in Mexico. Because of the threats they received in Mexico and their irregular immigration status in the United States, they experience constant stress and fear. They mistrust not only the people around them, but also social services, health providers, and non-governmental organizations. Many of them found it difficult to create any type of social connection with people including neighbors, store clerks, or support groups. Many refrained from using social, medical, or legal services in fear of being apprehended by U.S. Immigration and Customs Enforcement (ICE) to be sent back to the place they escaped from. This resulted in feelings of isolation and in some cases exacerbated symptoms of depression.

How does fear of being deported influence political migrants' mental health and daily lives? This chapter focuses specifically on families who fled Ciudad Juarez, Mexico because of threats, persecution, and violence toward them and their families and arrived in neighboring El Paso, Texas. It offers evidence supporting the claim that migrants experience severe mental and emotional stressors. Even among the majority Latin community in El Paso, immigrant families face stress related to emigration and acculturation. Unfortunately, the risk of being reported for their undocumented status is too great for the migrants to seek assistance or advice from others. Thus, they rarely talk about their sense of loneliness and fear with other undocumented migrant families or neighbors, who could show empathy for their situation.

NAMING MIGRANT POPULATIONS

Living as an undocumented immigrant means that one does not have the proper legal permission to live in a country. Some believe that undocumented immigrants are freeloaders who take advantage of America's wealth as a shortcut to a better life. However, immigrants earn their place in the United States through hard work and effort as they carve their niche in American communities through their many contributions to the economy, culture, and society. Furthermore, many U.S.-born citizens fail to realize the daily anxiety undocumented immigrants face, including the fear of being caught by ICE, jailed, and subsequently deported (Golash-Boza 2015).

People categorized as "illegal" simply have an irregular immigration status because they entered a nation-state outside of designated customs and immigration posts, or they overstay their visa term, and thus lack documents (residency permit, work visa, TPS, or any other authorization) allowing them to reside in the country (Cheliotis 2017). Millions of people live, work, and study in the United States without sanctioned immigration status. Citizens and pundits often make abstract moral judgments of "illegal" individuals. They incorrectly assume that any person who may "look Latin" may be "undocumented"; however, asking individuals about the subject is somewhat taboo. Thus, non-Latin people rarely take the time to ask individuals they interact with how their immigration status affects their everyday life, their goals, and their mental health.

Refugees are the migrants who were forced out of their country of origin. According to international law, refugees have a well-founded fear of persecution because of their race, politics, religion, sexual orientation, nationality, culture, or group affiliation. They flee armed conflict or persecution and cross international borders. Estimates show that by the end of 2014, 59.5 million individuals had been forcibly displaced across the world (Lloyd 2017). Because their migration is largely involuntary, and there is no guarantee that they will be returning home freely and safely, they seek asylum abroad. Being denied asylum may have deadly consequences (Stillman 2018).

Mexican immigrants have been entering the United States for a hundred years (Jiménez 2008; Massey, Durand, and Malone 2002; Garip 2017) and the ongoing violent drug war in Mexico means many are seeking refuge and political asylum in the United States for fear of their lives (Albuja and Rubio Díaz-Leal 2011, Olivares 2012, Morales et al. 2013, Lusk and Villalobos 2012, Calderón Chelius and Cornejo 2012, Mann 2012). The focus of this chapter is on migrants who fled their homes because they were being persecuted or threatened in Mexico. This chapter presents illustrative narratives of adults who have irregular migration status, or who in a few cases are waiting for a decision on their asylum cases, and it describes how this bureaucratic limbo affects their lives. Most legal and academic studies focus on either economic or political migrants, but, as we show below both these populations have more in common than what is often accepted by the state.

Living in the United States as an undocumented immigrant comes with many restrictions and complications, including limitations on purchasing private health insurance (Jerome-D'Emilia and Suplee 2012). Due to the lack of access to basic healthcare, undocumented immigrants are put at a higher risk of physical and mental health problems, including depression and anxiety (Garcini et al. 2016). Despite these challenges, they are often able to access community health centers or federally qualified health centers when such services are available.

Sporadically, undocumented individuals are actively searched for by immigration enforcement officials. The knowledge of this reality causes them great fear of being caught and deported, adding to the already present difficulties and stress of being an undocumented immigrant. This fear and panic of being sent back to potentially life-threatening situations in their countries of origin is a daily fear. Many are afraid to speak up against employers' abuse or discrimination, fearing retaliation by involving immigration authorities. Unfortunately, many employers, landlords, spouses, neighbors, and citizens are aware of this fear and take advantage of it. This extensive abuse and exploitation can also place undocumented immigrants at a higher risk of emotional distress (Garcini et al. 2016). Aside from the extensive discrimination they encounter, undocumented immigrants feel they have very few rights (Castañeda 2018b). With no plausible legal solution in the near future, many migrants and asylum seekers live in a constant, debilitating legal limbo (Castañeda 2013a). As a result, the undocumented are hypervigilant and are constantly looking over their shoulders (Joseph 2011), which can lead to long-term consequences that distress their mental state (Moya et al. 2016).

In this study, we evaluate a series of stressors and fears that the migrants and their families face every day, and how these stressors detrimentally affect the mental state and wellbeing of undocumented immigrants in the U.S.-Mexico border region.

Sending Country Conditions

In just three years (2008–2010), there were 7,319 homicides in Ciudad Juarez; 86.4 percent of the victims were men between 15 and 44 years old. The city had a homicide rate of 229 per 100,000 residents in 2010 (Martínez Toyes and Arellano Quiroga 2012, 47). Furthermore, in 2009, 17.5 percent of residents reported being victims of crime (Velázquez Vargas and Martínez

Canizales 2012, 71). In 2010, 21 percent of Juarez residents were victims of crime and 14.4 percent were victims of extortions, according to the Survey of Perception of Insecurity in Ciudad Juarez 2010 (a probability sample of 1,900) (Martínez Toyes and Arellano Quiroga 2012, 47). Also, 33 percent said that a family member had been a crime victim in 2010 (Velázquez Vargas and Martínez Canizales 2012, 71). It is estimated that around 62 percent of crimes in Juarez are not reported to the authorities (Martínez Toyes and Arellano Quiroga 2012, 46). Seventy-one percent of survey respondents said they passed a homicide crime scene in 2010 (Velázquez Vargas and Martínez Canizales 2012, 72). In 2010, 95.37 percent considered Juarez as a little safe or not safe at all (Velázquez Vargas and Martínez Canizales 2012, 73). Comparatively, 81.4 percent of Ciudad Juarez residents considered El Paso, Texas, safe or very safe (Velázquez Vargas and Martínez Canizales 2012, 75). Over 230,000 people left Juarez by 2010, mainly escaping the violence, with El Paso as the main destination (Martínez Toyes and Arellano Quiroga 2012, 58).

Data and Methods

The data used comes from 35 interviews carried out between 2014 and 2015 in the border city of El Paso as part of a research grant (Moya et al. 2016). While these respondents escaped violence in Mexico, they suffered psychological stress and trauma associated with their sudden departure from Mexico, and they often reported that their immigration status is the number one cause of their stress and anxiety. Respondents talked about the experience of illegality and the effects that this administrative status had on their mental health. These findings are compatible with arguments that migration can result in chronic stress and vulnerability to mental illness (Achotegui 2016, 2011). Pseudonyms are used for all interviewees to ensure that the respondents' identities remain anonymous.

Findings

Our findings from this one specific population in El Paso reveal many similarities in the struggles that migrants across the world experience, regardless of whether they left their home because of political or economic reasons. We find some symptoms that could be misdiagnosed as paranoia; yet, these seemingly paranoid thoughts are the products of real persecution and potential harm in the form of loss of income or employment, deportation, depression, and family separation. Some immigrants also experience chronic fear due to the uncertainty of their legal status, which could result in deportation and separation from their families at any moment (Castañeda and Buck 2014).

We found that undocumented administrative status causes immigrants to avoid talking with and trusting strangers, thus hindering the potential development of long-term supporting relations, social capital, and strong social ties that could aid them in their integration. Many of our participants developed feelings of mistrust and cynicism about the people around them. They found it difficult to develop social connections and refrained from using health, medical, or legal services for fear of being reported to immigration authorities. Every action they made—visiting the doctor, driving to work—became a life-threatening decision because of the risk of unexpectedly getting caught by ICE and sent back to a country from which they were escaping violence, corruption, and poverty. This further contributes to their high levels of isolation, depression, and feeling of living in limbo.

Over 75 percent of the 35 participants also reported that employers, landlords, and neighbors used their undocumented status against them. Some have had acquaintances and strangers threaten to call immigration authorities. Their marginal status left them vulnerable to exploitation and abuse, limited their educational and economic prospects, and exacerbated their post-traumatic stress symptoms. Furthermore, the following testimonies show the mental toll that experiencing illegality creates in the everyday lives of millions of undocumented individuals and their family members, who often are citizens and legal permanent residents.

Gloria, age 27, mentions that one of the biggest changes in her life in the United States is how much leisure time she spends outside. She and her children used to stroll casually through Ciudad Juarez, Mexico every afternoon as a family tradition. Today, she minimizes the amount of time she steps out of her own house unless it is for something imperative like work or a medical emergency. She explains,

> In Mexico we were used to walking. Even though we had a car, we tried to walk as much as we could. . . . But in the United States because of the fear of not having a legal status we are scared to even step out of the house. . . . I get very scared when I am out all day on the street because I am afraid a police officer can stop me at any time.

Diego, age 45, nostalgically reminisces about the numerous memories of group outings and big social gatherings in Mexico. Today his family barely leaves the house to go to a restaurant or a movie in fear of being stopped by someone from ICE:

We no longer go out, for example, to the movies or parties, it is very rare. We generally just attend church events because they are safer since they are very close by. We try to not travel large distances because of the fear that a police car or ICE could stop us at any time.

Because of the fear of deportation, families who were once social and engaged in various activities with other families are now leading introverted, isolated lives. They have been placed in a position where they feel forced to withdraw from society as a whole to protect their residence in the United States. Gabriela, age 30, admits that

> one often feels discouraged and alone, but you're not really alone it's just you don't really make the effort to meet people—do you know what I mean? It's more like you close yourself in at times.

Reclusiveness and isolation not only stem from remaining in the house in fear of encountering an ICE officer, but also from the fear of interacting with people who may at any point in time decide to call ICE on them if they know they are undocumented.

Trust No One

Because undocumented migrants constantly worry about deportation, they have a paranoid mindset, constantly looking over their shoulder and walking on eggshells around anybody they encounter. They recognize that anyone at any time has the power to call ICE and to alter their lives permanently. To minimize the probability of being reported to immigration authorities, undocumented immigrants are extremely cautious of whom they trust with their legal status. Many children of undocumented migrants are instructed to hold this life-threatening secret from as many people as possible including classmates, counselors, social workers, coworkers, and even best friends. This lack of honesty about their identities may create an impostor syndrome; the children learn that the revelation of this secret to the wrong person could create possible deadly consequences for themselves, their livelihood, and the well-being of their entire families. Ximena, age 42, admits her constant state of caution and distrust of those around her when she says,

> When one is an undocumented immigrant you try not to really talk about your problems with other people because of the terror inside of you. I mean some-times you even hear stories of immigrants themselves calling immigration en-forcement on fellow immigrants who were not to their liking.

This constant distrust of the intentions of those around them creates a permanent state of stress within the minds and bodies of many undocumented immigrants.

Regardless of how hard an undocumented immigrant may try to keep their legal status hidden, there are certain people in their lives, such as employers and landlords, who may become aware of their status. This puts the fate of the undocumented and their families at the mercy of these people. Participants mentioned cases of abuse by employers and landlords with the assumption that the undocumented are unlikely to report their mistreatment in fear of deportation. Gloria, 27, expresses her frustration when she recalls a negative experience she had with a prior employer:

> I worked a whole month without pay. . . . I got tired of going because I had to constantly ask my sister to borrow her car. The employer stopped answering my calls and when I did speak with him he would tell me to go collect the payment, referring to, I imagine, something about immigration. So, I just never went back.

Since the employer merely hinted at getting immigration involved, the interviewee immediately backed down out of petrifying fear of being taken away by ICE, and accepted that her hard work would not be remunerated.

Agustina, 47, shares how her landlord, who lives next door in a trailer park, carefully and cautiously observes her every move. The landlord notes whenever she leaves the house in the morning and at what time she comes back. The landlord reminds her of her undocumented status and the power that comes with this knowledge at any chance she gets. Agustina elaborates,

> Well I don't really step out of my trailer very often, the women who we rent from has me sick and tired because she knows we don't have papers. . . . And she constantly makes up stories and lies to get me into trouble. We cannot talk to any of our neighbors or anything. She gossips and lies. . . . She told my husband when he went to pay her the rent money that she saw me leave my trailer with a tattooed American man. . . . I am at her complete mercy.

Many undocumented migrants feel obliged to be overtly courteous and complacent with everyone who has knowledge of their legal status. They must ignore when they are discriminated or taken advantage of because at any point they may be summoned to immigration court, detained, or deported. Furthermore, depending on their security circumstances in their country of origin, they could possibly be killed; many of our informants have received direct death threats by organized crime for failing to pay extortions or partake in protection rackets.

People with an undocumented status also distrust hospitals, clinics, support groups, non-profits and refrain from using their services. Josefina, age 26, confesses that she

> was scared to go and visit the doctor. . . . I was scared to go here in this country because sometimes we come across people who give us incorrect information and tell us that we shouldn't go because there we could possibly be discovered by immigration and taken away, or maybe on the way to the doctor we could possibly be stopped and taken away.

We asked Luis, age 51, if he was part of any immigrant organizations, to which he replied,

> Well no, not really because I tell you if you are undocumented it's very hard to establish a friendship in this country with someone you don't know here. You never know with whom you are dealing with. I feel like I can't share anything because you never know what could possibly happen.

Refraining from going to the doctor or reaching out for necessary help from volunteer organizations is a reality that many undocumented immigrants face every day. It constricts them from being able to acquire useful social capital, and from establishing the relationships that they may need to be successful in the United States. The majority reported that they had received little to no information about how to apply for asylum or how to regularize their immigration status. This partly stems from their hesitation to interact with institutions, including immigrant support groups and legal organizations.

Running for Their Lives

For many of these immigrants, the decision to move was not their own. Many of the immigrants we interviewed were practically chased out of Ciudad Juarez by extortionists, con men, or gang members. Mario, age 32, had to think extremely fast when he came across a note one day on his car stating that if he did not pay $7,000 in less than 24 hours, there would be heavy consequences and that he would not necessarily be the one physically paying. He was immediately overcome with terror for his wife, children, and family; he knew he had to act fast. He fearfully and regretfully recalls the encounter:

> That day I woke up very early for my daily activities. Then I noticed on my car's windshield a note asking me for seven thousand dollars. I immediately came back in the house and told my wife to "Go and get all of our important papers, our passports, the important stuff, like the money" . . . and we left our house . . . I spoke to the person extorting me, and I told her that she was confusing me with

someone else, that I didn't have the amount of money she was asking for at that very moment, but that if she would give me the option of giving her 2 thousand dollars along with my cars. I told her, "I'll give you my cars, you can keep my cars. I will give you the 2 thousand dollars very soon. I don't want any trouble, I have a family I have cousins, brothers, I have a grandmother." I told her, "I don't want any trouble. I'll close down the business." But the extorter did not accept this, she said no, she said that she wanted the 7 thousand dollars and I said okay, "Give me an extra 24 hours so that I can give you these 7 thousand dollars." The extorter threatened me, she told me that if she had taken different actions my wife's family would have already given her all of the money, meaning she could have kidnapped my wife, who always stayed home alone. And in the moment the intensity of the situation rose to another level and I now saw that even if I gave her the money she would not be satisfied, she would always want more and more and more, and more.

Mario felt that the extortions would escalate and that his family would always be at risk. He could either 1) stay in Mexico and try to collect that amount of money as fast as he could while relying on the mercy of the extortionists not to kidnap and kill his family along with endless threats and requests, or 2) he could gather up the strength to leave behind everything he had ever worked for and achieved in Juarez to migrate to a safer place for the sake of his family's survival. Similarly, Ximena recalls the encounter with her extortionist:

They took away my husband's truck at gunpoint along with various other documents that he had in his portfolio [with our personal information]. . . . Fortunately they did not take away his phone since it was not anywhere visible. . . . They told him to sit still and not do anything because there was another car following him. . . . Later they called because in those portfolio documents, well they had everything about us. They called me and started extorting me, telling me that they had my husband, and to sit still and not do anything, that they would later be in communication with me, using words that were very obscene and aggressive. As I was trying to communicate with my husband well of course in that moment he was panicking, he was shocked, he was not answering any of my calls because of the fear and terror that he had. When he returned home he said to me, "Well, they took everything, they took away my truck, they took everything." Fortunately, we had another vehicle that we used to immediately go pick up the girls together, with a lot of fear within us. Afterwards the extorters started to call our cell phones where they were trying to extort more money from us, where they told us that we had to give to them ten thousand pesos a week or else they would kill me or one of my daughters.

Ximena found herself in a similar situation, where she and her family were put through a series of life-threatening events that must be handled with extreme care as one wrong move could have resulted in death.

Because most of the families interviewed used to live in Ciudad Juarez, they immediately thought that their safest bet for their survival was to cross the border. Some of our participants were business owners and upper-middle-class individuals who had never planned to live in the United States but were chased out of their own country by criminals. They do this to show to other families that there are consequences to not paying them off.

Joana, age 40, becomes visibly upset when she recounts her 24-hour kidnapping, which she says felt like an eternity. She uneasily recalls how her abductor originally kidnapped her husband and nephew and then brought them back to the house where she was. The kidnapper then left them there and took her instead. She shudders as she remembers how the captor took her to an abandoned lot with a gun in his hand and said terrifying things like,

> "Here is where I will shoot you." He would put the gun to my face and I would try and swat it, but he would then get real close and say, "Do not touch the gun because if you touch the gun I will pull the trigger." He would also drive me out to abandoned roads and say things like, "This is where your family will find you laying dead."

She talks about a turning point when she told her assailant, "If you want to kill me, then kill me." The kidnapper responded with, "Are you not afraid to die?" and she said, "No, you have me in the palm of your hands, you can kill me at any time you please." She said she attributed these sudden outbursts of courage to her faith.

Extortion, kidnapping, and murder threats are enough to trigger people into moving to the United States because the Mexican government is unlikely to prosecute these crimes and offer protection to these citizens. Several interviewees reportedly tried to reach out to local enforcement officials, but in the end, no justice was done. For example, when Ximena was asked why she crossed the border immediately after being threatened with extortion, she responded,

> More than anything, to save my family, also because of the close proximity of Juarez to El Paso. We felt that looking for bus tickets to return to our city of origin would take too much time and we would run the risk of something bad happening to my husband or to my daughters. So, at that moment we immediately crossed over. Plus, a bad policy [war on drugs] has caused a lot of insecurity in Mexico.

Linda, age 46, recalls an incident where Mexican federal officials victimized her son in Chihuahua. She explains that one day her son and his friends were lost in the roads of Chamizal looking for a baptism he had been invited to, when suddenly federal enforcement officers flooded the area and yelled at everyone to get down on their stomachs while they searched them. She was informed soon after that her son was in the hospital because he had been brutally beaten up by federal officers. Linda was thankful that her son returned with only bruises, as several others had much more serious injuries. The mother emphasizes that she was threatened to remain silent about the incident; otherwise, there would be consequences.

It is terrifying to live in a time when someone can threaten to kidnap you and kill your family with impunity. The extremity of these cases and the existence of many similar ones demonstrate that while crossing the U.S. border without proper documentation or overstaying a visa is not ideal, many of these immigrants do not have much choice. They must accept that while living undocumented in the United States is extremely difficult, it is often their only hope. Many Mexican and Central American citizens do not enjoy the level of security that most Americans do.

Because of the extreme violence, terror, and constant threat of murder that many of the families showing up at the U.S. border are running away from, the stakes of keeping their identity and legality a secret are that much higher. The mere thought of having to go back to a country that they were practically chased out of is a constant stressor along with the many other worries undocumented immigrants live with.

Linda explains the panic and terror she felt when she first moved to the United States. She was constantly watching her back and looking over her shoulder to make sure she was safe. She had just recently escaped a horrendous situation in Mexico where she was being stalked and extorted and was afraid of running into the people who almost killed her family:

> When I first arrived to El Paso, I would look at people driving motorcycles and say "you see how they hide their face like that? Oh my, no! That's them coming after me" I mean I had such a fear and panic. . . . Also my daughter—my daughter can't even physically go to the center of Juarez, she can't go because she is terrified of it. Because days before, like two months before, we had physically witnessed a young man being killed in the market. They had shot to the air and the bullets hit the young man. They asked a young man to go get some CDs; and when he returned with the CDs they killed him right then and there, right in front of us.

It was hard for her to lead a normal life because of this trauma. She escaped alive, but she knew that she could never live free of worry again. The possibility of encountering her blackmailers was still very real because at any moment the truth about her legality could be uncovered, forcing her back to Ciudad Juarez, which created this fear that she says is with her at all times.

Figure 8.1. Highway sign in El Paso for the exit to Ciudad Juarez, Mexico. Photo by Valeria Mejia.

Camila, 41, was threatened, robbed, and extorted in Mexico. She feels a chilling terror every time she even sees a road sign for Ciudad Juarez, which are common through El Paso's main highways,

> Notice, that's why I got lost, because by simply seeing the road sign for Ciudad Juarez, I got petrified. That is why I drove in circles and circles around the sign because I entered a state of hysteria. I told my son, "I really don't want to go back to Juarez!"

Camila was triggered when she saw the exit sign for Juarez while driving in El Paso. These are just a few examples of how undocumented immigrants experience post-traumatic stress. The undocumented constantly worry about maintaining a low profile, limiting their social life, confining themselves to their own homes as much as possible, and being extremely careful about who they trust with information about their legal status. These factors cause them to refrain from using services from hospitals and support groups. Migrants are always aware that one wrong move could mean being sent back to the place where they were threatened and attacked. Luckily, threats and extortion do not follow them to El Paso. The worry of going back is largely about fearing that the perpetrators they escaped from may await them.

Anxiety for the Safety of Loved Ones

Many refugees, asylum seekers, and undocumented individuals feel that the safety of their children and spouses rests entirely in their hands, adding on to the ever-growing list of stressors. They also fear that if ICE suddenly takes a loved one who may be incarcerated and later deported, they would be unable to see them for years. This nightmare is all too likely.

Ximena emphasizes just how much her children and her husband mean to her. She explains the twists and turns her stomach takes anytime one of them leaves the house:

> Every time my husband leaves the house, I fear that he won't return. Not because I think he is going to abandon us but because I fear he might be detained and deported. That is my constant angst and uncertainty. Every time he leaves, I'm left with great worry until we speak on the telephone and he reassures me, "I've made it to work" and only then do I feel a certain tranquility. Then when he calls and tells me, he has left work and is on his way home, the feeling of worry and angst returns. I often go and open all of the windows and sit and wait until I see his car on the driveway. Only then is when I think, "Oh thank the Lord, he's home."

Her constant state of worry and anxiety for her husband's safety every time he leaves the house may seem somewhat irrational and paranoid to some individuals, but the reality is that any time an undocumented immigrant is on the road they run the risk of being stopped by a law enforcement officer and being unable to hide their immigration status. This reality is all too common throughout the undocumented community; this happened in El Paso to the father of one of my former students (Castañeda and Buck 2014).

Ximena also explains how she has consciously made the personal decision to become a stay-at-home mother to better monitor her daughters' whereabouts and security:

> We both came to the decision that he would work and I would stay home and be in charge of the girls' safety, so that we wouldn't have to put them at risk of anything dangerous like gangs or anything of that nature. We feel that they are at a very risky stage in life.

This extra concern for the safety of loved ones is an important stressor for our respondents. Their chronic stress about the safety of children and spouses takes a toll on their mental health.

Mental Health State of Terror and Hopelessness

More than 75 percent of the Latin individuals we interviewed claimed to have some sort of anxiety or depression while living in the United States because of the stress and worry that comes with being undocumented. Over 75 percent of the participants also claimed to have irregular sleep patterns. Ximena explains it best when she recalls the horrific mental state she and her spouse fell into when first arriving to this country due to the fear of being sent back to Mexico, where she received gruesome threats about kidnapping their daughter. She states,

> When we first arrived here my husband and I fell into a really deep depression. We came with a lot of fear and terror. We went to sign our daughters up for school, which we live in front of. My husband would go and take our daughters to school early in the morning, and when he would come back we would both go to bed and go to sleep. Neither of us had any motivation to do anything. We were both terrified of everything. It always made us jump when our landlord would come to knock at our door because my first thought was always "My daughters! Where are my daughters?" We lived in great fear, I mean everyone we met we assumed had bad intentions. It was an overwhelming feeling that we slowly had to try and overcome.

When you live a life of constant worry and anxiety imagining every time you leave the house, your loved ones go to work or to the local grocery that you may never see your children or spouse again, you develop feelings of helplessness, suffocation, and entrapment. Not only do many simply not have the option of going back to a country where harm or even death awaits them, but also many do not have the option of being legalized as citizens in the United States either. At this point, many feel as if they have lost complete control over their lives because at any moment their lives could completely change by no conscious choice of their own. These extreme levels of terror, fear, worry, and anxiety occur at all hours of the day with no resolve to look forward to. For many, this may prove to be too much. There is a point of dehumanization where they may no longer see the point of living.

Isabella, age 41, shares the story of how she got to the United States and how a series of extremely unfortunate events caused her to get sick. For years, she endured domestic violence from her abusive husband in Ciudad Juarez, until she decided to move to the United States. However, he soon followed her and continued the abuse. Caught by ICE, she was sent back to Juarez and was forced to leave her two daughters with her abusive husband in El Paso. She feared for the safety of her daughters because she knew that her husband was a drug addict and an alcoholic. Through much determination to be reunited with her daughters, she made it back to the United States. However, by this time her mental health had deteriorated significantly. She explains,

Unfortunately, I arrived at a time when I was very ill, when I crossed the border I immediately suffered a convulsion downtown. I stayed in the center plaza for two days because I was very psychologically ill; I was very traumatized. I had no idea where to go or anything. . . . I felt like an extreme failure, I had the thought that if I couldn't get anything done I would place myself in the middle of the train tracks.

The stress and angst turned into depression, which because of neglect and violence had led to other serious health problems such as epilepsy and seizures. She had reached a point where she told us she no longer saw the purpose of living. She could no longer rationalize what the point of continuing was. She felt she had no one to turn to because she was undocumented, and any decision she made could land her back in Mexico.

A woman we interviewed was afraid to call the police on her husband when he would beat her because she was afraid the police would deport the whole family. When we asked, "Were you a victim of any crime in the U.S.?" she said,

Domestic violence, the only thing I fear is that I left his apartment. . . . I fear his family will call immigration on me. My husband would even tell me that if I ever left him, he would kill me or something, and I am extremely scared.

This fear of deportation forced her to put up being beaten by her husband for the sake of her daughters' stay in the United States.

Millions of undocumented immigrants face excruciating circumstances every day, whether it is escaping violent perpetrators, or being separated from their family, children, sisters, grandparents, and having to leave everything behind. It is a cycle of never-ending terrors and stressors that keep piling on with a lack of hope that they will ever be remediated because of the limited avenues to legal residence. For many, there is no happy conclusion because wherever they go, they are blocked by walls of intolerance and indifference.

Agustina, 47, explains how all the frustration and constant state of angst became so unbearable that she very seriously contemplated suicide: "One day I sat myself on my chair and I grabbed a bunch of sleeping pills and I said, 'I'm going to take all of these and that's it, I'm not going to wake up. I won't wake up and continue to live with this constant fear.'" This occurred after hearing that a neighbor had been deported.

Andrea, 56, also claimed she had contemplated taking her own life after leaving her sick father in Mexico and not being able to visit him or bring him to the United States. He then died. Andrea explains,

After my kids, my dad was my only support, my counselor, my friend. So, I was no longer with him I thought, "What am I doing?" and I know that it's really bad to think this way because it goes against God's teachings, but I really did get to a point where I thought to myself, "Why am I alive?"

These feelings of pain continue to build with no solution in sight. As a result, situations like these arise where people become severely depressed and develop suicidal thoughts.

Changing Lifestyles: Forced Reclusion

Undocumented immigrants are aware of the repercussions that may occur if they are caught by immigration authorities. They know that at any moment —regardless of how long they have lived in the United States, or how much they have worked—their whole lives may be disrupted once again. Hundreds of fathers, mothers, caretakers, or providers are abruptly taken and detained by ICE. Every day children come home from school to find their siblings, parents, or grandparents missing because they have been caught and taken away, altering their whole lives forever.

A lot of the hate and contempt for undocumented immigrants stems from the mistaken idea that they have an easy life in the United States, and unfairly benefit by taking jobs away from Americans (Cochrane and Nevitte 2014). In contrast, more than half of the interviewees claimed that how they led their lives was negatively impacted after arriving into the United States. Undocumented individuals often lack U.S. forms of identification, so a minor traffic violation can lead to arrest and deportation. The mere thought of any type of encounter with a law enforcement officer instills a paralyzing fear into the minds and bodies of the undocumented and their documented loved ones. Certain officers and sheriffs in the United States like Sheriff Joe Arpaio of Arizona have become notorious for stopping people who merely "look" like immigrants and requesting proper residential identification on the spot. As a result, several of the participants we interviewed testified to doing everything in their power to avoid entering any type of situation that could put them at risk including leaving the house for leisure.

CONCLUSION

The violent and traumatic events that force families to migrate and the fear of deportation have negative effects on their mental and physical health. Revamping deportation policies, anti-immigrant legislative proposals, and public discourse can exacerbate immigrants' stress and anxiety. Unfortunately, immigrants who are not considered as refugees or as asylum seekers by law, judges, or researchers often have the same profiles and traumatic experiences as approved refugees and asylees, especially given the recent spikes in violence in Mexico and Central America. Despite these patterns of violence in the countries of origin, the current U.S. government refuses to grant or extend temporary protective status (TPS) or deferred action from deportation (DACA) (Tilly, Castañeda, and Wood 2019; Menjívar 2017; Rathod, Hershberg, and Stinchcomb 2017).

As described in several of these testimonies, having an undocumented immigration status means living with a secret that often fills these individuals with shame and guilt as they internalize the social stigma against illegals. Many individuals and their families cross international borders to escape violence, extortion, abuse, and murder. Migrants face higher rates of physical and mental illness compared to native populations due to a multitude of stressors experienced before, during, and after migration (Fellmeth, Fazel, and Plugge 2017). They migrate in hopes of survival. But this comes with a price because of entrenched xenophobia, anti-immigration expression, and unsympathetic politicians. Therefore, millions of undocumented immigrants are stuck in a state of uncertainty and their fate depends on whether they are caught by ICE and are deported, something that could prove deadly.

Despite migrants' similar experiences with anxiety, depression, stress, and fear, they are unable to rely on one another as a support system through community groups or organizations because of the risk of deportation. The contradiction of feeling so isolated while being surrounded by others who are enduring similar emotions and frustrations reflects the harm that immigration policies have on migrants' well-being. Uncertain about speaking with people outside of their immediate family, most migrants we interviewed in El Paso did not seek medical help for their mental health problems or seek counseling. Instead, they suffered in silence.

Migrants are resilient (Lusk and Chavez-Baray 2017), but current xenophobic discourse scapegoating immigrants reinforces social boundaries, creates dangerous stereotypes of criminal immigrants, and increase stress and anxiety among immigrants. Many live in a state of panic and fear of being turned in to immigration authorities. Every decision they make, whether visiting the doctor or driving to work, becomes a life or death decision. The paralyzing thought of being sent back to a country where they feared for their lives or lived in poverty is enough to make anyone lie awake at night while cautiously analyzing every decision and relationship they make. These individuals felt fatally threatened enough to risk crossing into the United States without resident papers, often losing everything they once had and starting from scratch; and they would have to start all over again if deported, trying to reconstruct a life elsewhere or trying to come back to the United States and risking imprisonment or death in the desert (De León 2015).

Chapter 9

Invisible New Yorkers

Boundaries, Interethnic Networks, Immigrant Integration, and Social Invisibility

Much of the academic literature on urban sociology and immigration focuses either exclusively on immigrant collectives and intraethnic solidarity or on interethnic conflict. Data used in this chapter comes from interviews, field notes, and over a decade of participant observation, as well as from illustrative survey data. This chapter describes the social ties that individuals of different backgrounds have with individuals of Mexican origin who live, work, and study in the New York metropolitan area. This chapter argues that interethnic ties at the individual level can coexist with social boundaries. It introduces the concept of social invisibility to describe how although these migrant groups exist in large numbers within a society, they are still treated by the media and the majority population as if they do not exist. Findings show that while keeping in touch with people in their hometowns, Mexicans living in New York City interact with individuals of other ethnicities, acculturate quickly, feel at home, and through time become New Yorkers. However, they experience a social invisibility because although they self-identify as New Yorkers, others do not see them as such.

SOCIAL NETWORKS, INTERETHNIC RELATIONS, AND BOUNDARY PROCESSES

This chapter takes a relational approach (Mische 2011) to understand the actual interactions between individuals in small groups in urban settings (Simmel 1964, 1971; Tilly 1984; White 2009 [1965]). In this theoretical approach, "interpersonal transactions compound into identities, create and transform social boundaries, and accumulate into durable ties" (Tilly 2005, xiii), and, in turn, social networks are the sets of ties between different social

165

sites (Tilly 2005). The empirical question posed by this chapter is about how the aggregation of social ties translates into the social visibility or invisibility of an immigrant group in a city.

Initially, immigrant groups will settle in specific destinations because of historical influences such as colonialism or labor recruitment. The migration literature has established the importance of chain migration, family reunification, and social networks in fostering migration between particular sites (Aguilera 2003, Massey et al. 1993, Massey 1990, Tilly and Brown 1967). This cumulative concentration of people from the same hometown in the same cities and neighborhoods often results in their being concentrated in niche jobs, occupations, and work sites (Massey et al. 1987, Tilly 2005, 1998b). Some studies document how co-ethnic solidarity in ethnic enclaves may provide employment and upward mobility to some (Valenzuela-García et al. 2014, Wilson and Portes 1980, Zhou 1992). This phenomenon helps migrants with low levels of education and no immigration papers to gain employment, but it may also limit their social mobility and economic prospects in the long term (Aguilera 2003). Non-desirable jobs are more likely to be open to new immigrants, and occupations that become categorized as "immigrant jobs" will often become low paid and undesirable (Karjanen 2008, Tilly 1998b). Catanzarite and Aguilera (2002, 113) found that men with mostly Latino co-workers earn less than those who work in more diverse environments. Whether immigrants live and work in diverse environments can impact their integration prospects and transnational behavior (Castañeda, Morales, and Ochoa 2014; Marcelli and Lowell 2005). Working alongside other ethnic groups has positive effects in terms of acculturation and higher income for migrants, but it also has the potential to increase racial tensions in conflictive work environments (Karjanen 2008).

Interethnic ties among individuals can theoretically coexist along with social boundaries (Bail 2008, Barth 1969, Lamont and Molnár 2002, Tilly 2005, Zelizer and Tilly 2006). Boundary-making is the process of differentiation between "us" and "them" (Bail 2008, Barth 1969). Categorical boundaries result from a bidirectional process of identification where group X defines itself in relation to group Y and vice versa (Tilly 2005). Each group will have a certain shared story, which can include national myths, official histories, and stereotypes that present them as different from others. The boundary between X and Y increasingly reinforces or creates this distinction as a self-fulfilling prophecy. If groups coexist in the same location, boundary work is necessary to maintain this separation of relations across the X and Y (Gieryn 1983). If successful, categorical inequalities become affixed to the two groups and maintained over time (Tilly 1998b). Boundary-making is often related to exploitation and opportunity hoarding, which is when groups in power monopolize resources and exclude others (Tilly 1998b). One can use the concept of boundaries to study ethnic relations (Wimmer 2008, Massey 2007, 146).

There are numerous immigrant enclaves and communities across the United States. This chapter looks specifically at Mexicans in New York to show how immigrants navigate and even challenge existing symbolic boundaries and anti-immigrant discourses. The theoretical and methodological challenge is to empirically represent the social worlds of migrants by focusing on social capital and ties in both sending and receiving societies. Cutting-edge quantitative work on migration and binational social networks succeeds in concurrently measuring immigrant social ties to their place of origin as well as to co-nationals in the place of destination (Parrado and Flippen 2014), but fails to describe immigrant ties to other individuals from different ethnoracial groups. Sociologist Ted Mouw and colleagues (Mouw et al. 2014) map a binational social network, but while they do include co-ethnic ties in the sending and receiving communities, they do not discuss the ties with non-Mexicans in the United States. This chapter calls attention to this important theoretical and methodological omission. Studying the integration of immigrant individuals, dynamics between contexts of reception and sending communities, as well as social ties between co-nationals, natives, and immigrants from other places can allow us to better understand how transnationalism, exclusion, integration, and acculturation work together (Castañeda, Morales, and Ochoa 2014; Snel, 'T Hart, and Van Bochove 2016).

Despite the widespread anti-immigrant rhetoric in the public discourse, many positive interactions occur at work and in public places among New Yorkers. Mexicans and Latin people feel a sense of urban belonging in New York City (Castañeda 2018b). Nonetheless, the public at large may not openly accept or recognize such belonging. Ultimately, this chapter focuses on how migrants experience a feeling of social invisibility in the cities they migrate to. I use the term social invisibility because there is a considerable number of Mexicans in New York, yet non-migrants and media portrayals often act as if they do not exist. This can happen in parallel as city residents talk abstractly about the nation's "immigration problem." This is another way to build symbolic and social boundaries.

Mexicans in Immigrant New York

Over 37 percent of New York City inhabitants are foreign born (Foner 2013). Among the many countries of origin represented, the largest immigrant groups are Dominicans, Chinese, and Mexicans (Lobo and Salvo 2013). In contrast with Texas or California, where Mexican-origin individuals have a long historical presence, in New York, the term Latino was originally used to denote Puerto Ricans (Aranda 2008, Bourgois 1996, Dávila 2004, Marwell 2007). Yet in the last several decades, the term now includes Dominicans, Mexicans, and those from Central and South America (Fuentes 2007; Grasmuck and Pessar 1991; Jones-Correa 1998; Kasinitz, Mollenkopf, and Waters 2004; Kasinitz et al. 2008).

New York City's government prides itself on a history of receiving immigrants from all corners of the world as symbolized by the Statue of Liberty, the Ellis Island museum, and the city's Office of Immigrant Affairs (Foner 2000, 2005). The city's government recognizes this reality, as reflected by Mayor Bloomberg signing a law that mandated that services and paperwork be conducted in any language needed. In 2015, Mayor de Blasio launched a city ID program largely to provide an opportunity for the undocumented population to receive an official identification (Berlinger et al. 2015).

Mexicans live in New York because there is high demand for their labor at both extremes of the labor market, ranging from delivery boys to Wall Street traders with experience in Latin American financial markets. Mexicans in New York come from all social classes and have relatively high levels of education (Suro 2005), including hundreds of Mexican professionals and students enrolled in institutions of higher education. Mexican-origin students are increasing in public schools (Martinez 2016). New York residents of Mexican origin come from various parts of Mexico, yet a majority come from the Mixteca region, which connects the states of Puebla, Guerrero, and Oaxaca; others come from Mexico City and the State of Mexico (Massey, Rugh, and Pren 2010; Smith 2006, 2013). Many Mexicans in New York have indigenous roots and speak indigenous languages (Rivera-Sánchez 2004).

According to the 2010 census, there were 319,263 Mexican-origin individuals living in New York City (U.S. Census Bureau 2010); adding Long Island and Northeastern New Jersey, the count goes up to 607,503 (Bergad 2013). However, Mexican-origin residents are a population hard to grasp from official census and household surveys because of their continuous mobility (including new immigration, return migration, and migration within the United States), overcrowded housing, long working hours, language barriers, undocumented status, and the desire to stay under the radar (Nuño 2013). The Mexican Consulate estimates that there are around 1.2 million Mexicans in the tri-state area of New York, New Jersey, and Connecticut (Semple 2010), based on services provided and applications for consular identification cards (Massey, Rugh, and Pren 2010; Suro 2005). Mexicans have one of the highest numbers of births in New York City (Bernstein 2007, Nuño 2013, Smith 2006).

Like Italians and other immigrants (Orsi 2002), Mexicans from the same hometowns re-create many of their pre-migration social relationships and cultural practices abroad. Ethnographic studies of transnationalism describe how Mexican migrants in New York City organize, communicate, worship together, and send money to family and friends in their hometowns (Gálvez 2009, Ibarra Mateos and Rivera Sánchez 2011, Smith 2006). An important set of organizations and individuals have worked on behalf of Mexicans in New York, resulting in a slowly increasing political voice (Gálvez 2006, Smith 2013). Despite their population size, Mexicans are dispersed across the urban area (Castañeda, Beck, and Lachica 2015).

Mexican immigrants in New York engage in transnational practices and often communicate with family members and friends who stayed back (Castañeda, Morales, and Ochoa 2014). However, the purpose of this chapter is to go back to the earlier theoretical emphasis on the importance of ties outside of the ethnic community as a sign of integration (Brubaker 2001, Gordon 1964). The larger theoretical argument is that the building of social boundaries around Mexicans in New York happens alongside the formation of interethnic ties. The question is whether Mexicans residing in New York City have many meaningful relationships with non-Mexicans and whether their intra-group connections inhibit their experience of belonging to New York City as New Yorkers.

Methodology

This chapter is part of a larger research agenda where I show the co-existence of exclusionary and inclusionary processes in cities using a mixed-methods comparative design (Castañeda 2018b). Results come mainly from ethnographic fieldwork and in-depth interviews and are triangulated with a maximum variability sample of a hard-to-reach population of documented and undocumented New York residents of Mexican origin. I have conducted fieldwork and participant observation within the Mexican community in New York intermittently since 2003. Living in the city for seven years (Manhattan and the Bronx), I was an active participant in several Mexican initiatives and organizations in New York. As a Mexican in New York, it was relatively easy for me to gain the trust of undocumented informants. Since 2010, I have routinely done ethnographic revisits (Burawoy 2003).

During three consecutive semesters (spring 2009 to spring 2010), students enrolled in a course I taught at Baruch College of the City University of New York carried out nonparticipant observation, ethno-surveys, and in-depth interviews of immigrants in New York. Around 100 students chose to participate in the project after months of training on interviewing techniques, safety, and human subjects research ethics. The ethno-surveys contained both closed-ended and open-ended questions (Massey and Zenteno 2000, Massey 1987). Purposive sampling of survey respondents was used to capture the heterogeneity among migrants in New York City. Partial data collected was analyzed often to maximize variation across education, age, and immigrant generation.

The respondents lived in different boroughs and neighborhoods of New York City, with a slight intentional oversampling of residents of El Barrio in East Harlem to capture more Latin immigrants. Surveys were not conducted in the interviewees' place of residence, but in public places so that respondents would not fear being traced back to their addresses. No identifying information from respondents was collected to ensure confidentiality. This is especially important given the undocumented status of many interviewees. Since the interviewer did not have to write down last names, phone numbers, or addresses, it was easier for respondents to talk about their undocumented status, suffering due to migration, and family separation. Most of the students were of immigrant origin and bilingual and often worked in small teams. Whenever preferred by the respondent, the interviewing was conducted in Spanish. The response rate was over 80 percent, which was likely due to similar ethnic backgrounds, the ability to communicate in Spanish, and, in many cases, long-term relationships between the interviewer and interviewees. Using local students as researchers makes reaching hard populations easier, and it also increases data reliability because some interviewers may know enough to know if the respondent is truthful or not, and lying is not the socially desirable behavior in an in-person interview for a university class project (Smith and Castañeda 2019).

Surveys and narratives from 410 Latin New Yorkers were collected. This chapter focuses on Mexican respondents ($N = 85$). The survey data were analyzed using the Statistical Package for the Social Sciences (SPSS 21). Census data and secondary sources were also used. Fragments from in-depth interviews conducted in Spanish by the author are presented. A few sections of field notes and student memos concerning ethnic relations in the workplace are also presented here. The quotes used were selected because they represent common experiences. All names used are pseudonyms.

Social Networks

The demographic profile of the sample of Mexican New Yorkers surveyed is 54.1 percent male (see table 9.1). More than half of the participants were legal residents, while 46.3 percent were undocumented when interviewed. The sample includes many men in their mid-30s, the typical demographic for first-generation economic migrants from Mexico (Massey et al. 1987). Because this migration stream has been active for over 30 years, the number of women is close to reaching parity, and we also begin to see individuals from the 1.5 (immigrated before turning 16 years old), second (born in the United States to a foreign-born parent), and third (parents born in the United States) immigrant generations.

Table 9.1. Demographics of sample of Mexicans in New York

Mean Age (StdDev)	32.4 (10.2)
Male	54.1%
Mean Years of Education (StdDev)	11.8 (3.5)
Legal Status	
Undocumented	46.3%
U.S. Citizen	31.3%
Lawful permanent resident	10%
Visa	8.8%
Refugee	3.8%
Immigrant Generation	
1st	60%
1.5	24.7%
2nd	14.1%
3rd	1.2%
Socioeconomic Status	
Low	69.9%
Middle	24.1%
High	6%
N	85

In terms of transnational behavior, not every respondent is active in transnational activities such as sending money, visiting, or planning to move back to the family's country of origin (see table 9.2). Many respondents are in communication with people in their places of origin but do not plan to return, and they would like to remain in the United States (Castañeda, Morales, and Ochoa 2014). First-generation immigrants remit more and have a higher desire to move back to their place of origin; however, only 34 percent had visited their place of origin in the previous eight years. Because of their undocumented status, many of them cannot visit as often as they would like to. Yet, it is noteworthy that 64 percent of the second-generation immigrants have visited their parents' hometowns in Mexico. U.S.-born children of migrants may be sent to visit grandparents and extended family to learn more about their ethnic culture.

Some of the Mexican immigrants surveyed reported having been helped in New York by a social worker, teacher, or professor, most of whom are non-Mexican. Few of the respondents are members of social clubs, hometown associations, or immigrant organizations. The second generation is more likely to participate in social organizations, but many of these groups may not have a transnational or ethnic orientation. The majority (66.7 percent) of the interviewees felt part of a community in New York City. Despite legal challenges and prejudice, most respondents do not feel isolated and see themselves as part of a larger group and belonging in New York City. Tellingly, the great majority of respondents reported having friends of different racial, ethnic, national, religious, or class backgrounds.

Social Boundaries

Elucidating social boundaries is another approach to discovering the lack of social ties between social groups. As Charles Tilly writes, "A close relation exist[s] between who 'we' say we are and which others we identify as

Table 9.2. Transnationalism and the interaction of Mexicans in New York City with other ethnic groups (affirmative answers reported in percentages)

	Immigrant Generation			
TRANSNATIONALISM	1	1.5	2	All*
Do you go back to visit your hometown?	34	52.4	63.6	42.5
Do your parents/siblings go back to visit?	25.6	28.6	27.3	27.6
Do you send remittances?	30	47.6	66.7	40.5
Do you plan to move back?	56.3	47.6	33.3	50.6
SOCIAL AND RACE RELATIONS				
Helped by a social worker	25.5	27.8	11.1	24
Helped by a teacher/professor	22	35	66.7	32.5
Part of a social club	6.1	14.3	16.7	10.8
Feel like they belong to a community	67.3	70	54.5	66.7
Have friends who are different in terms of race, class, religion, or nationality	82.4	81	100	84.7
Friends of different race/ethnicity	60.8	55	50	58.3
Friends of different nationality	58.8	57.9	66.7	60.2
Friends of different religion	33.3	30	50	34.5
Friends of different political views	31.4	30	33.3	31
Friends of different class	29.4	30	66.7	34.5
Partner of different race/ethnicity/ nationality	11.8	30	66.7	21.6
N	51	21	12	85

*The All column includes 1 respondent from the third generation, not shown separately.

'not us.'" Tilly's (2005) work on narratives, identities, social ties, and social boundaries asks the responses to the questions "Who are you?" and "Who is not us?" inspired me to add the survey question "With whom do you have nothing in common with?" Almost half (47 percent) could not think of any groups or individuals to name, answered "no one," mentioned phrases like "we are all humans," or refused to answer this open-ended question (see table 9.3). These answers were categorized and then grouped together. Among those who named an out-group, the most commonly named were criminals and uneducated people. This can be understood as a rhetorical device to increase personal worth by drawing symbolic boundaries and distancing one-self from categorical groups widely seen as negative and from characteristics often applied to immigrants (Lee and Fiske 2006, Tilly 2005), thus, portraying themselves as hardworking, good-mannered immigrants and minorities.

Table 9.3. Out-groups

| With whom do you feel you have nothing in common? (percentages) | *Immigrant Generation* | | | |
	1	1.5	2	All
No one (e.g., we are all humans)	45.1	57.1	41.7	47.1
Black	13.7	4.8	8.3	10.6
LGBT	5.9	/	/	3.5
People with different religious beliefs	5.9	/	/	3.5
White people	3.9	/	/	2.4
Uneducated/ignorant people	2	5.8	/	2.4
Criminals	3.9	4.8	/	3.5
Rich people	3.9	4.8	8.3	5.9
Other	15.7	23.8	41.7	21.2
N	51	21	12	85

The other groups named may originate in the respondents' perception of being rejected by those groups. This categorical grouping can be due to homophily because of individuals' desires to associate with those who are like them. It can also originate among some first-generation immigrants due to a lack of familiarity with those of a different ethnicity, religion, or gender orientation. On the positive side, we see that for the 1.5 and second generations many of those symbolic boundaries disappear. The only boundary that remains present across generations is the perception of rich New Yorkers as different. This is not surprising given the growing class inequality in New

York (Sassen 2001). A boundary between Mexicans and African-Americans could be a reflection of the low position that blacks are perceived to occupy in American society, and sporadic conflicts at work and in the streets (Karjanen 2008, Portes and Zhou 2003). Friendship across racial groups decreases as generations increase. This trend may be due to different definitions of friendship, and racialization taught to the young in neighborhoods and school settings (Flores-González, Aranda, and Vaquera 2014). Later generation respondents are younger, and their friendships are derived from schools rather than purely from work. Therefore, while their interaction with members of different ethnicities may be higher, the racialized understandings of difference may be higher.

Table 9.4. Strong ties by race or ethnicity for up to five relationships

	Five closest individuals (%)				
	Relation 1	Relation 2	Relation 3	Relation 4	Relation 5
Mexican	78.3	79.6	69.7	83.3	70
Latin (non-Mexican)	5.8	7.4	15.2	11.1	10
White (non-Mexican)	4.3	5.6	6.1	5.6	0
Black (non-Mexican)	4.3	1.9	3	0	10
Non-Latin Immigrant	7.2	5.6	3	0	10
Other	0	0	3	0	0
N	69	54	33	18	10

Even though first-generation immigrants are often dehumanized as "illegal," they also draw social boundaries. They mainly have strong interethnic ties, given their recent migration and dependence on trust networks (Flores-Yeffal 2018). The respondents were asked to name the five individuals closest to them and to describe their type of relationship and their ethnicity. We used the same questions from the General Social Survey: "From time to time people discuss important matters with other people. Looking back over the past six months, who are the people with whom you discussed matters important to you?" along with "List 1–5 people's initials, relationship, ethnicity/race, and how often do you see each other?" Not all respondents could think of five strong relationships in New York. The most common relationships were parents, wives, siblings, cousins, and children. Thus, an important percentage of subjects' social ties are indeed of Mexican origin. Yet, we see that among family members, closest friends, and associates, there are often non-Mexicans showing important relationships across categorical groups. Furthermore, 20 percent of those in a romantic relationship reported that their partner or spouse was of a different race, ethnicity, or nationality than them. Even if most close friends and family are co-ethnics, only one respondent provided five Mexican-origin individuals. All others named at least one person of a different race/ethnicity/nationality among their five closest relationships in New York. This is noteworthy, especially for a sample with a high number of undocumented and recently arrived immigrants. These results demonstrate that Mexicans in New York interact with non-Mexicans at home, school, work, and during leisure time, and have strong ties to at least one non-Mexican. Still, most of their socialization and solidarity happens within their ethnic group.

Beyond Demography: Commercial Visibility versus Social Visibility

New York has more than three million immigrants, over 37 percent of the population (Foner 2013, Lobo and Salvo 2013). Latin individuals and families make up over 30 percent of the New York population, yet they often are missing from the image that New York projects outside of its city limits. A symbolic boundary underplays much of the culture produced by Latin New Yorkers. Similarly, the population estimate of Mexicans in New York may be over one million when including new arrivals, students, and the undocumented, who are all unlikely to answer the census. But despite their significant number, Mexican lives often remain invisible, relegated to the back rooms of stores and restaurants (Thompson 2007). Mexicans are just one ethnic group in the city, and their presence is often underappreciated by other New Yorkers. While the Mexican-origin residents of New York constitute a heterogeneous group with different professions, many do work as cooks and restaurant staff (Bergad 2013); it has been argued that by working in the back of restaurants, homes, and sweatshops, Mexicans are an invisible labor force (Thompson 2007). On the other hand, Mexican busboys, deliverymen, and grocer assistants are physically visible and frequently interact with the public, yet they inhabit very low-status jobs, and often are what I call "socially invisible" because many people act as if they do not exist as a collective terrorized by federal anti-immigrant policies. Before the election of city council member Carlos Menchaca in 2013, Mexicans held no visible positions of political power in New York City. Menchaca is a Mexican-American born in El Paso who represents a multiethnic coalition of residents in Brooklyn.

The ways in which ethnic communities are most visible to outsiders is through "ethnic" storefronts and restaurants. The growth of the Mexican community can be perceived indirectly through the increasing availability of tortillas and many other Mexican food products in supermarkets and corner stores, specifically catering to the tastes of recent Mexican immigrants and others who have acquired a taste for their food (Selee 2018). A related indirect indicator of the Mexican presence in New York is the increase in the number of Mexican restaurants, although most of these restaurants are not owned by Mexicans, and do not prepare "authentic" Mexican food. Many small, informal restaurants are owned by Mexicans and were opened originally to cater to other Mexican immigrants. The recent broad geographic spread of Mexican restaurants in New York can be seen by both residents and visitors.

The most visible Mexican religious practices are the torch runs from Mexico to New York that culminate with the celebration of the Virgin of Guadalupe on December 12 (Castañeda 2018b, Chapter 5). The prominently Irish hierarchy of New York's Catholic church has embraced these festivities as their pastoral duty. Incorporating Mexican New Yorkers into the otherwise declining membership of the New York Catholic church brings new blood into the church. Still, most of these religious activities remain within church walls.

Findings about El Barrio

While at first glance Manhattan's East 116th Street in East Harlem would appear to be the heart of a New York Mexican enclave or even a "Little

Figure 9.1.   Mexican-owned businesses in Spanish Harlem. Photo by author, 2013.

Mexico," most Mexicans living in New York do not live in "El Barrio" (Bergad 2013). El Barrio is still the cultural heart of the Puerto Rican community in the New York metropolitan area, but it is not a closed ethnic enclave. From the ethno-surveys conducted there, we found that most of the business owners and those who work in El Barrio do not live there, but commute from all over the city. Similarly, most of the residents of El Barrio do not work there. Indeed, 79 percent of respondents who lived in El Barrio report leaving the neighborhood often for work or leisure. Yet, one of the effects of the extensive underground subway network in New York is that it allows residents to transport themselves from their place of residence to their place of work or recreation while ignoring the areas in between. In contrast, when one walks or drives, it is impressive to see, for example, the transition from all the luxury shops along Fifth Avenue or Madison Avenue until one arrives to El Barrio, where one observes large numbers of public housing and a steep decline in luxury retail. One also sees an increase in the people of color in Harlem, reinforcing the idea of homogenous neighborhoods.

Nevertheless, the data show that El Barrio and Harlem have a mix of ethnicities living in them (Castañeda, Beck, and Lachica 2015). Table 9.5 shows the composition of Manhattan's Community Board 11, which is bounded by East 96th Street in the south and East 142nd Street in the north, Fifth Avenue to the west, and the Harlem River to the east, and includes Randall's and Ward's Island Parks.

Table 9.5. Population of East Harlem by race and ethnicity

Population of East Harlem (%)	1990	2000	2010
White (Non-Hispanic)	7.1	7.3	12
Black (Non-Hispanic)	38.9	35.7	31.2
Hispanic	51.9	52.1	49.2
Asian	1.4	2.7	5.6
Native American	.2	.2	.2
Other	.4	2	1.8
Total Population	110,508	117,743	120,511

Source: U.S. Census Bureau, 2000 and 2010 Census PL and SF1 Files and 1990 Census STF1.

Population Division as reported in "Profile of Manhattan Community District 11" in New York City Department of City Planning (2011).

East Harlem has seen a decrease in its African-American population and a slight decrease in Hispanics, along with a slight increase in white and Asian residents (see table 9.6) (New York City Department of City Planning 2012). Census tract 188, the heart of El Barrio, has 3,988 Hispanics out of 6,008 residents, 66 percent of the population. Furthermore, Hispanics can be separated as Puerto Rican, Dominican, Mexican, and Central and South American. Thus, while El Barrio is often stigmatized by outsiders as a dangerous area full of undocumented immigrants, it is indeed a very diverse neighborhood (Castañeda 2012, Castañeda, Beck, and Lachica 2015).

Table 9.6. Population of East Harlem by race, ethnicity, and nationality (not mutually exclusive)

Population of East Harlem	Population	Percentage Total
Hispanic/Latino	61,164	49.8
Puerto Rican	32,973	26.8
Mexican	11,686	9.5
Other Hispanic	16,505	13.5
Black/African-American	38,885	31.6
White	14,117	11.5
Asian	6,763	5.5
Total Population	122,920	98.4

Source: U.S. Census Bureau, 2006–2010 American Community Survey (5 Year Estimates for Public Use Microdata Area 03804 in New York), as reported in "Profile of Manhattan Community District 11" in New York City Department of City Planning (2012).

The people who live and spend time in the geographic boundaries of El Barrio are rather diverse, with no one group as an absolute majority. According to official data, white residents of El Barrio made up around 11.5 percent in 2010, Puerto Ricans 26.8 percent, Mexicans 9.5 percent, Asians 5.5 percent, and Blacks 31.6 percent, with only 26 percent of residents being foreign born (New York City Department of City Planning 2012). Mexican populations are widespread throughout the New York metropolitan area (Bergad 2013). They participate in many different communities and have interactions with other ethnoracial groups. For example, Robert Smith describes the importance that many Mexican-origin youths in New York place on socializing, identifying, and acculturating to black culture, which may end up helping these individuals to achieve social mobility in adulthood (Smith 2014).

Mexican New Yorkers not only interact with blacks, but recent immigrants themselves are surprised by the diversity of the United States, as an immigrant told anthropologist Judith Hellman:

Before you get to New York, Los Angeles, or wherever it is you may end up, you have a picture of yourself . . . wandering around a place full of tall blond people . . . and the boss is going to be someone who squints at you through cold blue eyes like in a film. But when you get here the boss turns out to be an Italian or a Greek, or an Armenian, or a Chinese or a Korean, or maybe someone from the Middle East or from Pakistan. And some of these people talk about how they are immigrants just like you or how their father was an immigrant just like you. And some treat the workers very well, and others [don't]. . . . [Customers] would come into the market who worked in hospitals or schools or places where they couldn't do their job if they couldn't speak some Spanish, and you could have a real conversation with them: [they would ask] "Where are you from?" "How long have you been here?" "Do you have children?" "Are they in school?" Stuff like that. (Hellman 2008, xx–xxi)

Thus, while the literature includes some evidence of interethnic interactions, most of the work focuses on single ethnic groups or on interracial conflict. Researchers know that Mexicans constantly interact with other ethnic groups in the city, but this is often overshadowed by the rhetorical, theoretical, and methodological focus on migrant communities, diasporic relations, and transnational social fields. This could be described as a half-full or half-empty glass type of argument, yet it is important to describe the interactions that Mexicans have with other New Yorkers. Without this important clarification, non-specialist readers may wrongly interpret studies of transnationalism and Mexican neighborhoods as evidence that Mexican immigrants "only socialize with other Mexicans," "prefer to speak Spanish, and do not want to learn English," or that "they self-segregate and do not want to be American," as some scholars have done when misrepresenting immigration research (Huntington 2004b). All these common stereotypes are disproved by countless empirical social science studies. Mexican New Yorkers maintain many elements of their culture, yet interactions with other ethnic groups are not rare. As the data shows, Mexicans in New York form ties with non-Mexicans and are eager to learn English for business and practical reasons while continuing to speak Spanish or Indigenous languages among co-ethnics. Propinquity at neighborhoods, work, and school allows for many acquaintances across ethnic lines.

Mexican Immigrant Embeddedness in the City

Daniel is a well-educated and connected Mexican immigrant who has been waiting for decades for his family reunification application to be reviewed. He left as a minor to accompany his parents (Dreby 2010, Massey et al. 1987) through social ties connecting Puebla and New York. Today, Daniel knows how to navigate through the New York metropolitan area; he has learned English and has made many friends of different ethnic, class, and religious backgrounds. He held different jobs and started a couple of businesses, but he cannot fully plan for the long term, as he is always anxious about being deported (Castañeda 2013b). Daniel identifies as a New Yorker but is unable to work in the formal economy since his student visa has expired, and he was unable to find a sponsor for a work visa. At times, Daniel feels socially invisible; although he has established himself in the city, he is treated by the law as if he does not exist. When most people think of a New Yorker, they do not picture someone like Daniel. Nonetheless, the city is full of immigrant entrepreneurs with and without citizenship papers.

Thousands of Mexicans live, study, and work in New York. They feel attached to their neighborhoods. They work to pay their expenses and remit to family in their places of origin. They speak Spanish and engage in cultural celebrations and public events. They experience urban belonging and culturally assimilate while keeping their traditions (Castañeda 2018b). But many are in a legal limbo that affects their further integration into the social fabric of New York, and the United States (Castañeda 2013a). These New York residents can open bank accounts, send remittances home, and have local identification cards, but they cannot vote. Furthermore, native New Yorkers and visitors rarely notice their presence. Most concrete interactions between Americans and Mexicans typically happen at work.

Coworkers' Views of Mexican New Yorkers

The most important interactions that first-generation labor migrants have with members of other ethnic groups occur in the workplace. The great majority of Mexicans in New York are hired to work for non-Mexicans. The fairness and generosity of employers, or the lack thereof, has a significant effect on how Mexican workers perceive the United States (Hellman 2008). Mexicans are preferred by employers because they are seen as hard workers (Fuentes 2007, Moss and Tilly 2001) and because they can be paid less than other groups.

It is also through workplace interactions that Americans and other immigrants dispel the stereotypes they have about Mexicans. For example, individuals from Jalisco and other regions in central Mexico work in "Country Club" (CC) in one of the most affluent counties in the New York metropolitan area. They work as landscapers, custodial staff, waiters, bartenders, hostesses, and receptionists. Workers live, eat, and sleep on the club grounds and range in age from 16 to their late 40s.

The perspective of Britney, a non-Hispanic white in her 20s, who worked in the club, illustrates the reproduction of hierarchies and the partial dispelling of stereotypes, as well as the confluence of cultures that sometimes happens in the workplace:

> I have known Pablo for almost six years now from when I first started working at the club as a snack bar waitress. For my entire time of employment, I always

went to him if I needed anything. Pablo is like the father of the family. He knows everyone by name and face and is as high up in rank as any of the immigrant workers have ever made it. . . . If Pablo is the father figure in the CC community, the "Mama" is a woman who emigrated from Jamaica when she was seven. . . . Pablo and all the other Mexican immigrants at the CC have influenced the menu that the members dine on and have added their own flare to the choices at the bar. . . . Mary, a second-generation Mexican-American woman, told me, "I don't know if I really feel Mexican anymore. I did when I was little but by the time I hit middle school I spoke better English than Spanish and all of my friends were white."

This account provides evidence of the ethnic job stratification that exists in many American workplaces and depicts the interactions that occur across class and ethnic groups, including the development of close personal relationships and fictive kinships. Mary, a young Mexican-American lady, identified with mainstream society as a function of the neighborhood where she resides, schools she attended, individual tastes in fashion or music, and her ability to physically pass as non-Mexican and the privilege this affords her in getting access to a better job in the club.

In another example, Alvin, an Albanian student writes,

Jorge is the assistant chef at the restaurant [where I work]. He is one of my closest friends with whom I hang out often after work. He lives on East 115th Street. . . . The other guys in the kitchen were working at least six days a week. Yet we used to play soccer [in a park in East Harlem]. Marco, a busboy from Ecuador that I work with, his English isn't good at all. . . . I tried in Spanish too, but my Spanish is very weak. However, having worked in Italian restaurants for a while, Marco was able to understand most of what I was asking him in Italian. . . . He told me that he came to the United States through the Mexican border and that he paid $2,500 to do so. Marco wasn't shy at all about his experience as an undocumented immigrant. . . . Jesus is a cook from Mexico that works at the restaurant and Enrique a 35-year-old Ecuadorian dishwasher that came in the U.S. a few months ago, lives in East Harlem and is fluent in Italian. . . . Every single one of them was sending money back to Mexico or Ecuador on a regular basis. What was unfortunate is that even though they weren't complaining much, their apartments were in very poor condition.

Alvin describes a workplace where Mexicans, Ecuadorians, Albanians, and Italians work side by side. Alvin is connected to other Albanians in New York, yet his best friend is Latin. The fact that the common language of this group is Italian demonstrates the multicultural nature of New York. Learning English is not the only way to integrate into the local society or assimilate with the cultural practices of neighbors, employers, and coworkers.

Britney openly expressed her opposition to "illegal migration" at the same time that she had formed close ties with undocumented co-workers and classmates. This shows how individuals can express anti-immigrant views in conversation and opinion polls yet have concrete friendships with undocumented individuals. These vignettes show individuals from different ethnic, geographic, religious, and class backgrounds interact and get to know each other in the workplace. Through interaction within these different social circles, the stereotypes that others had of Mexicans may have changed by getting to know some members of this categorical group. At other times, their interactions reinforce the stereotypes of Latin people as hardworking, undereducated, poor, and living in slum-like conditions, as if they were personal choices, rather than resulting from their social position. These interactions both challenge and reinforce the social boundaries established between Mexicans and other groups living in New York.

Ties are the basis for networks, and superimposed networks may build up to categorical networks (catnets), yet once social boundaries are in place, they tend to remain despite relationships across categories (Tilly 2005). Some of the literature on racial formations has shown for some time that views of immigrants as despised outgroups can prevail even though individuals might have ties with select immigrants (Omi and Winant 2015). In other words, racialized generalizations of immigrants can prevail even when one might have a few immigrant friends (Golash-Boza 2017).

CONCLUSION

Many new Mexican immigrants often do not want to be noticed because they lack papers and fear deportation (Hellman 2008, Thompson 2007). The ties with other racial groups previously described vary in type, are often hierarchical, and do not imply equality. There is a social distance between natives and immigrants, especially those newly arriving and those from stigmatized groups. Nevertheless, this distance is often overcome by the third generation —when ethnicity is overtaken by other characteristics such as class, gender, and education as a predictor of life chances as it is for the rest of Americans (Kasinitz, Mollenkopf, and Waters 2004; Kasinitz et al. 2008).

Mexicans in New York are proud of their origin and maintain connections and social ties in Mexico, yet they have an impact on the economic, political, cultural, and social spheres of New York City. They adapt to their new neighborhood, city, and country. Like previous immigrant waves of Italian, Irish, and Jewish immigrants to New York, Mexicans maintain ties with their homeland and may form a symbolic ethnic identity (Gans 1979). They can use telephones, e-mail, Skype, cell phones, and social media that previous waves of immigrants lacked, yet their undocumented status and the implications that this has had in recent decades in blocking physical and social mobility leave undocumented immigrants more trapped than ever (Núñez and Heyman 2007). Despite their undocumented status and ethnic pride, they are also New Yorkers. As Brooklyn Borough President Eric Adams said to Brooklyn residents of Mexican origin in a public event on April 12, 2015, "You don't have to stop being Mexican in order to be a proud New Yorker."

Most Mexicans in New York are at the bottom of the social hierarchy, yet they identify as New Yorkers. Mexican individuals living and working in New York have an important influence on the city and the people who live there. At the same time, Mexican immigrants who are studying, living, and working in New York are changed forever by the experience as they assimilate into new cultural practices and languages. Mexican New Yorkers have an ethnic origin just like Italian-American or Irish-American New Yorkers (Tilly 1976, 1989). A demographic report by the New York City Department of City Planning about the foreign-born population is appropriately titled "The Newest New Yorkers" (Lobo and Salvo 2013). As one of the fastest growing ethnic groups in New York, Mexican-origin residents are indeed among the newest New Yorkers, even if they remain socially invisible to many. This is another example of a self-identity that has not been matched in the mainstream due to the low social status of an out-group. Mexicans in New York suffer from the national stigmatization of being, or presumed to be, undocumented immigrants and are visible as a faceless social problem, yet they are socially invisible as individuals while working behind the scenes and interacting mainly with coworkers.

Chapter 10

Why Walls Won't Work

Interactions between Latin Immigrants and Americans

Ernesto Castañeda and Maura Fennelly

Our families, friends, the news, and what the state tells us all shape many of our views regarding immigration. It is impossible to avoid being influenced by them, but it is important to be reminded of the biases and prejudices that come from them. The various voices and topics included in this book provide an opportunity to challenge preconceived notions and presuppositions. While the media may only use sound bites from a handful of politicians or interview experts and spokespeople, this book allows readers to witness the nuance surrounding the inclusion and exclusion of immigrants and minorities in the United States. The chapters presented various perspectives pertaining to the relationship between Mexican migrants, Latin citizens, and white Americans.

The objective of this book is to analyze the building of symbolic boundaries and physical walls between Americans and Latin people, particularly Mexicans. The consequences of these barriers on Mexican migrants and their communities are discussed in Part III. Concepts like "social invisibility" help explain the feelings of exclusion and isolation that Mexican immigrants feel even in the most inclusive cities in the United States.

Income inequality, stagnant wages, increased costs of higher education, and other economic barriers impact millions of Americans. Immigrants, refugees, and asylees also endure all of these challenges while dealing with feelings of exclusion and judgment from many American citizens, along with fearing detainment or deportation at any moment. This is not to suggest that undocumented migrants' struggles are more significant than those of American citizens. In fact, recognizing the similar economic and financial struggles that lower- and middle-income Americans and migrants face would reflect the lack of social mobility in the United States. Unfettered models for producing growth in the American economy continue to depend on free-market policies that continue to exacerbate inequalities, allowing only the truly well off to benefit.

The rise of neoliberalism across the world since the 1980s encouraged global trade, free markets, and multinational corporations, but it did not support open borders for people. Instead, narratives focusing on immigrants stealing jobs, being violent, and abusing the welfare system became the main talking points of political campaigns. Despite studies showing that immigrant workers' impact on overall native workers' wages is minimal or negligible, politicians and news pundits claim the opposite. Also, immigrants have almost no effect on the overall employment rates for U.S.-born workers. In fact, demographic and economic experts Francine D. Blau and Christopher Mackie state how

> immigration is integral to the nation's economic growth. The inflow of labor supply has helped the United States avoid the problems facing other economies that have stagnated as a result of unfavorable demographics, particularly the effects of an aging workforce and reduced consumption of housing and consumer durables by older residents. (Blau and Mackie 2017)

No matter how much evidence proving immigrants' positive impacts on America's economy and society is presented, prejudice and xenophobia still exist.

Why is there so much animosity against Mexican and Central American migrants seeking safety and opportunity in America, even with evidence showing that they benefit our economy more than they harm it? As discussed in several chapters, feelings of nationalism are strongly related to desires for a homogenous culture. Categorical groupings separating individuals into national identities are supported by states around the world. The standardization of American identity through citizenship, patrolling of borders, and deportation illustrates the government's active attempt to control who does or does not belong in the country.

The push for a homogenous society does not just stem from the U.S. government. Some academics also claim that multiculturalism and a diverse U.S. population will only cause problems, as they fail to recognize the ability of diverse individuals to live harmoniously together. While there is prejudice against immigrants in America, there are still millions of Americans who support refugees and actively protest the deportation and detention of migrants. It is apparent that there is a large split on immigration issues in America today, but multiple opinion polls show that over half of the population of the United States is open to immigration and diversity.

The best way to understand how Americans and Mexicans feel about one another is to ask them, which is one of the things this book does. Firsthand experiences from undocumented migrants themselves are included in order to give a platform for the voices of individuals who are often misunderstood and stereotyped by popular narratives. Interviews, discourse analyses, macro-level theoretical discussions, case studies, ethnographies, and other fieldwork provide context to understand the perspectives that communities have on the relationship between Americans and Latin migrants.

The everyday interactions, theory, and policies on migration discussed in this book show us how physical and symbolic boundaries between people are created, supported, and challenged. These boundaries are also enhanced by categorical inequalities that Mexican migrants, and most other migrants, face in the United States. Economic inequality and the lack of social mobility in the United States only enhance these categorical inequalities. Unless immigrants appear white, are wealthy, and are highly educated, they will face discrimination and adversity when adjusting to life in the United States.

The trope of "a nation of immigrants" is entirely accurate, but it does not assuage any concerns, dislike, and hatred that many Americans hold toward migrant populations throughout the country. Charles Tilly notes,

> The history of American immigration therefore combines the general and the particular in a compelling way. On one side, it is everyone's history, a history in which chains of migrants formed over and over again to link distant places to the United States. On the other, its precise form differs from group to group, even from person to person; each of us has his own tale of migration to tell, ending networks and receiving networks could hardly be more specific, yet their junction and transformation follow well-defined general rules. . . . In examining the history of immigration as individual experience of collective phenomenon, we are probing the roots, and the broken branches, of American democracy. (Castañeda and Schneider 2017, 323)

Western Europeans came to the United States in large numbers from the 1600s up through the early 1900s. Although many groups faced discrimination (the Irish or Italians, e.g.), they molded with the American identity and became white, and a new homogenous America was celebrated. Immigrant groups from Africa, Asia, Latin America, and the Middle East are not able to easily fit in because they are perceived to challenge the whiteness of the United States. There is a strong narrative claiming that cohabitation and shared communities with certain groups are not possible or desirable. Instead, nationalist rhetoric, calls for a border wall, the formation of groups like the Minutemen, barring refugees, and deporting migrants are suggested and implemented as solutions.

This book encourages readers to think critically about their own views about the border and projections into it. Interviews with undocumented migrants in El Paso and New York City offer two cases of the effects of social invisibility on the groups' well-being and identity. The more macro-level discussions of theory and boundary-making show how the individual cases happen within a larger socio-historical context. The Minutemen and their protestors illustrate both the persistence of nationalist movements in the United States as well as active resistance against them.

The discourse analysis of news articles' online comments offers insight into how strong anti-immigrant sentiment is across the United States. The Trump administration has taken a hard-line stance against Mexican migrants. Stories of ICE separating parents from their children and arresting workers in the middle of the day are heard often. Calls to build a border wall and deport even more migrants continue.

Empathy must be used when addressing this topic. Empathy is needed for the migrants, their families, and misunderstood Americans. As citizens, it is our responsibility to engage with those who hold divergent viewpoints and even opposite moral understandings than our own.

This book shows how hard it will be to solve the tension between heterogeneity and homogeneity, between open and closed borders, and between support for immigrants and xenophobia. Many of the xenophobic and hate-filled comments posted on news articles and forums show that misunderstandings and false information associated with Latin immigrants must be addressed promptly. Fortunately, the boundaries that separate Latin migrants from their American counterparts are permeable and transient. Students' interactions with the border fence increased their sense of empathy for individuals crossing into the United States. This shows that understandings and views on the matter can change through education, awareness, and firsthand interactions with immigrants. Cultural, economic, and personal ties are not determined by social or political boundaries.

Interaction and openness is a better alternative because in the long run walls will not work.

In his book *Why Walls Won't Work* Berkeley geographer Michael Dear shows how misinformed and futile is the policy of building walls on the border. The book concludes that walls will not work because

1. the border has long been a place of connection;
2. the wall is an aberration in the context of the border region's history;
3. the prosperity of the border's sets of twin cities requires that there be few barriers between them;
4. people always find ways over, under, through, and around walls;
5. government and private interests continue opening doors in the wall;

6. a cultural mix of Mexican and American traditions exists in the minds and habits of border residents;
7. mobility and demographic realities trump the border industrial complex;
8. Mexico is increasingly global and democratic; and
9. walls always come down.

Dear writes, "Nevertheless, we should preserve sections of the Wall to commemorate that fraught moment in history when the US lost its moral compass" (Dear 2013, 177). The book also cites the widespread practice, between 1917 and 1950, of forcing legal border crossers to enter disinfection areas where their clothes would be fumigated, and if suspected of carrying lice, they would be bathed with kerosene, vinegar, gasoline, sulfuric acid, DDT, or Zyklon-B, which was later used by the Nazis in their death camps (Dear 2013, 64). Will future generations see the building of the fence the way we now see the past fumigation of border crossers?

It is incumbent upon all of us to learn from history. We must critically understand how we have created social boundaries. Individuals are not born with an understanding of who belongs or who does not. Anti-immigrant sentiment is acquired; therefore, it can and must be changed.

In the midterm elections of 2018, over 280,000 anti-immigration political ads were used against Democratic candidates—containing terms like gangs, open borders, sanctuary cities, and the migrant caravan as threats to America (Moran and Gourevitch 2018). Nevertheless, the most anti-immigrant candidates lost, and many Democratic incumbents targeted for their pro-immigration views were re-elected (Moran and Gourevitch 2018). In the 2014 House elections, Democrats got over 60 million votes while Republicans got less than 51 million (Wasserman and Flinn 2018). Latin people voted in large numbers in the 2018 elections, and in 2019 there are a record 42 Latin Representatives in both chambers (Gambino 2018). Despite gerrymandering and other dynamics, one could read the 2018 mid-term results partly as a rejection of anti-immigrant policies. It seems that welcoming immigrants and providing asylum to those facing persecution for their ideas, religion, or identity has again become a moral issue. The number of xenophobes and open racists may have reached a ceiling which is below half of the voting-age population. There is no longer a hegemonic bipartisan consensus that used to feel free to criticize the moral character of Latin individuals, whether because they may speak Spanish, look indigenous, be Catholic, or be suspected of being undocumented. Talking and spending time with people from different categorical groups can dispel many of the negative stereotypes associated to their group. As social boundaries and physical walls have been constructed, walls can be breached, and bridges can be built, too.

References

Achotegui, Joseba. 2011. *How to Assess Stress and Migratory Mourning: Scales of Risk Factors in Mental Health*. Llançà, España: Ediciones El Mundo de la Mente.

Achotegui, Joseba. 2016. "La Atención a La Salud Mental de los Inmigrantes y Demandantes de Asilo." *Advances in Relational Mental Health* 15 (1).

Agamben, Giorgio. 1998. *Homo Sacer: Sovereign Power and Bare Life*. Stanford, CA: Stanford University Press.

Agamben, Giorgio. 2005. *State of Exception*. Chicago, IL: University of Chicago Press.

Agamben, Giorgio. 2017. *The Omnibus Homo Sacer*. Stanford, CA: Stanford University Press.

Aguilera, Michael Bernabé. 2003. "The Impact of the Worker: How Social Capital and Human Capital Influence the Job Tenure of Formerly Undocumented Mexican Immigrants." *Sociological Inquiry* 73 (1):52–83.

Akhtar, Salman. 1999a. "The Immigrant, the Exile, and the Experience of Nostalgia." *Journal of Applied Psychoanalytic Studies* 1 (2):123–30.

Akhtar, Salman. 1999b. *Immigration and Identity: Turmoil, Treatment, and Transformation*. Northvale, NJ: Jason Aronson.

Alberti, Gabriella. 2014. "Mobility Strategies, 'Mobility Differentials' and 'Transnational Exit': The Experiences of Precarious Migrants in London's Hospitality Jobs." *Work, Employment & Society* 28 (6):865–81.

Albuja, Sebastián, and Laura Rubio Díaz-Leal. 2011. "Los Olvidados de la Guerra contra el Narcotráfico en México." *Foreign Affairs Latinoamérica* 11 (4):23–31.

Anderson, Benedict. 2006. *Imagined Communities: Reflections on the Origin and Spread of Nationalism*. Rev. ed. London: Verso.

Anzaldúa, Gloria. 1987. *Borderlands: The New Mestiza = La Frontera*. San Francisco: Spinsters/Aunt Lute.

AOL. 2017. "Federal Government Solicits Design Proposals for Border Wall with Mexico." AOL. https://www.aol.com/article/news/2017/03/19/federal-government-solicits-design-proposals-for-border-wall-wit/21902558/#.

AP. 2011. "Arizona: Border Activist Sentenced to Death." *New York Times*. https://www.nytimes.com/2011/02/23/us/23brfs-BORDERACTIVI_BRF.html.

Appadurai, Arjun. 1996. *Modernity at Large: Cultural Dimensions of Globalization*. Minneapolis, MN: University of Minnesota Press.

Aranda, Elizabeth M. 2008. "Class Backgrounds, Modes of Incorporation, and Puerto Ricans' Pathways into the Transnational Professional Workforce." *American Behavioral Scientist* 52 (3):426–56.

Aranda, Elizabeth, and Elizabeth Vaquera. 2015. "Racism, the Immigration Enforcement Regime, and the Implications for Racial Inequality in the Lives of Undocumented Young Adults." *Sociology of Race and Ethnicity* 1 (1):88–104.

Arendt, Hannah. 1958. *Origins of Totalitarianism*. Cleveland, OH: The World Publishing Company.

Armenta, Amada. 2017. "Racializing Crimmigration: Structural Racism, Colorblindness, and the Institutional Production of Immigrant Criminality." *Sociology of Race and Ethnicity* 3 (1):82–95.

Ash, Timothy Garton. 2004. "The Great Powers of Europe, Redefined." *New York Times*, December 17.

AZBR. 2016. "Arizona Border Recon." https://www.arizonaborderrecon.org/.

Babones, Salvatore J. 2014. *Methods for Quantitative Macro-comparative Research*. Thousand Oaks, CA: SAGE Publications.

Bail, Christopher A. 2008. "The Configuration of Symbolic Boundaries against Immigrants in Europe." *American Sociological Review* 73 (1):37–59.

Baker, Zeke. 2018. "Meteorological Frontiers: Climate Knowledge, the West, and US Statecraft, 1800–50." *Social Science History* 42 (4):731–61.

Barth, Fredrik. 1969. *Ethnic groups and boundaries: The social organization of culture difference*. London, UK: George Allen and Unwin.

Bebout, Lee. 2016. *Whiteness on the Border: Mapping the US Racial Imagination in Brown and White*. New York: New York University Press.

Belew, Kathleen. 2011. "An America for Brisenia Flores." History News Network. https://historynewsnetwork.org/article/135967.

Benton-Cohen, Katherine. 2018. *Inventing the Immigration Problem: The Dillingham Commission and Its Legacy*. Cambridge, MA: Harvard University Press.

Bergad, Laird W. 2013. "Demographic, Economic and Social Transformations in the Mexican-Origin Population of the New York City Metropolitan Area, 1990–2010." *Latino Data Project—Report 49*. New York: Center for Latin American, Caribbean & Latino Studies, Graduate Center, City University of New York.

Berlinger, Nancy, Claudia Calhoon, Michael K. Gusmano, and Jackie Vimo. 2015. *Undocumented Immigrants and Access to Health Care in New York City: Identifying Fair, Effective, and Sustainable Local Policy Solutions: Report and Recommendations to the Office of the Mayor of New York City*. New York: The Hastings Center and the New York Immigration Coalition.

Bernstein, Nina. 2007. "A Mexican Baby Boom in New York Shows the Strength of a New Immigrant Group." *New York Times*, June 4.

Bernstein, Richard. 2004. "A Continent Watching Anxiously Over the Melting Pot." *The New York Times*, December 14. http://www.nytimes.com/2004/12/15/international/15letter.html.

Binder, Amy J., and Kate Wood. 2014. *Becoming Right: How Campuses Shape Young Conservatives*. Princeton, NJ: Princeton University Press.

Blau, Francine D., and Christopher Mackie. 2017. "The Economic and Fiscal Impact of Immigration in the US." *NIUSS*, March 27.

Block, Fred L., and Margaret R. Somers. 2014. *The Power of Market Fundamentalism: Karl Polanyi's Critique*. Cambridge, MA: Harvard University Press.

Bonilla-Silva, Eduardo. 1997. "Rethinking Racism: Toward a Structural Interpretation." *American Sociological Review* 62 (3):465–80.

Bonilla-Silva, Eduardo. 2006. *Racism without Racists: Color-Blind Racism and the Persistence of Racial Inequality in the United States*. 2nd ed. Lanham, MD: Rowman & Littlefield Publishers.

Bonilla-Silva, Eduardo. 2017. *Racism without Racists: Color-blind racism and the persistence of racial inequality in America*. 5th ed. Lanham, MD: Rowman & Littlefield Publishers.

Bourdieu, Pierre. 1984 [1979]. *Distinction: A Social Critique of the Judgement of Taste*. Cambridge, MA: Harvard University Press.

Bourdieu, Pierre. 1991. *Language and Symbolic Power*. Cambridge, MA: Harvard University Press.

Bourdieu, Pierre. 1994. "Rethinking the State: Genesis and Structure of the Bureaucratic Field." *Sociological Theory* 12 (1):1–18.

Bourdieu, Pierre. 1996 [1989]. *The State Nobility: Elite Schools in the Field of Power*. Oxford, UK: Polity Press.

Bourdieu, Pierre. 1998. *Practical Reason: On the Theory of Action*. Stanford, CA: Stanford University Press.

Bourdieu, Pierre, and Loïc Wacquant. 2000. "The Organic Ethnologist of Algerian Migration." *Ethnography* 1 (2):173–82.

Bourgois, Phillipe. 1996. *In Search of Respect: Selling Crack in El Barrio*. Cambridge: Cambridge University Press.

Brooks, David. 2000. *Bobos in Paradise: The New Upper Class and How They Got There*. New York: Simon & Schuster.

Brubaker, Rogers. 1992. *Citizenship and Nationhood in France and Germany*. Cambridge, MA: Harvard University Press.

Brubaker, Rogers. 2001. "The Return of Assimilation? Changing Perspectives on Immigration and Its Sequels in France, Germany, and the United States." *Ethnic and Racial Studies* 24 (4):531–48.

Brubaker, Rogers. 2004. *Ethnicity without Groups*. Cambridge, MA: Harvard University Press.

Brubaker, Rogers, Margit Feischmidt, Jon Fox, and Liana Grancea. 2006. *Nationalist Politics and Everyday Ethnicity in a Transylvanian Town*. Princeton, NJ: Princeton University Press.

Budnitskii, Oleg. 2012. *Russian Jews between the Reds and the Whites, 1917–1920*. Translated by Timothy J. Portice. Philadelphia: University of Pennsylvania Press.

Burawoy, Michael. 1976. "The Functions and Reproduction of Migrant Labor: Comparative Material from Southern Africa and the United States." *American Journal of Sociology* 82 (5):1050–87.

Burawoy, Michael. 2003. "Revisits: An Outline of a Theory of Reflexive Ethnography." *American Sociological Review* 68 (5):645–79.

Calderón Chelius, Leticia, and Andrea González Cornejo. 2012. "Rastros del Duelo: Exilio, Asilo Político y Desplazamiento Forzado Interno en la Frontera Norte de México." In *Migrantes, Desplazados, Braceros y Deportados: Experiencias Migratorias y Prácticas Políticas*, edited by Dolores Paris Pombo, 30. México, DF: COLEF.

Calhoun, Craig J. 1997. *Nationalism: Concepts in Social Thought*. Minneapolis: University of Minnesota Press.

Calhoun, Craig J. 2003. "The Class Consciousness of Frequent Travelers: Toward a Critique of Actually Existing Cosmopolitanism." *South Atlantic Quarterly* 101 (4):869–97.

Calhoun, Craig J. 2007. *Nations Matter: Culture, History, and the Cosmopolitan Dream*. London: Routledge.

California Commission on Civil Rights. 1971. *Political Participation of Mexican Americans in California*, edited by California State Advisory Committee to the United States Commission on Civil Rights, Sacramento, CA.

Campbell, Howard. 2009. *Drug War Zone: Frontline Dispatches from the Streets of El Paso and Juárez*. Austin, TX: University of Texas Press.

Caplan, David. 2017. "CBP Issues Requests for Border Wall Proposals: It Will 'Be Physically Imposing in Height." ABC News, accessed 2017. http://abcnews.go.com/Politics/cbp-issues-requests-border-wall-proposals-physically-imposing/story?id=46218945.

Carranza, Rafael. 2017. "Border Wall Materials: Concrete, 'Other.'" USA Today, accessed April 16. https://www.usatoday.com/story/news/nation-now/2017/03/15/border-wall-materials-concrete-other/99198014/.

Castañeda, Ernesto. 2012. "Places of Stigma: Ghettos, Barrios and Banlieues." In *The Ghetto: Contemporary Global Issues and Controversies*, edited by Ray Hutchison and Bruce D. Haynes, 159–90. Boulder, CO: Westview Press.

Castañeda, Ernesto. 2013a. "Living in Limbo: Transnational Households, Remittances and Development." *International Migration* 51 (s1):13–35.

Castañeda, Ernesto. 2013b. *Waiting for Real Reform: How Half-Way Measures Leave Immigrants in Limbo and Deprive America of Their Talents*. Cambridge, MA: Scholars Strategy Network.

Castañeda, Ernesto. 2018a. *Immigration and Categorical Inequality: Migration to the City and the Birth of Race and Ethnicity*. New York, NY: Routledge.

Castañeda, Ernesto. 2018b. *A Place to Call Home: Immigrant Exclusion and Urban Belonging in New York, Paris, and Barcelona*. Stanford, CA: Stanford University Press.

Castañeda, Ernesto. 2018c. "Understanding Inequality, Migration, Race, and Ethnicity from a Relational Perspective." In *Immigration and Categorical Inequality: Migration to the City and the Birth of Race and Ethnicity*, edited by Ernesto Castañeda. New York: Routledge.

Castañeda, Ernesto, and Kevin Beck. 2018. "Stigmatizing Immigrant Day Labor: Boundary-Making and the Built-Environment in Long Island, New York." In *Immigration and Categorical Inequality: Migration to the City and the Birth of Race and Ethnicity*, edited by Ernesto Castañeda. New York, NY: Routledge.

Castañeda, Ernesto, Kevin Beck, and Josue Lachica. 2015. "Walking through Contemporary North American Barrios: Hispanic Neighborhoods in New York, San Diego, and El Paso." In *Walking in Cities: Quotidian Mobility as Urban Theory, Method, and Practice*, edited by Evrick Brown and Timothy Shortell. Philadelphia, PA: Temple University Press.

Castañeda, Ernesto, and Lesley Buck. 2011. "Remittances, Transnational Parenting, and the Children Left Behind: Economic and Psychological Implications." *The Latin Americanist* 55 (4):85–110.

Castañeda, Ernesto, and Lesley Buck. 2014. "A Family of Strangers: Transnational Parenting and the Consequences of Family Separation due to Undocumented Migration." In *Hidden Lives and Human Rights in America: Understanding the Controversies and Tragedies of Undocumented Immigration*, edited by Lois Ann Lorentzen. Santa Barbara, CA: Praeger.

Castañeda, Ernesto, and Josiah M. Heyman. 2012. *Is the Southwestern Border Really Unsafe?* Cambridge, MA: Scholars Strategy Network.

Castañeda, Ernesto, Cristina Morales, and Olga Ochoa. 2014. "Transnational Behavior in Comparative Perspective: The Relationship between Immigrant Integration and Transnationalism in New York, El Paso, and Paris." *Comparative Migration Studies* 2 (3):305–34.

Castañeda, Ernesto, and Cathy Lisa Schneider. 2017. *Collective Violence, Contentious Politics, and Social Change: A Charles Tilly Reader*. New York: Routledge.

Castañeda, Jorge G. 2007. *Ex Mex: From Migrants to Immigrants*. New York: New Press.

Castles, Stephen, and Alastair Davidson. 2000. *Citizenship and Migration: Globalization and the Politics of Belonging*. New York: Routledge.

Catanzarite, Lisa, and Michael Bernabé Aguilera. 2002. "Working with Co-Ethnics: Earnings Penalties for Latino Immigrants at Latino Jobsites." *Social Problems* 49 (1):101–27.

CEA. 1882. Chinese Exclusion Act.

Cepeda, Esther J. 2013. "The Arizona Minutemen, Lost in a Changing America." September 4. http://nbclatino.com/2013/09/04/opinion-the-arizona-minutemen-lost-in-a-changing-america/.

Cervantes-Soon, Claudia. 2014. "The U.S.-Mexico Border-Crossing Chicana Researcher: Theory in the Flesh and the Politics of Identity in Critical Ethnography." *Journal of Latino/Latin American Studies* 6 (2):97–112.

Chatterjee, Partha. 1986. *Nationalist Thought and the Colonial World: A Derivative Discourse?* London, UK: Zed Books.

Chatterjee, Partha. 2004. *The Politics of the Governed: Reflections on Popular Politics in Most of the World.* New York: Columbia University Press.

Chávez, Ernesto. 2002. *Mi Raza Primero! Nationalism, Identity, and Insurgency in the Chicano Movement in Los Angeles, 1966–1978.* Berkeley, CA: University of California Press.

Chavez, Leo R. 2001. *Covering Immigration: Popular Images and the Politics of the Nation.* Berkeley, CA: University of California Press.

Chavez, Leo R. 2008a. *The Latino Threat: Constructing Immigrants, Citizens, and the Nation.* Stanford, CA: Stanford University Press.

Chavez, Leo R. 2008b. "Spectacle in the Desert: The Minuteman Project on the U.S-Mexico Border." In *Global Vigilantes*, edited by David Pratten and Atreyee Sen. New York: Columbia University Press.

Cheliotis, Leonidas K. 2017. "Punitive Inclusion: The Political Economy of Irregular Migration in the Margins of Europe." *European Journal of Criminology* 14 (1):78–99.

Chou, Vivian. 2017. "How Science and Genetics Are Reshaping the Race Debate of the 21st Century." Harvard University, accessed November 29. http://sitn.hms.harvard.edu/flash/2017/science-genetics-reshaping-race-debate-21st-century/.

Cochrane, Christopher, and Neil Nevitte. 2014. "Scapegoating: Unemployment, Far-Right Parties and Anti-Immigrant Sentiment." *Comparative European Politics* 12 (1):1–32.

Collins, Patricia Hill. 2015. "Intersectionality's Definitional Dilemmas." *Annual Review of Sociology* 41 (1):1–20.

Collins, Patricia Hill, and Sirma Bilge. 2016. *Intersectionality*. Cambridge, UK: Polity.

Corbett, Erin. 2018. "'Today' Show Faces Backlash for Giving a Platform to White Supremacist Group." *Fortune*. http://fortune.com/2018/10/17/today-show-backlash-white-supremacist-group/.

Daniels, Roger. 2004. *Guarding the Golden Door: American Immigration Policy and Immigrants since 1882.* New York, NY: Hill & Wang.

Dávila, Arlene M. 2004. *Barrio Dreams: Puerto Ricans, Latinos, and the Neoliberal City.* Berkeley, CA: University of California Press.

Dávila, Arlene. 2012. *Latinos, Inc: The Marketing and Making of a People.* Berkeley, CA: University of California Press.

Dear, Michael J. 2013. *Why Walls Won't Work: Repairing the US-Mexico Divide.* New York: Oxford University Press.

De Genova, Nicholas. 2004. "The Legal Production of Mexican/Migrant 'Illegality.'" *Latino Studies* 2004 (2):160–85.

De Heer, Hendrik, Eva M. Moya, and Romel Lacson. 2008. "Voices and Images of Tuberculosis Photovoice in a Binational Setting." *Cases in Public Health Communication and Marketing* 2:55–86.

Delano, Alexandra. 2018. *From Here and There: Diaspora Policies, Integration, and Social Rights Beyond Borders.* New York: Oxford University Press.

De León, Jason. 2015. *The Land of Open Graves: Living and Dying on the Migrant Trail*. Oakland, CA: University of California Press.

Delgado, Richard, and Jean Stefancic. 2017. *Critical Race Theory*. New York: New York University Press.

DeMarche, Edmund. 2017. "Trump to Order Construction of US-Mexico Border Wall; Expected to Suspend Refugee Program." Fox News. http://www.foxnews.com/politics/2017/01/25/trump-to-order-construction-us-mexican-border-wall-reportedly-to-suspend-refugee-program.html.

Dentice, Dianne. 2018. "The Escalation of Trump: Stormfront and the 2016 Election." *Theory in Action* 11 (3):37–57.

DHS. 2016. 2015 *Yearbook of Immigration Statistics*, edited by Office of Immigration Statistics. Washington, DC: Department of Homeland Security.

Díaz-Cepeda, Luis Rubén, and Ernesto Castañeda. n.d. "Motivations and Activist Typologies: Core Activists in Ciudad Juarez." *Interface: A Journal for and About Social Movements*.

Dickinson, Gerald S. 2017. "The Biggest Problem for Trump's Border Wall Isn't Money. It's Getting the Land." *Washington Post*. https://www.washingtonpost.com/posteverything/wp/2017/03/03/the-biggest-problem-with-trumps-border-wall-isnt-money-its-getting-the-land/?utm_term=.7d9f0297f0ad#comments.

Dowling, Jonathan Xavier, and Julie A. Inda. 2013. *Governing Immigration through Crime: A Reader*. Stanford, CA: Stanford University Press.

Dreby, Joanna. 2010. *Divided by Borders: Mexican Migrants and Their Children*. Berkeley, CA: University of California Press.

Dunn, Timothy J. 2009. *Blockading the Border and Human Rights: The El Paso Operation That Remade Immigration Enforcement*. Austin: University of Texas Press.

Eisenstadt, Todd A., and Cathryn Thorup. 1994. *Caring Capacity versus Carrying Capacity: Community Responses to Mexican Immigration in San Diego's North County*. San Diego, CA: Center for U.S.-Mexican Studies, University of California, San Diego.

Elias, Norbert. 2000 [1939]. *The Civilizing Process*. Oxford, UK: Blackwell.

Eyal, Gil. 2006. *The Disenchantment of the Orient: Expertise in Arab Affairs and the Israeli State*. Stanford, CA: Stanford University Press.

Fact-Finding Committee. 1930. *Mexicans in California; Report of Governor C. C. Young's Mexican Fact-Finding Committee*. California State Printing Office.

Fanon, Franz. 2007 [1963]. *The Wretched of the Earth*. New York: Grove.

Feagin, Joe R., and José A Cobas. 2015. *Latinos Facing Racism: Discrimination, Resistance, and Endurance*. New York: Routledge.

Fellmeth, Gracia, Mina Fazel, and Emma Plugge. 2017. "Migration and Perinatal Mental Health in Women from Low- and Middle-Income Countries: A Systematic Review and Meta Analysis." *BJOG: An International Journal of Obstetrics & Gynaecology* 124 (5):742–52.

Fikes, Bradley. 2018. "Gathering Aims to Relaunch Minuteman Project, Fortify Border, in Response to Central American Caravan." *Los Angeles Times*.

Fish, Stanley. 2006. "There's No Business Like Show Business." *New York Times,* October 15. https://opinionator.blogs.nytimes.com/2006/10/15/theres-no-business-like-show-business/.

Fitzgerald, David. 2009. *A Nation of Emigrants: How Mexico Manages Its Migration.* Berkeley, CA: University of California Press.

Flores, René D. 2017. "Do Anti-Immigrant Laws Shape Public Sentiment? A Study of Arizona's SB 1070 Using Twitter Data." *American Journal of Sociology* 123 (2):333–84.

Flores, René D., and Ariela Schachter. 2018. "Who Are the Illegals? The Social Construction of Illegality in the United States." *American Sociological Review* 83 (5):839–68.

Flores-González, Nilda. 2010. "Immigrants, Citizens, or Both? The Second Generation in the Immigrant Rights Marches." In *¡Marcha! Latino Chicago and the Immigrant Rights Movement!,* edited by Amalia Pallares and Nilda Flores-González, 198–214. Urbana, IL: University of Illinois Press.

Flores-González, Nilda. 2017. *Citizens but Not Americans: Race and Belonging among Latino Millennials.* New York: New York University Press.

Flores-González, Nilda, Elizabeth Aranda, and Elizabeth Vaquera. 2014. "'Doing Race': Latino Youth's Identities and the Politics of Racial Exclusion." *American Behavioral Scientist* 58 (14):1834–51.

Flores-Yeffal, Nadia Y. 2018. "Migration-Trust Networks: Unveiling the Social Networks of International Migration." In *Immigration and Categorical Inequality: Migration to the City and the Birth of Race and Ethnicity,* edited by Ernesto Castañeda. New York, NY: Routledge.

Foley, Neil. 2014. *Mexicans in the Making of America.* Cambridge, MA: The Belknap Press of Harvard University Press.

Foner, Nancy. 2000. *From Ellis Island to JFK: New York's Two Great Waves of Immigration.* New Haven, CT: Yale University Press; Russell Sage Foundation.

Foner, Nancy. 2005. *In a New Land: A Comparative View of Immigration.* New York, NY: New York University Press.

Foner, Nancy. 2013. *One out of Three: Immigrant New York in the Twenty-First Century.* New York: Columbia University Press.

Foucault, Michel. 2003. *Society Must Be Defended.* New York: Picador.

Fox, Cybelle. 2004. "The Changing Color of Welfare? How Whites' Attitudes toward Latinos Influence Support for Welfare." *American Journal of Sociology* 110 (3):580–625.

Fox, Cybelle. 2012. *Three Worlds of Relief: Race, Immigration, and the American Welfare State from the Progressive Era to the New Deal*: Princeton, NJ: Princeton University Press.

Fox News. 2017a. "Dershowitz: If Obama Issued Trump's Travel Ban, It Would've Been Upheld." Fox News, accessed April 16. http://insider.foxnews.com/2017/03/18/alan-dershowitz-if-obama-issued-trump-travel-ban-would-not-been-blocked-upheld-court.

Fox News. 2017b. "Trump Notes 'Dangerous' Uptick in Refugees Since Courts Ruled Against Travel Ban." Fox News, accessed March 19. http://www.foxnews.com/politics/2017/02/11/trump-says-77-percent-refugees-from-dangerous-coun tries-since-court-halted-his-travel-ban.html.

Frank, Thomas. 2004. *What's the Matter with Kansas? How Conservatives Won the Heart of America*. New York: Metropolitan Books.

Friedman, Thomas L. 1999. *The Lexus and the Olive Tree: Understanding Globalization*. New York: Farrar, Straus, Giroux.

Friedman, Thomas L. 2005. *The World Is Flat: A Brief History of the Twenty-First Century*. New York, NY: Farrar, Straus and Giroux.

Fuentes, Norma. 2007. "The Immigrant Experiences of Dominican and Mexican Women in the 1990s: Crossing Boundaries or Temporary Work Spaces?" In *Crossing Borders and Constructing Boundaries: Immigration Race and Ethnicity*, edited by Caroline Brettell, 94–119. New York, NY: Lexington Books.

Gálvez, Alyshia. 2006. "La Virgen Meets Eliot Spitzer: Articulating Labor Rights for Mexican Immigrants." *Social Text* 24 (88).

Gálvez, Alyshia. 2009. *Guadalupe in New York: Devotion and the Struggle for Citizenship Rights among Mexican Immigrants*. New York: New York University Press.

Gambino, Lauren. 2018. "Latino Turnout Up 174% in 2018 Midterms Elections, Democrats Say *Guardian*, November 14. https://www.theguardian.com/us-news/2018/nov/14/latino-turnout-up-174-in-2018-midterms-elections-democrats-say.

Gannon, Megan. 2016. "Race Is a Social Construct, Scientists Argue." *Live Science*. http://www.livescience.com/53613-race-is-social-construct-not-scientific.html.

Gans, Herbert J. 1979. "Symbolic Ethnicity: The Future of Ethnic Groups and Cultures in America." *Ethnic and Racial Studies* 2 (1):1–20.

Garcini, L. M, K. E. Murray, A. Zhou, E. A. Klonoff, M. G. Myers, and J. P. Elder. 2016. "Mental Health of Undocumented Immigrant Adults in the United States: A Systematic Review of Methodology and Findings." *Journal of Immigrant & Refugee Studies* 14 (1):1–25.

Garip, Filiz. 2017. *On the Move: Changing Mechanisms of Mexico-U.S. Migration, Princeton Analytical Sociology Series*. Princeton: Princeton University Press.

Gaynor, Tim. 2009. *Midnight on the Line: The Secret Life of the U.S. Mexico Border*. New York: Thomas Dunne Books.

Gieryn, Thomas F. 1983. "Boundary-Work and the Demarcation of Science from Non-Science: Strains and Interests in Professional Ideologies of Scientists." *American Sociological Review* 48 (1):781–95.

Gobat, Michael. 2013. "The Invention of Latin America: A Transnational History of Anti-Imperialism, Democracy, and Race." *American Historical Review* 118 (5):1345–75.

Golash-Boza, Tanya Maria. 2015. *Deported: Immigrant Policing, Disposable Labor, and Global Capitalism, Latina/o Sociology Series*. New York: New York University Press.

Golash-Boza, Tanya Maria. 2016a. "A Critical and Comprehensive Sociological Theory of Race and Racism." *Sociology of Race and Ethnicity* 2 (2):129–41.

Golash-Boza, Tanya Maria. 2016b. "The Parallels between Mass Incarceration and Mass Deportation: An Intersectional Analysis of State Repression." *Journal of World-Systems Research* 22 (2):484–509.

Golash-Boza, Tanya Maria. 2017. *Race and Racisms: A Critical Approach*. New York: Oxford University Press.

Golash-Boza, Tanya Maria. 2018. *Race and Racisms: A Critical Approach*. 2nd ed. New York: Oxford University Press.

Gómez, Laura E. 2007. *Manifest Destinies: The Making of the Mexican American Race*. New York: New York University Press.

Gonzales, Roberto G. 2011. "Learning to Be Illegal: Undocumented Youth and Shifting Legal Contexts in the Transition to Adulthood." *American Sociological Review* 76 (4):602–19.

Gonzales, Roberto G. 2015. *Lives in Limbo: Undocumented and Coming of Age in America*. Oakland: University of California Press.

Goodwin, Liz. 2012. "The End of the Minutemen: Tea Party Absorbs the Border-Watching Movement." Yahoo News, accessed October 27. https://www.yahoo.com/news/blogs/lookout/end-minutemen-tea-party-absorbs-border-watching-movement-173424401.html.

Gordon, Milton Myron. 1964. *Assimilation in American Life: The Role of Race, Religion, and National Origins*. New York: Oxford University Press.

Grasmuck, Sherri, and Patricia R. Pessar. 1991. *Between Two Islands: Dominican International Migration*. Berkeley, CA: University of California Press.

Greenhouse, Linda. 2014. "Justices to Hear Case of Mexican on Death Row." *New York Times*, December 11.

Guidotti-Hernández, Nicole M. 2017. "Affective Communities and Millennial Desires: Latinx, or Why My Computer Won't Recognize Latina/o." *Cultural Dynamics* 29 (3):141–59.

Gutiérrez, Ramon A. 2016. "What's in a Name? The History and Politics of Hispanic and Latino Panethnicities." In *The New Latino Studies Reader: A Twenty-First-Century Perspective,* edited by Ramon A Gutiérrez and Tomás Almaguer. Oakland, CA: University of California Press.

Guzman, Ralph. 1971. "The Function of Anglo-American Racism in the Political Development of Chicanos." *California Historical Quarterly* 50 (3):321–37.

Habermas, Jürgen. 1989. *The Structural Transformation of the Public Sphere: An Inquiry into a Category of Bourgeois Society, Studies in Contemporary German Social Thought*. Cambridge, MA: MIT Press.

Hahn, Steven. 2016. *A Nation Without Borders: The United States and Its World in an Age of Civil Wars, 1830–1910, The Penguin History of the United States*. New York: Viking.

Hartman, Andrew. 2019. *A War for the Soul of America: A History of the Culture Wars*. Chicago: University of Chicago Press.

Haslip-Viera, Gabriel. 2010. "The Evolution of the Latino Community in New York: Nineteenth Century to Late Twentieth Century." In *Hispanic New York: A Sourcebook*, edited by Claudio Iván Remeseira. New York: Columbia University Press.

Hatewatch. 2018. "Anti-Immigrant Groups Clash with Sanctuary Policies in Six States." Southern Poverty Law Center. https://www.splcenter.org/hate watch/2018/05/21/anti-immigrant-groups-clash-sanctuary-policies-six-states.

Hattam, Victoria. 2007. *In the Shadow of Race: Jews, Latinos, and Immigrant Politics in the United States*. Chicago, IL: University of Chicago Press.

Hauser, Christine. 2016. "Minuteman Co-Founder Sentenced to 19½ Years for Molesting 5-Year-Old." *New York Times*, July 12. https://www.nytimes.com/2016/07/13/us/minuteman-christopher-simcox-sentenced-for-child-molestation.html.

Hawley, George. 2017. *Making Sense of the Alt-Right.* New York: Columbia University Press.

Hay, Andrew. 2019. "'Disgusting' razor wire must go, say U.S. border city residents." Reuters. https://news.yahoo.com/disgusting-razor-wire-must-u-border-city-resi dents-020205084.html.

Hellman, Judith Adler. 2008. *The World of Mexican Migrants: The Rock and the Hard Place*. New York: New Press.

Hernandez, Kelly Lytle. 2010. *Migra!: A History of the U.S. Border Patrol*. Berkeley, CA: University of California Press.

Hernandez, Salvador. 2017. "A Mexican Congressman Climbed a US Border Fencer to Show Trump How 'Totally Absurd' a Wall Would Be." BuzzFeed News, accessed 2017. https://www.buzzfeed.com/salvadorhernandez/a-mexican-official-sat-on-top-of-a-wall?utm_term=.vc7w1MMWKe#.ui8kKbbjMw.

Heyman, Josiah McC. 2013a. "Constructing a Virtual Wall: Race and Citizenship in the U.S.-Mexico Border Policing." In *Governing Immigration through Crime: A Reader*, edited by Jonathan Xavier Dowling and Julie A. Inda. Stanford, CA: Stanford University Press.

Heyman, Josiah McC. 2013b. "A Voice of the US Southwestern Border: The 2012 'We the Border: Envisioning a Narrative for Our Future' Conference." *Journal on Migration and Human Security* 1 (2):60–75.

Heyman, Josiah McC. 2018. "Immigration or Citizenship? Two Sides of One Social History." In *Immigration and Categorical Inequality: Migration to the City and the Birth of Race and Ethnicity*, edited by Ernesto Castañeda. New York, NY: Routledge.

Hing, Julianne. 2011. "Minuteman Vigilante Shawna Forde Convicted for Brisenia Flores' Murder: Forde Reportedly Planned Elaborate Heists in order to Fund her Anti-immigration Activism." *Colorlines*. https://www.colorlines.com/articles/minuteman-vigilante-shawna-forde-convicted-brisenia-flores-murder.

Hinman, George W. 1926. Report of the Commission on International and Interracial Factors in the Problem of Mexicans in the United States.

Hirvonen, Ari. 2017. "Fear and Anxiety: The Nationalist and Racist Politics of Fantasy." *Law and Critique* 28 (3):249–65.

Hochschild, Arlie R. 2016. *Strangers in Their Own Land: Anger and Mourning on the American Right*. New York: New Press.

Hollifield, James. 1992. "Migration and International Relations: Cooperation and Control in the European Community." *International Migration Review* 26 (2):568–95.

Hollifield, James. 2000. "The Politics of International Migration: How Can We 'Bring the State Back In'?" In *Migration Theory: Talking across Disciplines*, edited by James Hollifield and Caroline Brettell, viii. New York, NY: Routledge.

Holmes, Seth. 2013. *Fresh Fruit, Broken Bodies: Migrant Farmworkers in the United States*. Berkeley, CA: University of California Press.

Holthouse, David. 2005. "Minutemen, Other Anti-immigrant Militia Groups Stake Out Arizona Border." *Intelligence Report*, June 27.

Huntington, Samuel P. 2004a. "The Hispanic Challenge." *Foreign Policy*, 30–45.

Huntington, Samuel P. 2004b. *Who Are We? The Challenges to America's Identity*. New York, NY: Simon & Schuster.

Ibarra Mateos, Marcela, and Liliana Rivera Sánchez. 2011. *Entre Contextos Locales y Ciudades Globales: La Configuración de Circuitos Migratorios Puebla-Nueva York. Lupus inquisitor*. Puebla, México: Universidad Iberoamericana Puebla.

Ignatiev, Noel. 1996. *How the Irish Became White*. New York: Routledge.

Jerome-D'Emilia, Bonnie, and Patricia D. Suplee. 2012. "The ACA and the Undocumented." *AJN: The American Journal of Nursing* 112 (4):21–27.

Jiménez, Tomás R. 2008. "Mexican-Immigrant Replenishment and the Continuing Significance of Ethnicity and Race." *American Journal of Sociology* 113 (6): 1527–1567.

Jiménez, Tomás R. 2010. *Replenished Ethnicity: Mexican Americans, Immigration, and Identity*. Berkeley, CA: University of California Press.

Jiménez, Tomás. 2017. *The Other Side of Assimilation: Immigration and the Changing American Experience*. Berkeley, CA: University of California Press.

Johnson, Gene, and Sudhin Thanawala. 2017. "Trump Administration's Rhetoric about Islam Is Key in Travel Ban Rulings." *Chicago Tribune*, accessed April 16. http://www.chicagotribune.com/news/nationworld/politics/ct-trump-travel-ban-rulings-muslim-ban-20170318-story.html.

Jones-Correa, Michael. 1998. *Between Two Nations: The Political Predicament of Latinos in New York City*. Ithaca, NY: Cornell University Press.

Joppke, Christian. 1998. "Why Liberal States Accept Unwanted Immigration." *World Politics* 50 (2):266–93.

Joseph, Tiffany D. 2011. "'My Life Was Filled with Constant Anxiety': Anti-immigrant Discrimination, Undocumented Status, and Their Mental Health Implications for Brazilian Immigrants." *Race and Social Problems* 3 (3):170.

Karjanen, David. 2008. "Gender, Race, and Nationality in the Making of Mexican Migrant Labor in the United States." *Latin American Perspectives* 35 (1):51–63.

Kasinitz, Philip, John H. Mollenkopf, and Mary C. Waters, eds. 2004. *Becoming New Yorkers: Ethnographies of the New Second Generation*. New York: Russell Sage.

Kasinitz, Philip, John H. Mollenkopf, Mary C. Waters, and Jennifer Holdaway. 2008. *Inheriting the City: The Children of Immigrants Come of Age*. New York, NY & Cambridge, MA: Russell Sage Foundation; Harvard University Press.

Katz, Michael B. 1996. *In the Shadow of the Poorhouse: A Social History of Welfare in America*. 10th anniversary ed. New York: Basic Books.

Kelly, David. 2005. "Border Watchers Capture Their Prey—the Media." *Los Angeles Times*. http://articles.latimes.com/print/2005/apr/05/nation/na-minuteman5.

Kendi, Ibram X. 2016. *Stamped from the Beginning: The Definitive History of Racist Ideas in America*. New York: Nation Books.

Keohane, Robert O., and Joseph S. Nye. 1987. "Review: Power and Interdependence Revisited." *International Organization* 41 (4):725–53.

Kraut, Alan M. 1995. *Silent Travelers: Germs, Genes, and the Immigrant Menace*. Baltimore, MD: Johns Hopkins University Press.

Krieger, Zvika. 2008. "Time's Up." *New Republic*, November 19.

Lacayo, Celia. 2016. "Latinos Need to Stay in Their Place: Differential Segregation in a Multi-Ethnic Suburb." *Societies* 6 (3):25.

Lacayo, Celia. 2017. "Perpetual Inferiority: Whites' Racial Ideology toward Latinos." *Sociology of Race and Ethnicity* 3 (4):566–79.

Lamont, Michèle, and Virág Molnár. 2002. "The Study of Boundaries in the Social Sciences." *Annual Review of Sociology* 28:167–95.

LeDuff, Charlie. 2006. "Poised against Incursions, a Man on the Border, Armed and Philosophical." *New York Times*, August 14, American Album.

Lee, Tiane L. and Susan T. Fiske. 2006. "Not an Outgroup, but Not Yet an Ingroup: Immigrants in the Stereotype Content Model." *International Journal of Intercultural Relations* 30:751–68.

Lepore, Jill. 2018. "Is Education a Fundamental Right?" *New Yorker*, September 10.

Lévi-Strauss, Claude. 2007 [1952]. *Race et Histoire*. Paris: Folioplus.

Levitt, Peggy. 2001. *The Transnational Villagers*. Berkeley, CA: University of California Press.

Limón, José E. 1981. "The Folk Performance of 'Chicano' and the Cultural Limits of Political Ideology." In *And Other Neighborly Names: Social Process and Cultural Image in Texas Folklore*, edited by Rirchard Bauman and R. D. Abrahams, 197–225. Austin, TX: University of Texas Press.

Lloyd, Annemaree. 2017. "Researching Fractured (Information) Landscapes: Implications for Library and Information Science Researchers Undertaking Research with Refugees and Forced Migration Studies." *Journal of Documentation* 73 (1):35–47.

Lobo, Arun Peter, and Joseph J. Salvo. 2013. *The Newest New Yorkers: Characteristics of the City's Foreign-Born Population*. New York: New York City Department of City Planning.

Lomnitz, Claudio. 2001. *Deep Mexico, Silent Mexico: An Anthropology of Nationalism*. Minneapolis, MN: University of Minnesota.

Loveman, Mara, and Jeronimo O. Muniz. 2007. "How Puerto Rico Became White: Boundary Dynamics and Intercensus Racial Reclassification." *American Sociological Review* 72 (6):915–39.

Loza, Oralia, Ernesto Castañeda, and Brian Diedrich. 2016. "Substance Use by Immigrant Generation in a U.S.-Mexico Border City." *Journal of Immigrant and Minority Health*, 1–8.

Lusk, Mark W., and Chavez-Baray, Silvia. (2017). "Mental Health and the Role of Culture and Resilience in Refugees Fleeing Violence." *Environment and Social Psychology* 2(1), 1–13.

Lusk, Mark W., and Griselda Villalobos. 2012. "The Testimonio of Eva: A Mexican Refugee in El Paso." *Journal of Borderlands Studies* 27 (1):17–25.

Mann, Katy. 2012. "Reporters as Refugees: Applying United States Asylum Laws to Persecuted Journalists in Mexico." *Hastings International and Comparative Law Review* 35 (1):149–72.

Marcelli, Enrico A., and B. Lindsay Lowell. 2005. "Transnational Twist: Pecuniary Remittances and the Socioeconomic Integration of Authorized and Unauthorized Mexican Immigrants in Los Angeles County." *International Migration Review* 39 (1):69–102.

Martinez, Isabel. 2016. "Supporting Two Households: Unaccompanied Mexican Minors and Their Absences from U.S. Schools." *Journal of Latinos and Education* 15 (3):229–43.

Martínez Toyes, L. Wilebaldo, and Jaime A. Arellano Quiroga. 2012. "Movilidad Poblacional: Efecto de la Violencia e inseguridad en Ciudad Juárez." In *Seguridad y Violencia en Ciudad Juárez, México*, edited by Myrna Limas Hernández. Ciudad Juárez, Chihuahua: Universidad Autónoma de Ciudad Juárez.

Marwell, Nicole P. 2007. *Bargaining for Brooklyn: Community Organizations in the Entrepreneurial City*. Chicago, IL: University of Chicago Press.

Massey, Douglas S. 1987. "The Ethnosurvey in Theory and Practice." *International Migration Review* 21 (4):1498–522.

Massey, Douglas S. 1990. "Social Structure, Household Strategies, and the Cumulative Causation of Migration." *Population Index* 56 (1):3–26.

Massey, Douglas S. 2007. *Categorically Unequal: The American Stratification System*. New York, NY: Russell Sage Foundation.

Massey, Douglas S. 2008. *New Faces in New Places: The Changing Geography of American Immigration*. New York, NY: Russell Sage Foundation.

Massey, Douglas S. 2018. "Migration and Categorical Inequality." In *Immigration and Categorical Inequality: Migration to the City and the Birth of Race and Ethnicity*, edited by Ernesto Castañeda. New York, NY: Routledge.

Massey, Douglas S., Rafael Alarcon, Jorge Durand, and Humberto González. 1987. *Return to Aztlan: The Social Process of International Migration from Western Mexico, Studies in Demography*. Berkeley, CA: University of California Press.

Massey, Douglas S., J. Arango, G. Hugo, A. Kouaouci, A. Pellegrino, and J. E. Taylor, 1993. "Theories of International Migration: A Review and Appraisal." *Population and Development Review* 19 (3):431–66.

Massey, Douglas S., Jorge Durand, and Nolan J. Malone. 2002. *Beyond Smoke and Mirrors: Mexican Immigration in an Era of Economic Integration*. New York: Russell Sage Foundation.

Massey, Douglas S., Jacob S. Rugh, and Karen A. Pren. 2010. "The Geography of Undocumented Mexican Migration." *Mexican Studies* 26 (1):129–52.

Massey, Douglas S., and Rene Zenteno. 2000. "A Validation of the Ethnosurvey: The Case of Mexico-U.S. Migration." *International Migration Review* 34 (3):766–93.

Mayda, Anna Maria. 2004. "Who Is Against Immigration? A Cross-Country Investigation of Individual Attitudes toward Immigrants," in *IZA Discussion Papers*. Schaumburg, Germany: Institute for the Study of Labor.

M. de Onís, Catalina. 2017. "What's in an x? An Exchange about the Politics of Latinx." *Chiricù Journal: Latina/o Literature, Art, and Culture* 1 (2):78–91.

Melville, Herman. 1849. *Redburn: His First Voyage, Being the Sailor-Boy, Confessions and Reminiscences of the Son-of-a-Gentleman, In the Merchant Service*. New York: Harper & Brothers.

Menjívar, Cecilia. 2017. *Temporary Protected Status in the United States: The Experiences of Honduran and Salvadoran Immigrants*. Lawrance, KS: Center for Migration Research, The University of Kansas.

Milfeld, Becca. 2017. "An 'Abrazo' on the U.S.-Mexico Border Celebrates Unity, but Trump Has Laredo Worried." *Washington Post*, accessed April 16. https://www.washingtonpost.com/national/an-abrazo-on-the-us-mexican-border-celebrates-unity-but-trump-has-laredo-worried/2017/02/19/0bb247e2-f6a2-11e6-9845-576c69081518_story.html?utm_term=.c1ef560a0e70#comments.

Miller-Idriss, Cynthia. 2017. *The Extreme Gone Mainstream: Commercialization and Far Right Youth Culture in Germany, Princeton Studies in Cultural Sociology*. Princeton: Princeton University Press.

Mills, Charles W. 2008. "Racial Liberalism." *PMLA* 123 (5):1380–97.

Mische, Ann. 2011. "Relational Sociology, Culture, and Agency." In *The Sage Handbook of Social Network Analysis*, edited by John Scott and Peter Carrington, 80–97. London: Sage Publications.

Mora, G. Cristina. 2014a. "Cross-Field Effects and Ethnic Classification: The Institutionalization of Hispanic Panethnicity, 1965 to 1990." *American Sociological Review* 79 (2):183–210.

Mora, G. Cristina. 2014b. *Making Hispanics: How Activists, Bureaucrats, and Media Constructed a New American*. Chicago, IL: Chicago University Press.

Morales, Cristina, Oscar Morales, Angelica C. Menchaca, and Adam Sebastian. 2013. "The Mexican Drug War and the Consequent Population Exodus: Transnational Movement at the U.S.-Mexican Border." *Societies* 1 (3):80–103.

Moran, Tyler, and Nick Gourevitch. 2018. "Republicans Embraced Trump's Immigration Scare Tactics and Paid a High Political Price." *USA Today*, December 4. https://www.usatoday.com/story/opinion/2018/12/04/trump-immigration-scare-tactics-backfired-republicans-column/2142965002/.

Morning, Ann. 2011. *The Nature of Race: How Scientists Think and Teach about Human Difference*. Berkeley, CA: University of California Press.

Moss, Philip I., and Chris Tilly. 2001. *Stories Employers Tell: Race, Skill, and Hiring in America, A Volume in the Multi-City Study of Urban Inequality*. New York, NY: Russell Sage Foundation.

Mouw, Ted, Sergio Chavez, Heather Edelblute, and Verdery Ashton. 2014. "Binational Social Networks and Assimilation: A Test of the Importance of Transnationalism." *Social Problems* 61 (3):329–59.

Moya, Eva M., Silvia María Chávez-Baray, Oscar A. Esparza, Leticia Calderón Chelius, Ernesto Castañeda, Griselda Villalobos, Itzel Eguiluz, Edna Aileen Martínez, Karen Herrera, Tania Llamas, Marcela Arteaga, Laura Díaz, Maribel Najera, Nancy Landa, and Virginia Escobedo. 2016. "Ulysses Syndrome in Economical and Political Migrants in Mexico and the United States." *EHQUIDAD Revista Internacional de Políticas de Bienestar y Trabajo Social* (5):11–50.

Nail, Thomas. 2018. "The Political Centrality of the Migrant." In *Critical Perspectives on Migration in the Twenty-First Century*, edited by Marianna Karakoulaki, Laura Southgate, and Jakob Steiner, 15–27. Bristol, England: E-International Relations.

Neuhauser, Alan. 2017. "What's Next for Trump's Travel Ban?" AOL, accessed April 16. https://www.aol.com/article/news/2017/03/18/whats-next-trumps-travel-ban-supreme-court/21902470/.

Nevins, Joseph. 2002. *Operation Gatekeeper: The Rise of the 'Illegal Alien' and the Making of the U.S.-Mexico Boundary*. New York, NY: Routledge.

Nevins, Joseph. 2010. *Operation Gatekeeper and Beyond: the War on Illegals and the Remaking of the U.S.-Mexico Boundary*. 2nd ed. New York: Routledge.

New York City Department of City Planning. 2012. *Profile of Manhattan Community District 11*. New York: New York City Department of City Planning.

New York Times. 2014. "A New World Order." December 17.

Ngai, Mae M. 2004. *Impossible Subjects: Illegal Aliens and the Making of Modern America, Politics and Society in Twentieth-Century America*. Princeton, NJ: Princeton University Press.

Nietzsche, Friedrich Wilhelm. 1974 [1882]. *The Gay Science; with a Prelude in Rhymes and an Appendix of Songs*. Translated by Walter Arnold Kaufmann. New York: Vintage Books.

Noiriel, Gérard. 2000. *Etat, Nation et Immigration: Vers une Histoire du Pouvoir, L'Univers Historique*. Paris: Belin.

Núñez, Guillermina Gina, and Josiah McC. Heyman. 2007. "Entrapment Processes and Immigrant Communities in a Time of Heightened Border Vigilance." *Human Organization* 66 (4):354–65.

Nuño, Luis F. 2013. "Mexicans in New York City." *Societies without Borders* 8 (1):80–101.

Olivares, Emir Alonso. 2012. "La Guerra Antinarco Agravo El Problema Del Desplazamiento En Diversa Comunidades." *La Jornada*, September 18. http://www.jornada.unam.mx/2012/09/18/politica/010n1pol.

Omi, Michael, and Howard Winant. 2015. *Racial Formation in the United States*. New York: Routledge.

Orsi, Robert Anthony. 2002. *The Madonna of 115th Street: Faith and Community in Italian Harlem, 1880–1950*. 2nd ed. New Haven, CT: Yale University Press.

Osorio, Sandra L. 2018. "Border Stories: Using Critical Race and Latino Critical Theories to Understand the Experiences of Latino/a Children." *Race Ethnicity and Education* 21 (1):92–104.

Parrado, Emilio A., and Chenoa A. Flippen. 2014. "Migration, Social Organization, and the Sexual Partners of Mexican Men." *Social Problems* 61 (3):380–401.

Passel, Jeffrey S., and Paul Taylor. 2009. "Who is Hispanic?" *Pew Hispanic Center.* http://www.pewhispanic.org/2009/05/28/whos-hispanic/.

Payton, Brenda. 1997. "Blacks, Browns and Yellows at Odds." In *Multi-America: Essays on Cultural Wars and Cultural Peace*, edited by Ishmael Reed. New York: Penguin.

Perlmann, Joel. 2005. *Italians Then, Mexicans Now: Immigrant Origins and Second-generation Progress, 1890 to 2000*. New York: Russell Sage Foundation.

Phelan, John Leddy. 1968. "Pan-Latinism, French Intervention in México (1861–1867) and the Genesis of the Idea of Latin America." In *Conciencia y Autenticidad Históricas: Escritos en Homenaje a Edmundo O' Gorman*, edited by Juan Antonio Ortega y Medina. Mexico City: Instituto de Investigaciones Históricas UNAM.

Portes, Alejandro, and Robert D Manning. 1986. *The Immigrant Enclave: Theory and Empirical Examples*. https://pdfs.semanticscholar.org/433f/567bd158d95f0c26114 89d8294ab64b9a376.pdf.

Portes, Alejandro, and Rubén G. Rumbaut. 2014. *Immigrant America: A Portrait*. 4th ed., revised, updated, and expanded. Berkeley, CA: University of California Press.

Portes, Alejandro, and Min Zhou. 2003. "The New Second Generation: Segmented Assimilation and Its Variants." *Annals of the American Academy of Political and Social Sciences* 530:74–96.

Rathod, Jayesh, Eri Hershberg, and Dennis Stinchcomb. 2017. "Country Conditions in Central America and Asylum Decision-Making: Report from a January 2017 Workshop." In *CLALS Working Paper Series*. Washington, DC: Center of Latin American and Latino Studies.

Rios, Victor M. 2011. *Punished: Policing the Lives of Black and Latino Boys*. New York, NY: New York University Press.

Rippberger, Susan J., and Kathleen Staudt. 2002. *Pledging Allegiance: Learning Nationalism at the El Paso-Juárez Border*. New York: Routledge.

Rivera-Sánchez, Liliana. 2004. "Expressions of Identity and Belonging: Mexican Immigrants in New York." In *Indigenous Mexican Migrants in the United States*, edited by Jonathan Fox and Gaspar Rivera-Salgado. La Jolla, CA: Center for U.S.-Mexican Studies, UCSD/Center for Comparative Immigration Studies, UCSD.

Rizzo, Carolina. 2015. "Catch and Detain: The Detention Bed Quota and the United States' Overreliance on Detention as a Tool for the Enforcement of Immigration Laws." *Harvard Journal of Hispanic Policy* 27:39–50.

Robin, Corey. 2017. *The Reactionary Mind: Conservatism from Edmund Burke to Donald Trump*. New York: Oxford University Press.

Rodriguez, Gregory. 2007. *Mongrels, Bastards, Orphans, and Vagabonds: Mexican Immigration and the Future of Race in America*. New York: Pantheon Books.

Romero, Mary. 2011. "Are Your Papers in Order: Racial Profiling, Vigilantes, and America's Toughest Sheriff." *Harv. Latino L. Rev.* 14:337.

Rosenberg, Clifford D. 2006. *Policing Paris: The Origins of Modern Immigration Control between the Wars.* Ithaca, NY: Cornell University Press.

Roy, Beth. 1994. *Some Trouble with Cows: Making Sense of Social Conflict.* Berkeley: University of California Press.

Roy, Jody M. 2002. *Love to Hate: America's Obsession with Hatred and Violence* New York: Columbia University Press.

Saslow, Eli. 2018. *Rising Out of Hatred: The Awakening of a Former White Nationalist.* New York: Penguin.

Sassen, Saskia. 1996. *Losing Control? Sovereignty in an Age of Globalization.* New York, NY: Columbia University Press.

Sassen, Saskia. 2001. *The Global City: New York, London, Tokyo.* 2nd ed. Princeton, NJ: Princeton University Press.

Sassen, Saskia. 2006. *Territory, Authority, Rights: From Medieval to Global Assemblages.* Princeton, NJ: Princeton University Press.

Sayad, Abdelmalek. 2004. *The Suffering of the Immigrant.* Cambridge, UK: Polity Press.

Schmitt, Carl. 1988. *The Crisis of Parliamentary Democracy.* Translated by Ellen Kennedy. Cambridge, MA: MIT Press.

Schneider, Cathy Lisa. 2014. *Police Power and Race Riots: Urban Unrest in Paris and New York.* Philadelphia, PA: University of Pennsylvania Press.

Schrag, Peter. 2011. *Not Fit for Our Society: Immigration and Nativism in America.* Berkeley: University of California Press.

Schult, Anne. 2017. *A Common Sense of National Decline: Populist Pundits and the Immigration Debate in Germany and France.* New York: Association for the Study of Nationalities, Columbia University.

Scott, James C. 1998. *Seeing Like a State: How Certain Schemes to Improve the Human Condition Have Failed, Yale Agrarian Studies.* New Haven, CT: Yale University Press.

Selee, Andrew D. 2018. *Vanishing Frontiers: The Forces Driving Mexico and the United States Together.* New York: Public Affairs.

Semple, Kirk. 2010. "Immigrant in Run for Mayor, Back Home in Mexico." *New York Times*, June 1. http://www.nytimes.com/2010/06/02/nyregion/02mexican.html?pagewanted=all.

Sen, Rinku, and Fekkak Mamdouh. 2008. *The Accidental American: Immigration and Citizenship in the Age of Globalization.* San Francisco, CA: Berrett-Koehler Publishers.

Shapira, Harel. 2013a. "The Border: Infrastructure of the Global." *Public Culture* 25 (2):249–60.

Shapira, Harel. 2013b. *Waiting for José: The Minutemen's Pursuit of America.* Princeton, NJ: Princeton University Press.

Simmel, Georg. 1964. *Conflict & the Web of Group Affiliations.* New York: Free Press.

Simmel, Georg. 1971. "The Metropolis and Mental Life." In *Georg Simmel on Individuality and Social Forms*, edited by Donald N. Levine. Chicago, IL: The University of Chicago Press.

Smith, Curtis, and Ernesto Castañeda. 2019. "Improving Homeless Point-in-Time Counts: Uncovering the Marginally Housed." *Social Currents* 6 (2), 91–104.

Smith, Robert C. 2006. *Mexican New York: Transnational Lives of New Immigrants*. Berkeley, CA: University of California Press.

Smith, Robert C. 2013. "Mexicans: Civic Engagement, Education, and Progress Achieved and Inhibited." In *One out of Three: Immigrant New York in the Twenty-First Century*, edited by Nancy Foner. New York: Columbia University Press.

Smith, Robert C. 2014. "Black Mexicans, Conjunctural Ethnicity, and Operating Identities: Long-Term Ethnographic Analysis." *American Sociological Review* 79 (3):517–48.

Smith, Ryan. 2009. "Anti-Illegal Immigration 'Extremists' Murder Girl and Father, Say Police." In *CBS News*. https://www.cbsnews.com/news/anti-illegal-immigration-extremists-murder-girl-and-father-say-police/.

Snel, Erik, Margrietha 'T. Hart, and Marianne Van Bochove. 2016. "Reactive Transnationalism: Homeland Involvement in the Face of Discrimination." *Global Networks* 16 (4): 511–30.

Staudt, Kathleen. 1998. *Free Trade? Informal Economies at the U.S.-Mexico Border*. Philadelphia, PA: Temple University Press.

Staudt, Kathleen A., and Zulma Mendez. 2015. *Courage, Resistance and Women in Ciudad Juárez: Challenges to Militarization in Ciudad Juárez*. Austin, TX: The University of Texas Press.

Staudt, Kathleen, and David Spener. 1998. *The US-Mexico Border: Transcending Divisions, Contesting Identities*. Boulder, CO: Lynne Rienner.

Sterling, Terry Greene. 2011. "Minuteman Vigilante's Arizona Murder Trial." *Daily Beast*. https://www.thedailybeast.com/minuteman-vigilantes-arizona-murder-trial-brisenia-flores-mother-testifies.

Stiglitz, Joseph E. 2003. *The Roaring Nineties: A New History of the World's Most Prosperous Decade*. New York: W. W. Norton & Co.

Stillman, Sarah. 2018. "When Deportation Is a Death Sentence: Hundreds of Thousands of Immigrants in the U.S. May Face Violence and Murder in Their Home Countries. What Happens When They Are Forced to Return?" *New Yorker*, January 15.

St. John, Rachel. 2011. *Line in the Sand: A History of the Western U.S.-Mexico Border*. Princeton, NJ: Princeton University Press

Stoskopf, Alan. 2002. "Echoes of a Forgotten Past: Eugenics, Testing, and Education Reform." *The Educational Forum* 66 (2):126–33.

Strayer, Joseph R. 2016. *On the Medieval Origins of the Modern State*. Princeton: Princeton University Press.

Suro, Roberto. 2005. *Survey of Mexican Migrants: Part One: Attitudes about Immigration and Major Demographic Characteristics*. Washington, DC: Pew Hispanic Center.

Telles, Edward Eric. 2004. *Race in Another America: The Significance of Skin Color in Brazil*. Princeton, NJ: Princeton University Press.

Thomas, Steven M. 2008. "The Minutemen Reconsidered." *Orange Coast Magazine.* June: 22.

Thompson, Gabriel. 2007. *There's No José Here: Following the Hidden Lives of Mexican Immigrants.* New York: Nation Books.

Thompson, Gabriel. 2010. *Working in the Shadows: A Year of Doing the Jobs (Most) Americans Won't Do.* Boulder, CO: Nation Books.

Thorne, Barrie. 1993. *Gender Play: Girls and Boys in School.* New Brunswick, NJ: Rutgers University Press.

Tienda, Marta, and Vilma Ortiz. 1986. "Hispanicity and the 1980 Census." 67 (1):3–20.

Tilly, Charles. 1976. "Cities and Migration." In *Center for Research on Social Organization Working Paper/I147.* Ann Arbor, MI: University of Michigan.

Tilly, Charles. 1984. *Big Structures, Large Processes, Huge Comparisons, Russell Sage Foundation 75th Anniversary Series.* New York: Russell Sage Foundation. http://deepblue.lib.umich.edu/bitstream/2027.42/51064/1/295.pdf.

Tilly, Charles. 1989. *Cities and Immigration in North America.* New York, NY: Center for Studies of Social Change, New School for Social Research.

Tilly, Charles. 1992. *Coercion, Capital, and European States, AD 990–1992.* Cambridge, MA: Blackwell.

Tilly, Charles. 1996a. *Citizenship, Identity and Social History. International Review of Social History. Supplement 3.* Cambridge: Cambridge University Press.

Tilly, Charles. 1996b. *Introduction to the French Melting Pot: Immigration, Citizenship, and National Identity by Gérard Noiriel.* Minneapolis: University of Minnesota Press.

Tilly, Charles. 1998a. "Contentious Conversation." *Social Research* 65 (3):491–510.

Tilly, Charles. 1998b. *Durable Inequality.* Berkeley, CA: University of California Press.

Tilly, Charles. 1998c. "Stories of Social Construction." *Social and Political Change Series,* New York: Lazarsfeld Center at Columbia University.

Tilly, Charles. 2002. *Stories, Identities, and Political Change.* Lanham, Md.: Rowman & Littlefield.

Tilly, Charles. 2005. *Identities, Boundaries, and Social Ties.* Boulder, CO: Paradigm Publishers.

Tilly, Charles. 2007. *Democracy.* Cambridge: Cambridge University Press.

Tilly, Charles. 2008. "Memorials to Credit and Blame." *The American Interest,* May–June. http://www.ssrc.org/essays/tilly/creditblame.

Tilly, Charles, and Harold C. Brown. 1967. "On Uprooting, Kinship, and the Auspices of Migration." *International Journal of Comparative Sociology* 8 (2).

Tilly, Charles, Ernesto Castañeda, and Cathy Lisa Schneider. 2017. *Collective Violence, Contentious Politics, and Social Change: A Charles Tilly Reader.* New York, NY: Routledge.

Tilly, Charles, Ernesto Castañeda, and Lesley J. Wood. 2019. *Social Movements, 1768–2018.* New York: Routledge.

Trujillo-Pagán, Nicole. 2018. "Crossed Out by LatinX: Gender Neutrality and Genderblind Sexism." *Latino Studies* 16 (3):396–406.

U.S. Census Bureau. 2010. DP-1-Geography—New York City, New York: Profile of General Population and Housing Characteristics: 2010. In *US Census 2010*. Washington, DC: U.S. Census Bureau.

U.S. Census Bureau. 2018a. Table 2. Population by Sex, Age, and Hispanic Origin Type: 2016. In *Current Population Survey, Annual Social and Economic Supplement, 2016*. Washington, DC: U.S. Census Bureau.

U.S. Census Bureau. 2018b. Table 7. Nativity and Citizenship Status by Sex, Hispanic Origin, and Race: 2016. In *Current Population Survey, Annual Social and Economic Supplement, 2016*. Washington, DC: U.S. Census Bureau.

Valenzuela-García, Hugo, José Molina, Miranda Lubbers, Alejandro García-Macías, Judith Pampalona, and Juergen Lerner. 2014. "On Heterogeneous and Homogeneous Networks in a Multilayered Reality: Clashing Interests in the Ethnic Enclave of Lloret de Mar." *Societies* 4 (1):85–104.

Van Hook, Jennifer, and Frank D. Bean. 2009. "Explaining Mexican Immigrant Welfare Behaviors: The Importance of Employment-Related Cultural Repertoires." *American Sociological Review* 74 (3):423–44.

Vargas, Edward D., Nadia C. Winston, John A. Garcia, and Gabriel R. Sanchez. 2016. "Latina/o or Mexicana/o? The Relationship between Socially Assigned Race and Experiences with Discrimination." *Sociology of Race and Ethnicity* 2 (4):498–515.

Vasquez, Richard. 2005 [1970]. *Chicano: A Novel*. New York: Rayo.

Vaughan, Mary Kay. 1997. *Cultural Politics in Revolution: Teachers Peasants, and Schools in Mexico 1930–1940*. Tucson, AZ: University of Arizona Press.

Velázquez Vargas, María del Socorro, and Georgina Martínez Canizales. 2012. "La Inseguridad en Ciudad Juárez desde la Percepción de los Ciudadanos." In *Seguridad y Violencia en Ciudad Juárez, México*, edited by Myrna Limas Hernández. Ciudad Juárez, Chihuahua: Universidad Autónoma de Ciudad Juárez.

Verea, Mónica 2008. "Contradicciones entre las Expresiones Anti-inmigrantes y el Insaciable Apetito por Contratar Migrantes." In *La Migración y los Latinos en Estados Unidos: Visiones y Conexiones*, edited by Elaine Levine, 389–409. Ciudad de Mexico: Universidad Nacional Autónoma de México, Centro de Investigaciones sobre América del Norte.

Vidal-Ortiz, Salvador, and Juliana Martínez. 2018. "Latinx Thoughts: Latinidad with an X." *Latino Studies* 16 (3):384–95.

Vila, Pablo. 1998. "The Competing Meanings of the Label 'Chicano' in El Paso." In *The US-Mexico Border: Transcending Divisions, Contesting Identities*, edited by Kathleen Staudt and David Spener, 185–211. Boulder, CO: Lynne Rienner.

Vila, Pablo. 2000. *Crossing Borders, Reinforcing Borders: Social Categories, Metaphors, and Narrative Identities on the U.S.-Mexico Frontier*. Inter-America Series. Austin, TX: University of Texas Press.

Wang, Caroline, and Mary Ann Burris. 1997. "Photovoice: Concept, Methodology, and Use for Participatory Needs Assessment." *Health Education & Behavior* 24 (3):369–87.

Wasserman, David, and Ally Flinn. 2018. "2018 House Popular Vote Tracker." Cook Political Report. https://docs.google.com/spreadsheets/d/1WxDaxD5az6kdOjJncm Gph37z0BPNhV1fNAH_g7IkpC0/htmlview?sle=true#gid=0.

Waters, Mary C. 1996. "Optional Ethnicities: For Whites Only?" In *Origins and Destinies: Immigration, Race and Ethnicity in America*, edited by Pedraza Sylvia and Rumbaut Ruben, 444–54. Belmont, CA: Wadsworth Press.

Weil, Patrick. 2005. *La France et Ses Étrangers: l'Aventure d'une Politique de l'Immigration de 1938 à Nos Jours*. Nouv. éd. refondue. Paris: Gallimard.

Weil, Patrick. 2008. *How to be French: Nationality in the Making Since 1789*. Durham, NC: Duke University Press.

White, Harrison C. 2009 [1965]. "Notes on the Constituents of Social Structure." *Sociologica* 1.

Whitman, Walt. 1855. *Leaves of Grass*. Brooklyn, NY: Walt Whitman.

Wilson, Kenneth L., and Alejandro Portes. 1980. "Immigrant Enclaves: An Analysis of the Labor Market Experiences of Cubans in Miami." *American Journal of Sociology* 86:295–319.

Wimmer, Andreas. 2008. "The Making and Unmaking of Ethnic Boundaries." *American Journal of Sociology* 113 (4): 970–1022.

Wimmer, Andreas, and Nina Glick Schiller. 2002. "Methodological Nationalism and Beyond: Nation State Building, Migration and the Social Sciences." *Global Networks: A Journal of Transnational Affairs* 2 (4):301–34.

Zelizer, Viviana A., and Charles Tilly. 2006. "Relations and Categories." In *The Psychology of Learning and Motivation*, edited by Arthur Markman and Brian Ross, 1–31. San Diego, CA: Elsevier.

Zhou, Min. 1992. *Chinatown: The Socioeconomic Potential of an Urban Enclave*. Philadelphia, PA: Temple University Press.

Zolberg, Aristide R. 2006. *A Nation by Design: Immigration Policy in the Fashioning of America*. New York & Cambridge, MA: Russell Sage Foundation & Harvard University Press.

Index

acculturation, 147, 165, 166, 167, 178
Agamben, Giorgio, 40; on sovereignty,
    42, 43
Aguilera, Michael Bernabé, 166
Alt-Right, 89
amnesty: governmentality and, 39;
    opposition to, 42
Anchondo, Teresa, 132–34, *133*
Anderson, Benedict, 35
Anglos, 5, 13
anti-immigrant sentiment, 15, 67,
    69, 163, 182; as acquired, 189;
    nationalism and, 30; nativism and, 5,
    25, 54, 79; New Yorkers of Mexican
    origin and, 167. *See also* Minutemen
    Project; online comments, on Trump
    inauguration
anti-Semitism: media conspiracy
    and, 98; race-mixing and, 98, 99;
    Stormfront website and, 89, 97–99,
    108; white nationalism and, 89;
    Zionism and, 98
Antunez, Danny, 142–43
Arendt, Hannah: on crimes of
    undocumented immigrants, 43–44;
    on homogenization, 23, 26, 45
Arizona SB 1070 bill, 19
Arpaio, Joe, 162

assimilation: Civil Rights movement
    and, 64; in Germany, 37; Hinman on,
    56; U.S., 22, 37–38

El Barrio, 176, 179; diversity of, 177,
    177, 178, *178*
Bebout, Lee, 20
Beck, Kevin, 59
belonging, 8, 43; for children, 19, 20;
    for New Yorkers of Mexican origin,
    26, 167, 169, 172, 180
Benton-Cohen, Katherine, 5
biopower, 40; race and, 36
birther movement, 81
blacks, 8; New Yorkers of Mexican
    origin and, 173–74; Stormfront
    website and, 94, 95, 96, 99, 100,
    106, 108
black-white binary, 20
de Blasio, Bill, 168
Blau, Francine D., 186
Bloomberg, Michael, 168
Bollinger, Lee, 77
border cities: Anchondo on, 132–34,
    133; Antunez on, 142–43; border
    as arbitrary in, 134–35; Delgado
    on, 132, *132*; drug trafficking in,
    127; Duarte on, 125–26; fear of,

About the Author

Ernesto Castañeda is assistant professor of sociology at American University in Washington, D.C., where he is affiliated with the Metropolitan Policy Center, the Center of Latin American and Latino Studies, and the Center on Health Risk and Society. He holds a BA in interdisciplinary studies from the University of California, Berkeley, and a PhD in sociology from Columbia University. He has been a visiting scholar at the Sorbonne, Sciences Po Paris, Oxford, and the New School for Social Research. He is the author of *A Place to Call Home: Immigrant Belonging and Exclusion in New York, Paris, and Barcelona* (Stanford University Press 2018); editor of *Immigration and Categorical Inequality: Migration to the City and the Birth of Race and Ethnicity* (Routledge 2018); co-editor with Cathy L. Schneider of *Collective Violence, Contentious Politics, and Social Change: A Charles Tilly Reader* (Routledge 2017); and co-author with Charles Tilly and Lesley Wood of *Social Movements 1768–2018* (Routledge 2019).